EDITED BY GEORG M. GUGELBERGER

MARXISM AND AFRICAN LITERATURE

Africa World Press
of the Africa Research & Publications Project

P.O. Box 1892
Trenton, New Jersey 08608

AFRICA WORLD PRESS, INC.
P.O. Box 1892
Trenton, N.J. 08607

©In selection and editing Georg M. Gugelberger 1985

©Individual contributors 1985

First published in 1986 in the United States of America
by Africa World Press and in Great Britain by James Curry Ltd.

Library of Congress Catalog Card Number: 85-72994

ISBN: 0-86543-030-6 Cloth
      0-86543-031-4 Paper

CONTENTS

For Renate, who helped when there was
'no fire in the fridge.'

ACKNOWLEDGEMENTS

I am grateful to the London Institute of Race Relations for permission to reprint from their journal *Race and Class* the essay by Chris Searle, 'The Mobilization of Words: Poetry and Resistance in Mozambique' and to the *Canadian Journal of African Studies* for permission to reproduce Omafume F. Onoge's 'The Crisis of Consciousness in Modern African Literature: A Survey.' I am very grateful to Geoff Hunt from the University of Ife, Nigeria, for his support while I worked on this book over the last few years. I am thankful to the University of California, Riverside, for assistance in the form of a grant to type the manuscript of this book.

The Publishers are grateful to the following for permission to reproduce copyright material:

Canadian Association of African Studies for the article 'The Crisis of Consciousness in Modern African Literature: A Survey (1974)' by Omafume F. Onoge *Canadian Journal of African Studies* Vol 8:2 1974; The Institute of Race Relations for the article 'The mobilisation of words: poetry and resistance in Mozambique' by Chris Searle *Race & Class* Vol XXIII Spring 1982 No 4 (c) The Institute of Race Relations, London.

INTRODUCTION Georg M. Gugelberger

'. . . To render reality to men in a form they can master'

Bertolt Brecht

This collection brings together for the first time a significant number of radical essays on African literature, still a major omission in the growing field of African and Third World literary criticism.

I began this collection while teaching in Nigeria from 1976–1977 in response to an increasing frustration (shared by many) with the main trends of African literary criticism, and with its implicit privileging of bourgeois Western approaches to literature, which pushed radical alternatives to the back. During the years this project was under way, the original few essays I had collected (by Biodun Jeyifo, Geoffrey Hunt, Omafume Onoge) were joined by many others, which to me confirmed a significant turn in African literary criticism.

As a comparatist interested in literary theory and related issues, I had expected from African literature, and more so from African literary criticism, what so many writers and critics had merely taken for granted: a specific political relevance. I expected to find, with the transition from colonialism to 'independence', the kind of increasing politicization we unfortunately find less and less in experimental and avant-garde modernist and post-modernist Western literature. I quickly learned that a geographic definition of Third World literature does not necessarily imply a politically progressive attitude. By now it has become clear to me that we have to replace the old geographic definition by a class-based progressive definition as Peter Nazareth has offered it in his *The Third World Writer*:

> To belong to the Third World is therefore to accept an identity, an identity with the wretched of the earth spoken for by Frantz Fanon, to determine to end all exploitation and oppression.

This definition – if adhered to – clearly replaces not only the old geographic definition but at the same time the notion of ethnicity (race/Africaneity) with clear class consciousness. This permits us to expand the concept of Third World literature in truly international solidarity to include such writers as William Blake, Bertolt Brecht and others, i.e. authors who made the fight against all forms of oppression their main theme.

The paradox of many an African writer, and even more so of many African critics, is the fact that they oppose Euro- and Americo-centric literary views but at the same time perpetuate precisely such views. Obviously, this must have traumatic implications. Most African critics have confused geography and ethnicity with ideology.

When I first collected some of these essays, I was looking for critical works which were radical in the Marxist sense of going to the roots of the problem, which is man – works which, due to their inherent international solidarity, were relevant first of all for Africans themselves and secondly for progressive peoples everywhere. What I found instead were mostly echoes of first and second world literary views. If they were original at all, they were frequently pseudo-radicalized through the label of Africaneity. By necessity this implied looking for books and articles revealing 'no African stylistic features or patterns of expression ... even if written by an African' (*pace* Janheinz Jahn who made this statement while discounting Peter Abrahams). While looking for a criticism sympathetic to writers such as Alex La Guma, Ngugi wa Thiong'o, Sembène Ousmane, the van der Post of *In a Province* (a sadly unrecognized South African novel), Okot p'Bitek and others, what I found were mostly essays and books on Joyce Cary and the African novel, Negritude (over and over again , Senghor, Kafka and Camara Laye, Symbol and Meaning in X, Jungian archetypes in Y, The State of Criticism (always, needless to say, exclusive of radical criticism), survey attempts in Ghanaian or Nigerian poetry, Fagunwa, Tutuola, interviews, folklore, 'tradition', the Universal etc., *ad infinitum*.

What I missed furthermore, aside from more sympathetic and committed essays, was a familiarity with what was frequently attacked: European and/or American literary criticism. Most modes of present critical discourse are largely unacknowledged in Africa. Certainly there were exceptions, albeit not the most fruitful ones: There were structuralist attempts by Sunday O. Anozie and other contributors to the literary journal *Conch*. There was a semiotic reading of Yambo Ouologuem's *Le Devoir de Violence*. There were a few sociological studies (largely Mutiso and Emmanuel Obiechina).

But when books and/or essays were sociological, or claimed to be so, this obviously meant traditionally sociological, i.e. in the sense that traditional sociology (as anthropology) always sees society through the perspective of established social organization, which in the African case frequently implied satisfaction with the post-colonial transition without any awareness of its neo-colonial implications. Radical sociology, on the other hand, looks at things through the eyes of oppressed groups. With few exceptions, the shift from traditional sociology to radical sociology had not taken place, either in sociology proper or in its affiliate – literary sociology.

While this assessment may seem harsh, it could be toned down by repeating that the absence of critical 'schools' could have been advantageous for the African literary context. But when the absence is the result of simple minded fusions of the unacknowledged bourgeois modes of formalist discourse, the time has come to worry and to change this deplorable situation. Bourgeois African criticism seems to be content with impressionistic and interpretative coverings of increasingly difficult texts, which always have to be discovered (usually first in the West) rather than being situated in a specific historical, political and economic context for a change-facilitating purpose.

What I was looking for, then, were critical manifestations which were supportive of my assumed shift from traditional to radical modes of criticism, manifestations which give us hope for a more fruitful development of African criticism rather than continuing to shadow box with autelic structures and producing misleading exegeses. What is needed is a salvational or redeeming literary criticism, conscienticization rather than 'banking education' (to borrow Paulo Freire's terminology). Ngugi wa Thiong'o said about the African critic and writer:

> And when he woke up to this *task*, a little surprised that events in post-independent Africa could take the turn they had taken, he only tried to be a liberal referee, an interpreter, standing on the fence between the new men of power and the people.

The African Writer and his Past (my emphasis)

Marx's well known thesis on Feuerbach comes to mind – that the philosophers have only *interpreted* the world while the task is to *change* it. A change-facilitating mode of writing and criticism is what I had been looking for rather than the continuous 'standing on the fence' of interpretation. This kind of criticism has been described aptly by Terry Eagleton:

> Criticism is not a passage from text to reader: its task is not to redouble the text's self-understanding, to collude with its object in a conspiracy of eloquence. Its task is to show the text as it cannot know itself, to manifest those conditions of its making (inscribed in its very letter) about which it is necessarily silent. It is not just that its very self-knowledge is the construction of a self-oblivion. To achieve such a showing, criticism must break with its ideological prehistory, situating itself outside the space of the text on the alternative terrain of scientific knowledge.

Terry Eagleton, *Criticism and Ideology*

The aim of this book has been to stake out this 'alternative terrain' (art as a new science of improved living) for the African situation, expanding it while integrating it into an already existing tradition (by no means the African tradition). To do so, in the hope of raising the present state of African literary criticism or to at least fruition a debate of substantial relevance, it was necessary to come to terms with one of Africa's most outstanding literary figures, one who presently seems to hold (at least in the bourgeois world) a position only Léopold Senghor held before him: Wole Soyinka.

The reader of these essays might at first be startled by what appears to be an anti-Soyinka bias in some of the essays. Many of the contributors felt compelled to confront Soyinka and his implied aesthetics with an alternative writer/aesthetics. An almost Lukácsian either/or polarity can be observed. Georg Gugelberger confronts Soyinka with Amiri Baraka, Biodun Jeyifo with Ibrahim Hussein; Geoffrey Hunt contrasts Amilcar Cabral's view of 'the return to the source' (class based) with Soyinka's view of 'tradition' (myth based), and even Peter Nazareth, who evokes Soyinka less (but certainly had done so in the past), is compelled to admonish Soyinka to address himself to another audience and holds up – almost unexpectedly – Cyprian Ekwensi against him. Omafume F. Onoge holds up the American Don Lee against Soyinka, or a mode of writing which is to be associated with Soyinka, namely bourgeois modernism.

If the criticism of Soyinka is sometimes harsh, I hasten to add that not only Marxists are by now perturbed by Soyinka's position and some of his writings. Even less radical critics such as Lewis Nkosi could say that 'it is high time that a great number of Soyinka's solecisms are recognized for what they are: failure to communicate clearly' (*Tasks and Masks*). It seems it has become increasingly difficult to talk about the contemporary state of African literature without talking about, or perhaps even to, Wole Soyinka. In doing so, these essays should not be considered biased. They have nothing to do with propaganda. They rather account for a fact. They encourage and continue a dialogue which is deeply needed and which has gone on since the time when some few people held up the writings of Ngugi wa Thiong'o against the writings of Wole Soyinka. In reading, as in writing, choices have to be made. There is simply no way to avoid this. These choices are always and have always been class based. They are imminently and eminently political.

Looking at the African scene from a Marxist perspective obviously meant two things: encouragement and recognition for those who have started writing in this tradition, but at the same time a warning that African specificity (race/Africaneity) cannot any longer be privileged concepts once progressive internationalist positions are taken. To literary criticism in Africa this implies a conscious assessment of the historical development of Marxist literary theory from its beginning in the middle of the nineteenth century to the present.

It is a deplorable fact that in what concerns aesthetics Marxist literary critics only too frequently have been less progressive than their colleagues in fields such as economics, politics, sociology. Too often they were influenced by overly rigid Lukácsian if not Zdhanovist reductionism. Too often this has led (in Africa as elsewhere in the Third, Second and First Worlds) to misconceived attacks against formalist issues and to the abandoning of the fundamental principle of dialectics. It has therefore been necessary to place African literary criticism in its international context and to speak out against the hidden (albeit understandable) nationalism implicit in the concept of ethnicity. We are aware that ethnicity is a more progressive concept than Euro-centric views and that the European notion of universalism is a particularly deplorable trick of imperialism, but we are also aware that a misfounded (or overly long adhered to) notion of race could be easily as detrimental. Therefore part of this book presents the particular question of race versus class as a still on-going debate.

While covering writers and literary developments in West Africa, South Africa and East Africa as well as genres ranging from orature to poetry, drama and the novel, the essays in this collection basically fall into three groups:

1. Those discussing the development of African literary criticism, literary sociology, and the rise of radical theory (-ies) as exemplified by Gugelberger, Hunt and Onoge;

2. Radical readings of selected bourgeois and/or progressive literary texts of various genres or developments in specific countries, as exemplified in essays by Fatunde, Hamilton, Kamenju, Nazareth and Searle;

3. Those which already come to terms with the issues of Modernism and Realism, as in the previous group, but at the same time analyze the increasing tendency to account for the interest in populist literature from orature to populist writers to populist media (journals), praising this development to a certain degree while seeing at the same time its potentially limiting and system-enforcing aspects, as exemplified in the essays by Darah, Nazareth, Searle and Vaughan.

The first essay, by Georg M. Gugelberger, accounts for the historical development of Marxist aesthetics (plural!) in relation to modernism, realism and populism. Gugelberger makes the three major debates (Sickingen, Brecht/Lukács, Kafka) bear on the various debates in Africa, from the definitional to the Negritude debates, from Eurocentric African criticism to ethnocentric criticism to the so-called Transition debate and shows in what ways Brecht is of importance for an ethical aesthetics and in what way particularly Bertolt Brecht can be of importance to the literary development in Africa. An awareness of the so-called Marxist debates in the specific context of their genesis, as well as the continuing debates between Marxist critics and formalists/structuralists/deconstructionists, can provide an answer for the attempted foundation of a truly class-conscious African and/or Third World literary theory. This is the implication of the 'Fourth Debate', an implication more relevant than the mysticism and mythicism of the 'Fourth Stage' in Soyinka's famous Ogunist essay.

Marxist criticism in Africa has frequently been associated with two critics: the Tanzanian literary critic Grant Kamenju and the Nigerian sociologist Omafume F. Onoge. In his 'The Crisis of Consciousness in Modern African Literature: A Survey' Onoge makes the point that African literature and its reception by African critics was sociologically conditioned by the colonial milieu. This did not permit it to develop progressively but forced it to be 'reactive', becoming in a sense reactionary (obviously there are exceptions). Mystical affirmation, Negritude, non-Negritude realism based on a wrongly chosen precursor (Joyce Cary), in other words modernism, made an affirmative progressive literary consciousness very difficult. Onoge aptly discusses the place of Senghor and Césaire, showing that what at one point was progressive can easily become reactionary when adopted at a later point in history. Post-Negritudinist literature and criticism push for authenticity, advocate bourgeois individualism, and slow down the necessary literary demands for change. Indebted to the Austrian Marxist Ernst Fischer, Onoge points out that a progressive African literary criticism would have to be based on writers such as Ngugi wa Thiong'o and Sembène Ousmane and on thinkers such as Fanon and Rodney. Onoge comes to terms sharply with the illusions of an 'African socialism'. He criticizes the concept of ethnicity and pleads for a correct class analysis.

Onoge's second essay, a talk originally given at the University of Dar-es-Salaam, comes to terms with the old Ibadan school of criticism – Abiola Irele and Dan S. Izevbaye. Onoge points out that political interests have been crucial factors in the appraisal of African culture. In this sense all literature is political, even when it condemns politics as thematically irrelevant. The crucial question is always the Brechtian one: for whom does a writer write? Whose political interests are affirmed? The decision has to be a choice between the politics of oppression and the politics of liberation. Onoge claims that academic bourgeois criticism of African literature is unable to judge literature in any satisfactory way and instead proposes a Marxist sociological criticism. Literary criticism, including what has been termed sociological criticism (of the Mutiso kind), is even more backward than the literature it criticizes. Marxist criticism, on the other hand, 'goes beyond a formal and content analysis of artistic works, to a consideration of the very institutional processes of art creation and art criticism'.

The British Gramsci scholar Geoffrey Hunt provides us with a philosophical critique of Wole Soyinka's literary essays in *Myth, Literature and the African World* to contrast this mythocentric/ traditionalist position with Amilcar Cabral's famous *Return to the Source*, which did not imply an ethically rooted tradition, as is the case with Soyinka, but a Marxist source, i.e. class conflict. At times harsh but at the same time with logical consequence rare in Soyinka criticism, Hunt sees Soyinka's 'ideological elaborations as attempts to reconcile the subjective contradictions of the neocolonial agent torn between allegiance to the bourgeoisie of the neo-colonizing power and allegiance to millions of impoverished rural Africans'. Going beyond Peter Nazareth's 'The Politics of Wole Soyinka', Geoffrey Hunt speaks of Soyinka's 'politics of ambiguity' which Hunt traces back to romanticism.

He confronts Soyinka's scepticism of ideology with the words 'Ideology is not dispensable but is inescapable, inherent and internal to all our thoughts and actions. It need not "speak itself" but "reveal[s] itself" in the form of word and deed'. Hunt confronts Soyinka's 'radical conservatism' (which he associates with romanticism) with Cabral's dialectical and realistic outlook. Hunt uses the tools of Cabral's collective and determinate view to combat Soyinka's Ogunism and his at once individualistic and abstract (universal) conception of man. He deplores, as do most of the contributors of these essays, Soyinka's 'tactic of out-Marxing the Marxists'. Hunt sees the ethnic imperative as subordinate to class analysis: 'Race is a subjective response to an objective class situation.' To quote Cabral: 'Contradictions between class, even when they are only embryonic, are of far greater importance than contradictions between tribes.'

The following essay by Biodun Jeyifo, a leading Marxist drama critic in Nigeria, gives us a contrastive Marxist reading of Soyinka's *Death and the King's Horseman* and Ibrahim Hussein's *Kinjeketile*. Jeyifo demonstrates what can be learned from the famous Sickingen debate between Marx and Engels on the one hand and Ferdinand Lasalle on the other.

Contrasting Soyinka's superbly written play with *Kinjeketile* by the Tanzanian Ibrahim Hussein, a play which deals with the famous Maji-Maji rebellion in former German Tanganyika. The latter certainly does not have the aesthetic merits of Soyinka's play but Jeyifo demonstrates what dangers aesthetic success without ideological insight can bring, which is reminiscent of a Brecht line from 'Literature shall be Scrutinized': 'The delicious music of words will only relate/that for many there was no food.'

In the words of Femi Osofisan, one can observe in Soyinka's later plays 'an evident superiority of craftmanship over the earlier ones' and at the same time 'a lessening intimacy with socio-political reality'. What Femi Osofisan has aptly termed the 'new exotic' is here analyzed as one of the main dangers of the unpoliticized modernist/avantgardist direction of some African plays. Jeyifo comes to terms with the issues of aesthetic success and ideological failure (what Brecht termed 'culinary' theater) as well as ideological relevance and aesthetic failure. This is a central issue that African dramatists must face, an issue which only rarely has been solved successfully anywhere at any time. There was Brecht in Germany; there are a few others who write or make films in the Brechtian tradition; and there is the emergent anti-exotic/Brechtian drama in West Africa represented by Kole Omotoso and Femi Osofisan. Jeyifo can see two African dramatic schools: a bourgeois historical tragedy represented by Soyinka, Ola Rotimi, and Seydou Badian which is basically 'culinary' in Brecht's sense of the word; and a 'realist' or 'socialist' historical tragedy ('a minority tradition') represented by Hussein or Aimé Césaire's *A Season in the Congo*. The impulse of the latter kind of play is 'to demystify, to unify'. Jeyifo has in mind an ethical consciousness which is political, not a metaphysical moral consciousness. He speaks of 'that superior, secular ethical consciousness which welds the life of the individual combatant to the destiny of an embattled and battling collectivity'.

Onoge had already postulated one way of progressively reading/using a literary text, namely, foregrounding the question of the treatment of the working masses (secondary to the Brechtian question 'for whom?'). The Nigerian Tunde Fatunde approaches a novel written in French with a more recent novel from Nigeria and looks at the treatment of masses and of violence. Fatunde sees violence as being inherent in colonial structures. Using a Fanonian and Brechtian point of view (through Brecht's famous poem 'A Worker Reads History') Fatunde gives us a progressive reading of *Le Devoir de Violence* by Mali's Yambo Ouologuem. This work, as fascinating as it might be on formal grounds, unfortunately mystified the class approach to let French colonialism off the hook. In contrast to Ouologuem's novel the Nigerian Festus Iyayi's novel *Violence* is successful due to its clear class consciousness and solid presentation of the working masses.

The following two essays analyze one of the most significant novels which has come out of Africa in recent years, Ngugi wa Thiong'o's *Petals of Blood*. First Peter Nazareth, a former Leeds classmate of Ngugi wa Thiong'o, questions Ngugi wa Thiong'o's point of view, or rather sees two Ngugis struggling with each other: a Christian Ngugi and a politicized Ngugi. While this might be so, we feel that the Christian Ngugi is rather a Blakean Ngugi and that Blake and Brecht (through Ngugi's novel) can be seen as revolutionary precursors of the famous Kenyan novelist.

Grant Kamenju, one of the foremost radical critics of East Africa, provides us then with a Leninist reading of *Petals of Blood*, which he sees as a 'mirror of the African Revolution' and a solid attack on the new élite in post-independence/neo-colonial Africa 'preoccupied with unmasking the pornographic and obscene role of the comprador class spawned and groomed by imperialism in Africa so as to play the part of intermediary, pimping for imperialist finance capital'.

MARXISM AND AFRICAN LITERATURE

Russel G. Hamilton, author of *Voices from an Empire, A History of Afro-Portuguese Literature* (1975), gives us in 'Class, Race, and Authorship in Angola' an overview of literary and social developments before, during and after the Angolan revolution. He too comes to the conclusion, by analyzing the contributions by non-black Angolan writers, that class, not race, has been central: 'Among committed Angolan intellectuals, notions of class generally prevailed over race, although racism was a social reality with which the *Novos Intelectuais* necessarily had to contend.' He sees race as a secondary issue of understandable cultural revindication. Focusing on literary essays by Neto and others, he asks what literature should and could be like in independent Angola and reminds us thus that Neto was fully aware of Zdhanovist/socialist realist dangers and had therefore called – as did Brecht and Mao – for a literature for and of the people. Hamilton specifically examines the Kimbundu-flavored Portuguese as a carrier of the new ideas and concludes his analysis by showing how this literature is presently produced and how language mediates this effort.

Chris Searle, editor of a major anthology of Mozambican poetry in English, *Sunflower of Hope: Poetry from the Mozambican Revolution* (1982) gives us a view of a country where poetry inhabits almost every aspect of daily life. In 'The Mobilization of Words: Poetry and Resistance in Mozambique' Searle analyzes poems of combat, collective poems, and literacy poems. While we are accustomed (in capitalist countries) to see poetry and art generally as functioning negatively, Searle makes a case for a new poetry of affirmation. Uncomplicated use of words here creates a post-revolutionary populism designed for educating the masses, raising productivity, informing about the revolution, solidarizing with revolutionary movements in the rest of the world. Searle, too, comes to the conclusion that class not race is the main issue in Africa. With reference to a speech by Graça Machel, Mozambique's minister of Education and Culture, we see once again that Africaneity and Negritude have been wrongly privileged: 'Such theories as Negritude and African authenticity are nothing more than theories of the ruling classes of neo-colonialism, hence of imperialism.'

We have already spoken of Peter Nazareth's early and seminal essay on the 'Politics of Wole Soyinka'. In Peter Nazareth we have a critic who admires Soyinka as a writer but hesitates when facing his politics. Peter Nazareth has always been a stout defender of populist modes of writing, be they Robert Tressell's *The Ragged Trousered Philanthropist* or Okello Oculi's *Orphan*. He provides us here with an account of the frequently scolded (by traditional critics) Nigerian writer Cyprian Ekwensi, whom he calls 'the man most responsible for the growth and development of modern African literature'. Using the Biafra war as his theme, as Ekwensi does in his *Survive the Peace*, Peter Nazareth shows the necessity of class analysis for literary criticism. Class struggle, rather than tribalism, is seen as one of the causes of the war. The war is over by now, but it has become 'difficult to survive the peace'. Peter Nazareth believes, as did Brecht before him, that 'teaching is done by entertaining'. And Ekwensi is an entertaining writer. Both, writer and critic, are convinced that the themes for the African writer should not be based solely on tradition, ethnicity and Africaneity because 'at this particular moment of time we live in politics and economics'. In his conclusion

Peter Nazareth, too, is forced to speak to the dilemma of Soyinka, whom he contrasts with the aesthetically less meritorious artist Ekwensi: 'The weakness of Soyinka, for instance, is that in being profound, he becomes virtually incomprehensible. Soyinka could do with a little of Ekwensi's kind of relationship with his audience.'

One of the most notable aspects of African literature has always been the continent's rich orature. It is therefore virtually a must to include an essay on this genre and gratifying to have come across someone who does not write merely in the tradition of early oral scholars. Contrasting traditional praise songs with more recent versions, Godini G. Darah gives us a socio-economic reading of Urhobo song poetry. He stresses the increasing commodification of orature. The worn out bourgeois vocabulary of formula, catalogue, parataxis, and theme (Milman Parry, A. B. Lord) is here replaced by the economic causes underlying song production and proliferation. The only formula left is 'Igboo sh'emu sua' (with money all things are possible). And the new catalogues are big-shot catalogues of those who pay to become the *nouveaux riches* heroes of the singer of tales. It is common to pay up to 600 Naira to have one's name eulogized in the new panegyric. Since Victor Zirmunsky, very few scholars have taken up oral literature from a Marxist perspective, and none, to my knowledge, has applied it to African literature or has gone as far.

While analyzing the specific South African situation and a few recent South African authors (Mutloatse, Nthodi, Matshoba) who have published in the populist magazine *Staffrider*, Michael Vaughan not only presents a very specific case, a situation where progressive views seem to be identical with ethnic views, but at the same time summarizes most of the issues discussed so far; he clarifies some of them, and advances many. The journal *Staffrider* makes it very clear that art for art's sake implies art for apartheid's sake and therefore challenges the distinction between producer and consumer and invites as many people to contribute as possible. This populist emphasis at first appears radical. But we soon learn that 'Staffrider' figures (dropouts, survivors, individual folk heroes) emphasize largely individualist values and hardly ever give attention to the struggle of the black working class as a class. 'The people' is not – according to Vaughan – an entity identical to that of the 'working class'. A major question remains unasked: to what extent will the struggle against racial oppression involve a struggle also against capital? For Vaughan the 'Staffrider' figure is not so much a proletarian but rather a member of the lumpen proletariat. The strength of populist ideology within this literature means that class analysis is very undeveloped, that it virtually prevents class analysis. This reminds us of the situation of many Afro-centric aestheticians and supports an argument which runs throughout this book. We have to look at things dialectically. What at first appears progressive (ethnicity, populism) can easily turn into something less progressive, something which actually enforces the status quo. According to Vaughan ' "Staffrider" literature which is committed to an ideological assault upon the racism of the apartheid state, appears unwilling or unable to take on the capitalist system'.

Some of these essays display a healthy note of aggressiveness, but aggressiveness is the best antidote for fake bourgeois objectivity. Furthermore, aggressiveness is the door to discussion unless the bourgeois reader slams this door to hide in the autelic warm room of formalism putting his worm's eye view of history. Critical aggressiveness is in line with Walter Benjamin's first thesis that the 'critic is the strategist in the literary struggle' ('13 Theses on the literary critic').

While we have basically three kinds of criticism in Africa, a bourgeois criticism, a Marxist anti-imperialist criticism and a pan-Africanist tendency, we also have in Africa, as elsewhere, three fundamental radical developments in recent years: at first aesthetics was considered to be at the opposite pole from politics, then aesthetics and politics became connectable, and now we move from aesthetics to politics. This development is reflected not only in African literature but in African literary criticism as well. In this sense Ngugi wa Thiong'o's recent title *Writers in Politics* is more than symptomatic.

Since Ngugi wa Thiong'o's *Homecoming* (1972) and more so since his *Petals of Blood, Writers in Politics* (1981) and *Barrel of a Pen* (1983), since Okot p'Bitek's *Africa's Cultural Revolution*, since Peter Nazareth's *Literature and Society in Modern Africa*, and since the Transition debate, radical criticism in Africa has matured tremendously. With Onoge, Jeyifo, Hunt, Darah, Kamenju, Vaughan and others we can, for the first time, speak of a coherent alternative and radical tradition, 'a road through to action', to modify Kermode's statement. It is the aim of this collection to gather these critics and to present them as a unified and increasingly important voice. More and more debates take place in Africa which center around Marxist issues, witness the various recent conferences at the Universities of Ibadan, Dar-es-Salaam and Ife. It is hoped that this volume will strengthen Marxist criticism in Africa as well as abroad. It is further hoped that this on-going debate will not be brushed aside by Africa's 'leading writer' as another version of 'radical chic-ism'. (Soyinka's term at the 23rd meeting of the African Studies Association in Los Angeles, 1980) There is more at stake here if we truly wish to see in Africa's literature a tool for consciousness-raising rather than another invitation for tourists attracted to exoticism. Third World literature must come to terms with its inherent Fanonian nature. For Third World literature as for Third World criticism there is only one definition: 'to belong to the Third World is therefore to accept an identity, an identity with the wretched of the earth spoken for by Frantz Fanon, to determine to end all exploitation and oppression'.

Most of the essays in this collection have been written with this aim in mind. It is hoped that they may be helpful in liberating literature from wrong formalist colonization. It is hoped that in the words of Paulo Freire they may at least help to replace 'banking education' by 'conscienticization'.

George M. Gugelberger
University of California, Riverside
1983

CHAPTER ONE

MARXIST LITERARY DEBATES AND THEIR CONTINUITY IN AFRICAN LITERARY CRITICISM

Georg M. Gugelberger

> Poetisch freilegen, meine ich – nicht zu poetisieren.
> To expose poetically is what I mean – not to poeticize
>
> Hubert Fichte, author of *Xango* (1976)

1

The 'ethnic imperative'[1] most likely has been the strongest in post-independence Africa's search for a viable and non-Eurocentric aesthetics. This 'ethnic imperative' presents itself in various disguises from: authenticity, traditionalism, 'Ogunism' (Soyinka),[2] Munto (Jahn), 'weusi' (Mutiso),[3] 'abibimañ' (Soyinka),[4] and 'afrocentric liberationist' (Chinweizu).[5] Most of these are basically 'formalist' concepts of a dangerous intrinsic orientation, historically understandable, but not therefore less regrettable; and most frequently they lead to petrified models. In the long run they have to be subordinated to the *ethic imperative* if African literature and criticism are to be spared the pitfalls of Western art and literature which, for so long, have been based on the *aesthetic imperative* (from Kant's purposeful purposelessness via the Russian formalists to the dominant versions of American New Criticism, French structuralism, and beyond). In other words: how do we come closer to a realization of Lenin's prophesy that ethics are the aesthetics of the future,[6] and how are recent debates in Africa, which are sometimes to be connected with the three Marxist debates on aesthetics, relevant for such an aesthetics of the future?

In European art and literature the demand for the aesthetic as the dominant in the artistic product, since romanticism, has made it possible for one avant-gardism to replace another, from Alfred Jarry's 'mot de Cambronne' *merdre* on a Parisian stage to Duchamp's *urinoir* against a museum wall, and more recently from Happening to Fluxus art, from Concept to Earth and Eat art. I happen to agree that many of these attempts can be seen as attempts to de-auratize art (Walter Benjamin)[7] and socialize it, or at least argue that these attempts are not decadent (Stefan Morawski),[8] but rather foreshadow a new cultural epoch where the élitist concept of art and its increasing commodification is to be replaced by a more democratic and participatory art (sometimes even conscious of Marx's suggestion that in a future society 'there are no painters but at most people who engage in painting among other activities.'[9]). In capitalist countries, however, commodification of aesthetic products will hardly allow for the necessary process of socialization. We know that in Africa prior to colonization, art functioned and communicated. It was not something to be merely admired, collected and/or sold.[10] It is therefore irritating to see in post-independence Africa a basically commodified Eurocentric aesthetics re-enter through the backdoor of authenticity (alias anti-Eurocentrism, Africaneity, autonomy, etc.). On the other hand, this development shows again that the post-independence period with its anti- or at least de-colonizing intentions is nothing but a regression into a well disguised neocolonialism. And if it is not always this, it is at least a reflection of a profound ambivalence. Lewis Nkosi, the South African writer and critic, stated the problem in these words:

> . . . while independence has liberated enormous energies in terms of artistic production, it has also revealed unexpected hesitations and social ambivalence in writers who, by the nature of their education and professional interest, live too close to the social power of the new ruling class not to disclose certain social compulsions within their works that such a proximity engenders.[11]

These hesitations and ambivalences are often the cause of vacuous surface commitment (in terms of the text's message quality) or they lead to formalist aesthetic qualities which are to be associated with Western modernism.

African literature for quite some time now has struggled between modes of writing which are essentially modernist, Eliotic, and/or Poundian, longing for permanence and everlastingness (the increasing difficulty of Soyinka's style, particularly of his *Idanre*, 1967, and his modernist 'miniature' epic *Ogun Abibimañ*, 1978, are a case in point) and an aesthetic of resistance and commitment inherent in the writings of Okot p'Bitek, Ngugi wa Thiong'o, Sembène Ousmane, Alex La Guma and others, writers who are less formalistically achieved but politically more engaged, even if they are less modernist. African writers themselves are fully aware of this bifurcation as can be witnessed in Okot p'Bitek's *Song of Lawino* and *Song of Ocol*, works which, according to one of the founders of African radical aesthetics, Grant Kamenju, are 'the neo-colonial aesthetics of capitalism and subjugation' versus 'the aesthetics of black pride, black affirmation, resistance and ultimate liberation'.[12] In order to come to terms with this apparent bifurcation not only in literature but in literary criticism, it is necessary to look at a specific tradition (by no means the African tradition) to which Marxism and its outlook towards realism, modernism, post-modernism and populist modernism' might very well provide the only answer on this long and troublesome journey from aesthetics to ethics.

The bifurcation observable in African literature (increased difficulty and quest for authenticity in modernist writers such as Soyinka and others, and decreasing difficulty, realistic mode of writing and socialist orientation in Ngugi wa Thiong'o and others) for a long time has been less felt in mainstream African literary criticism. While D. S. Izevbaye could speak of an 'orientation of African criticism towards sociology'[13] (without defining what he meant by literary sociology), the same critic expressed the need for an African criticism and went so far as to claim that it is literary criticism which could shape a truly African literary tradition:

> The power of criticism to shape a literary tradition was recognized by African critics, as may be seen in the rejection of European critical concepts and the *debate* about setting up African standards of criticism which would lead to the establishment of an African critical tradition.[14] (italics added)

Immediately we again have – this time in criticism – the haunting notion of authenticity; and while it is certainly possible to write a literature which is specifically African (due to specific traditions, existing languages, political circumstances, different readers' expectations, etc.) it is doubtful that we can ever arrive at what Izevbaye seems to think of as a criticism based on the rejection of European critical concepts. Criticism, philosophy, logic, ethics, etc. can hardly be reduced to black and white, Europe versus Africa, but can be conceived as being class related, i.e. supportive of one class while being harmful to another. Contrary to the tendency of the majority of African literary works toward durability and artistic everlastingness (art-for-art's sake) Izevbaye claimed that: 'Many English-speaking African writers accept the notion that African art is functional, and that therefore the concept of art for art's sake should not be allowed to take root in African critical thought.' While the majority of African works might not be precisely art for art's sake, the dangers of a mode of writing which is a final analysis leads to the same social impotence as art for art's sake can be observed. Let us not forget that one of the most politically and socially oriented poets of modernism, Ezra Pound, (one of the few who based his poetics on economics but at the same time refused to take into consideration the lessons of Marxism and instead opted for a personally constructed tradition) became a supporter of Italian fascism.[15] Walter Benjamin's aphoristic conclusion with regard to extreme modernism and fascism, *fiat ars pereat mundi*,[16] still holds: the more refined and successful in aesthetic terms a work of art becomes, the more it lacks moral and social integrity. Copying Pound by itself is not the cause. Copying, however, what is wrong in Pound, often is. Witness Soyinka as a writer who fell into the Poundian trap. Witness the Nicaraguan poet Ernesto Cardenal, Pound's Spanish translator, who did not.

This essay then is concerned with looking at the development of modernism in relation to Marxism while extending the implications of this development to Africa where increasing dissatisfaction with post-independent aesthetic developments has given birth to a radical criticism. Most critics in Africa who are quick in using terms such as functionality and politicization have done so without coming to terms with Marxism. Obviously there are exceptions and the number of exceptions increases every year, but until very recently African literary criticism has been bourgeois in its orientation, i.e. it has been clearly affiliated with Western formalism (the critical response to increasingly difficult literary works) despite the fact that this mode of thinking has been attacked by the same critics who have practised this type of criticism. To say the least, this development is a far cry from Abiola Irele's demand that African criticism 'must grow with our literature.'[17]

The debates over commited versus autonomous literature which presently rage in Africa have been going on at least since the mid-nineteenth century in Europe. These debates become clearer within the context of the development of Marxist aesthetics, and this is the approach that we will pursue here, despite the fact that ultimately the final question might be based on the analysis of a fundamental opposition between Marxism and aesthetics. We can agree with Tony Bennett that 'in its attempt to produce an aesthetic, Marxism has responded not to its own theoretical and political needs but to the ideological demands placed on it by the need to compete with bourgeois criticism.'[18] If we discuss in the following pages various aesthetic debates, emphasizing the so-called three Marxist debates and their implications for African literary criticism we are doing so because we believe that Marxist criticism can only be discussed in the entirety of its developmental process rather than by singling out one or two Marxist critics. This is particularly important since in Africa, on the few occasions when radical criticism has been formulated, adherence to a single spokesman rather than to the development of Marxist aesthetics can be observed. In Terry Eagleton's words it can be re-stated that 'The most valuable way of discussing Marxist criticism, then, would be a historical survey of it from Marx and Engels to the present day'[19] without losing sight of the fact that Marxism is and always has been an open theory which continually transforms itself.[20]

We believe that these debates bear on what has been going on in the various Negritude debates; in the debates between form versus commitment; in the debate between Soyinka and Chinweizu (the so-called Transition debate); and in the debates between Soyinka and what he unfortunately has termed the 'radical chic-ists'.[21]

2

Although Marx and Engels were highly interested in literary issues they never arrived at what could be called a systematic aesthetics nor is it likely to be argued that the establishment of such a systematic study on their part is really a necessity for the development of a Marxist aesthetics. Such an aesthetics would have led invariably to precisely the kind of specialized thinking that Marxism is opposed to. Marx and Engels were observant of the literature of their time as well as of the literature of the past which largely meant the acknowledged great masterpieces of Western Europe. They were particularly fond of Balzac's novels; Marx even planned to write a book on this French writer of the nineteenth century, a writer we normally associate with realism; which might account for the reason why Marxist critics have placed realism, for so long, at the centre of their literary discussions. Seldom has the praise for the value of literature been stressed as much as with Engels when he said that the had learned more from Balzac than 'from all of the professed historians, economists and statisticians of the period together'.[22] While we are by no means sure what Marxist aesthetics might have meant for Marx and Engels, we do know that their basic methodology was historical, materialist, dialectical: a methodology which certainly can be applied to literature once we learn to refrain from merely citing their statements out of context to back up a particular point of view that we want to make. Marxism is clearly teleological, its goal must be the amelioration of a given society. It is class conscious and anti-metaphysical. As we know from the *German Ideology*, we always have to set out from *real* active men and from the basis of their real life-process. The real life-process for Marx clearly has priority and literature and philosophy are secondary. This, however, does not negate the possibility of literature as a reflecting device of socio-economic development and/or regress, nor does it exclude literature's instigative and admonitory potential since the truth of art is for Marx synonymous with the self-awareness of the human species. While having made numerous albeit mostly marginal statements about literature, Marx and Engels always wondered what it is that constitutes the staying power of certain works of art, why do they continue to afford us aesthetic pleasure. A reference from the 1857 *Introduction to the Critique of Political Economy* hints at the possibility that there might be something which has to do with the formal achievement which is not easily accounted for by Marxist methodology. And it was Engels who, after Marx's death, stressed this apparent neglect of formal issues in a letter to Franz Mehring:

> ... there is only one point lacking, which, however, Marx and I always failed to stress enough in our writings and in regard to which we are all equally guilty. That is to say, v e all laid, and *were bound* to lay, the main emphasis, in the first place on the *derivation* of political, juridical and other ideological notions, and of actions arising through the medium of these notions, from basic economic facts. But in so doing we neglected the formal side – the ways and means by which these notions, etc., come about – for the sake of content.[23]

Here we have for the first time what amounts to – in a commited aesthetics – the apparent contradiction between formal issues and issues of reflection: between realism and modernism. This later became the basis for a total revision of Marxist aesthetics in the 1930s when Lukács and Brecht discussed their notions of modernism and realism. Marx and Engels themselves, however, never dealt with the issue. They gave us instead, in a few personal letters, what later critics have refered to as the Sickingen debate, which was conducted in the spring of 1859 between Ferdinand Lasalle and Marx and Engels. In these letters the two founders of Marxism claimed that Lasalle selected the wrong and unrepresentative Sickingen for the protagonist in his work instead of the progressive and representative Thomas Münzer. They objected to Lasalle's *Schillerism*, i.e. they objected to using characters as mouthpieces of ideas which they viewed as tendentious. (In an African context Biodun Jeyifo's comparison of Soyinka's *A Dance of the Forests* and *The King's Horseman* with Hussein's *Kinjeketile* come readily to mind.) Here we have for the first time concepts relevant for a definition of 1) realism; 2) typology; and 3) selection of characters representative of pro-

5

gressive forces. These terms Engels, rather than Marx, defined at a later point and these concepts are central to Lukács' theory of realism. Engels referred to these concepts in letters to Minna Kautsky (1885) and to Margaret Harkness (1888). Engels' definition of realism – rather cautiously formulated – is:

> Realism, *to my mind*, implies, besides truth of detail, the truthful reproduction of typical characters under typical circumstances.[24]

This is by no means the only definition of realism as Engels clearly implies through the qualifier 'to my mind', but for an age which had just read Balzac extensively, the definition may hold. It is another thing, however, to use this definition undialectically and give it the status of paradigm as Lukács and others have done.

The years prior to the Russian Revolution did not see a particular deepening of Marxist literary issues. In Germany and Russia, Mehring and Plekhanov critically applied for the first time some of the critical insights suggested by Marx and Engels to literature. In 1905 Lenin wrote his famous *partignost* manifesto, 'Party Organization and Party Literature', which if dialectically read (as it was written) by no means implies that the party has a right to direct the themes and forms of writers as this was later construed by Stalin's cultural Minister Zdhanov. Zdhanovism or socialist realism as it became known was a far cry from Lenin's intentions and had very little to do with either literature or socialism. Lukács still deserves to be praised for having arrived at more significant and opposing views on socialist realism.

In the years following 1905, largely due to the relative facility with which bourgeois critics could attack Marxist ignorance of formal issues, a significant and careful study of literature as a science came into being. The Russian formalists defined for the first time the study of literature not as the study of individual texts but the study of what truly constitutes literariness (Jakobson's famous *literaturnost*). *Literaturnost* versus *partignost* – if we are willing to go to an extreme condensation of the issues – became the two dominant opposing views on literature. The Russian formalists tried to account for the devices which constitute literariness, Shklovsky coined the concept of the *priem ostranenija* or strange-making device and argued that the task of literature is to make you see, to work against familiarity and habitualization. This is achieved by strange-making, rearrangement, and deconstruction. Works of 'increasing difficulty' were becoming central, and Russian formalism can be seen as the appropriate literary criticism for the increasing vogue of modernist works. While the Russian formalists by no means were as conservative as later Marxists have attempted to make them (since social issues could be as much a *dominant* as literary issues), and while they – as romantics and modernists prior to them – reflect a bifurcation between proper formalism of a bourgeois tendency (Opoyaz and other groups) and left wing (LEF) critics, both camps had a difficult time in the years after the Russian Revolution. The fact that these issues are not as simple as some Marxists saw them becomes clear in a marvellous dialectical piece of writing by Leon Trotsky who both attacked and praised the Russian formalists at the same time. In *Literature and Revolution* (1923) he said:

> It is quite true that a work of art should never be judged, accepted, or rejected on the basis of Marxist principles. The products of artistic creation must be evaluated first and foremost on the basis of their own laws, that is to say the laws of art. But only Marxism is capable of explaining why and how a certain orientation of art came about at a certain period, that is to say the origin and the reason for such an orientation and not some other.[25]

By the early twenties the issue became one of priority. To describe the 'laws of art' was precisely what the formalists tried to do. The fact that they never went further was due to political circumstances, as previously Marx and Engels were unable to get to the formal issues. Whatever the flaws, it must be repeated that the discussions by Marxists and formalists in the twenties in Russia furthered Marxist literary theory tremendously. Without this development the second major Marxist debate between Lukács and Brecht would not have been as fruitful since Brecht, as Trotsky before him, saw some positive elements in modernist/formalist modes of writing. Lukács begins with Marxist writings which he treats catechistically. Brecht starts out with some of the left wing formalists (due to his own attachment to expressionism and other modernist modes of writing) such as Tretjakov and Boris Arvatov.[26] Brecht is basically able, via formalist insights, to advance Marxist aesthetics while Lukács, in his vehement objection to formalism which he equated with modernism, refuses to take even Brecht seriously and often reduces Marxist literary theory to a petrified and rather undialectical theory. The aesthetics that they develop are basically a static aesthetics of reflection (Lukács) versus a dynamic aesthetics of social commitment (Brecht).

The general literary canon of Georg Lukács is by now relatively well known. His basic concept of realism or 'great' and 'critical realism' goes back to the previously quoted definitions of Engels. His thorough understanding of the past, without bothering about contemporary literary phenomena (including Brecht's own writings which Lukács misunderstood to the degree that he saw in the epic theatre a continuation of Aristotelian theatre) made it impossible for him to come to terms with expressionism, futurism, Russian formalism, and what he himself termed 'modernism'. Attacking the entire line of development from romanticism to naturalism, expressionism, and 'wrong' socialist realism (while defending the healthy Goethian line of classicism via critical realism to a not yet existing socialist realism based on the classical models), he published in January 1934, an essay in *Internationale Literatur* entitled 'Größe und Verfall des Expressionismus'. Since Brecht had started out as an expressionist in the 1920s he came immediately to the defense of expressionism backed up by the philosopher Ernst Bloch. But Lukács was not willing to stop debating and he published two years later his perhaps richest and certainly most seminal essay of the period, 'Erzählen oder Beschreiben' ('To Narrate or to Describe'). The either/or fallacy from that point on was to be characteristic of Lukács' polemicism. The conjunction 'and' drops out of his writings and we are faced with 'description' (negative) or 'narration' (epic, realistic, positive), 'reportage' or 'fictional representation', later on 'existentialism of Marxism' to which Sartre answered brilliantly in his 'Existentialism and Marxism' until the fallacy reaches its full dead end in the essay 'Franz Kafka or Thomas Mann':

> Between these methods, between Franz Kafka and Thomas Mann, the contemporary bourgeois writer will have to choose.[28]

The Kafka model (according to Lukács' misconception) is identical with descriptive detail ('realism of detail negates the reality described'), formalism, schematism, chaos, modernism, and *Angst*. The Thomas Mann model, based largely on an admittedly thorough analysis of *Dr Faustus*, is presented as the model for all socialist writers. This leads Lukács to the absurd position that supports the concept of a 'slow' revolution after first strengthening bourgeois concepts which can easily be seen in the statement:

> Mann envisages the perspective of socialism without abandoning the position of a bourgeois, and without attempting to portray the newly emergent socialist societies or even the forces working towards their establishment.[29]

Brecht, in his typical way of rhetorical overstatement to drive his point home, no longer bothered to analyse this kind of Marxist model-building in the name of Marx but merely jotted down:

> Don't ask me to try to understand *The Magic Mountain* (I am singling Mann out only because he is the epitome of the parvenu bourgeois producer, the author of artificial, pointless, useless books). I frankly confess that I would be willing to make financial sacrifices if it would enable me to prevent the publication of certain books.[30]

Brecht's works and position by now are at least as equally well known as Lukács' and it is a hopeful sign that Brecht has been more and more frequently referred to in African literature and criticism. He has been referred to in various speeches by Soyinka who, however, seems to consider the pre-Marxist Brecht of the *Three Penny Opera* more important that the polemical and radical Brecht. But in his speech on 'Modern Negro-African Theater' he has also referred to *Arturo Ui* and to *Galileo Galilei*. Alioum Fantouré's *Le Cercle des Tropiques* (1972) is significantly indebted to the Brecht poem 'Burial of the Trouble-Maker in a Zinc Coffin'; the Cameroonian playwright Alexandre Kuma N'dumbe has been influenced by Brecht; and Ngugi wa Thiong'o quotes, in an essay in *Writers in Politics*, Brecht's famous poem 'A Worker reads History' in connection with his work *Petals of Blood*.[31] These are significant indicators not for Eurocentric influence studies but for a significant new direction and understanding of the way forward to a truly international African aesthetics. Third World writers and critics can learn a great deal from Brecht, as opposed to Lukács, because he was one of the first Marxist writers to bring modernism and realism into a fruitful dialectical relationship.

After reading the various anti-modernist essays by Lukács, Brecht wrote 'The formalist in me is at work.'[32] The formalist in him made it possible to see in Lukács' Marxist aesthetics signs of formalism and doom. Brecht wrote four significant essays against Lukács: 'The Essays of Georg Lukács', 'On the Formalist Character of the Theory of Realism', 'Remarks on an Essay', and 'Popularity and Realism'. What he objected to in Lukács was:

> It is the element of capitulation, of withdrawal, of utopian idealism which still lurks in Lukács' essays ... It gives the impression that what concerns him is enjoyment alone, not struggle, a way of escape, rather than a march forward.[33]

While Lukács adhered to aesthetic notions of enjoyment, Brecht based his theory and practice on Marx's eleventh thesis on Feuerbach (without giving up enjoyment) which argued that the philosophers have only interpreted the world while the true task is to change the world. Literature as a 'change-oriented activity'[34] from that point on became the centre of Marxist aesthetics, quite a development from Marx' and Engels' praise for authors who hide their views. From a Brechtian perspective literature has to become outspoken, militant, committed and should use whatever is useful, modernist and/or realist, experimentation or its opposite, if it is successful in promoting the struggle for change. Formalism then is not necessarily bad, but a specific kind of formalism is unwarranted. 'Formalism on the one side – contentism on the other. That is surely too primitive and metaphysical.'[35] We have to understand what formalism is exactly, and we will not learn this from literature alone. We have to learn to ask different questions and step outside of literature:

> We have to look aside from literature for a moment and descend into 'everyday life'. What is formalism there? Let us take the expression: 'Formally he is right'. That means that actually he is not right, but he is right according to the form of things and only according to the form. Or: 'Formally the task is solved' means that actually it is not solved. Or: 'I did it to respect the forms'. That means that what I did is not very important; I do what I want, but I preserve outward forms and in this way I can best do what I want to do. When I read that the autarky of the Third Reich is perfect on paper, then I know that this is a case of political formalism. National Socialism is socialism in form – another case of political formalism.[36]

The best example of what we can learn from formalism is Brecht's own adoptation of Shklovsky's autonomous strange-making device (*priem ostranenija*) into the V-Effekt (*Verfremdungseffekt*, strange-making effect). The English translation into 'alienation effect' is an obvious misnomer since Brecht's entire notion of writing was not based on alienating the spectator – the spectator has already been alienated. The task is to de-alienate him and society. Brecht was never a pure formalist, he did not believe, for instance, in the 'self-development' of literature as it was postulated by many of the Russian formalists (e.g. Boris Eikhenbaum). He was fully aware that 'Literature, to be understood, must be considered in its development, by which I do not mean self-development.'[37] But we also have to know why we want to understand literature and what we want to understand when we claim to understand literature. The task is always, according to Brecht, to master reality: 'We shall use every means, old and new, tried and untried, derived from art and elsewhere, to render reality to men in a form they can master . . .'[38] Since reality constantly changes, in order to represent it the modes of representation must also change. This demands not an aesthetic concept of realism nor a concept of formalism and/or modernism, but a political concept of realism 'sovereign over all conventions'.[39] In this sense Brecht arrived at a definition of realism which fully bears upon the African scene:

> Realistic means: discovering the causal complexes of society/ unmasking the prevailing view of things as the view of those who rule it/ writing from the standpoint of the class which offers the broadest solutions for the pressing difficulties in which human society is caught/emphasizing the element of development/ making possible the concrete, and making possible abstractions from it.

To this we have to add his definition of 'popularity' from the same text:

> Popular means: intelligible to the broad masses, adopting and enriching their forms of expression/ assuming their standpoint, confirming and correcting it/ representing the most progressive section of the people so that it can assume leadership, and therefore intelligible to other sections of the people as well/ relating to traditions and developing them/ communicating to that portion of the people which strives for leadership the achievements of the section that at present rules the nation.[40]

The third Marxist debate is less significant for African literature and criticism, but it shows the tremendous influence of Brecht's thinking over the domination of the literary landscape by Lukács. Kafka had been literally banned in East European countries due to what Lukács saw as his modernism and therefore decadence. In the 1960s – during the Kafka symposium at Prague – Goldstücker (a Kafka scholar), the Austrian Marxist Ernst Fischer, Roger Garaudy, Jean Paul Sartre and others defended Kafka. They saw in his writings an accurate mirror of the society in which he lived. Since then – without making Kafka a radical – new light has been shed on Kafka scholarship and many of the problems posed by modernism (and even Lukács, before he died, had to admit that Kafka was a realist). That this could have occured is largely due to Brecht.[41]

3

Since the 1960s many of the issues discussed in the various Marxist debates have been systematized and unfortunately frequently complexified. Scholarship (again largely due to the increasingly complex mode of dominant bourgeois criticism) took over where populous issues had reached larger masses before. The debates were carried on largely in the institutions of higher learning. In France, structuralism (its non-genetic as well as its genetic Goldmannian version) triumphed. In England where, aside from Christopher Caudwell and Raymond Williams, little was known about German Marxism (which may explain why English-speaking African countries have come so late to these debates), Terry Eagleton introduced German Marxist criticism. In the United States, where radical criticism had been very strong during the 1930s, Fredric Jameson bypassed his own radical tradition and turned to France and Germany for critical models. At the present time post-structuralism, Tel Quelism and de-constructionism are discussed by Marxists throughout Western Europe and the United States. Relevant as all these discussions are, the issues of the 1930s have become academicized and de-popularized. A certain élitism can be observed which irritates some of the more populist oriented Marxist critics. Michael Ryan formulated this irritation quite honestly when he stated that: 'For a time, I was worried that deconstruction's critical impact on Marxism would be politically disabling',[42] and to a certain degree it has been. Recent developments try to bring too many contradictory issues together; but nonetheless, the issues which are more competently discussed than in the 1920s and 1930s are still connected with the modernism/realism dialectics.[43]

In Africa literary criticism has developed quite differently. Due to the continent's particular historical development and due to liberationist imperatives, literary criticism has been less concerned with its definitional duties and therefore has allowed outdated European and American modes of criticism to enter. But, more and more this outdated Eurocentric criticism is revised, combated and a truly African Marxist aesthetics is in the making.

The search for a Marxist aesthetics within an African context (the fourth Marxist debate?) is what we are striving towards in the following pages. The main tendencies of post-independence African criticism are:

Larsonist cristics
Larsony[44] as Ayi Kwei Armah has called this phenomenon of European critics who write on African literature and constantly compare it to European literature. Critics such as Larson, Palmer, Roscoe and others.

African Euro-centric critics
African critics who have been trained in Europe and largely apply European criteria to African literature such as Irele, Echeruo, and even such structuralists as Sunday O. Anozic and contributors to the journal The Conch.

Bolekaja critics
Bolekaja[45] critics such as Chinweizu et al. who rebel against obscurantism and Eurocentrism in African

literature and criticism and demand an autonomous African aesthetics based on Africa's orature. The *Ogunists* call them *Tarzanists*.

Ogunist critics

Pseudo-traditionalists such as Soyinka and his followers who claim that they are traditionalists but
they are basically individualists writing in the tradition of European modernism. They tend to call
the polemical *Bolekaja* critics pseudo-traditionalists
or *Tarzanists* while defending mythopeic/Euro-
centric formalist and neo-Negritudinist modes of
writing under the mask of *Ogunism*.

Marxist critics

Marxist critics, such as Onoge, Kamenju, and others (called "radical chic-ists" by Soyinka) look at
literature's function in society and demand social
change and amelioration.

There is one addition to this, a type of criticism that we do not want at this
point to label, a criticism practised by writers who do not claim to be Marxist but who are aware of and interested in Marxism and generally arrive
at rather objective observations such as the essays by Lewis Nkosi, Peter
Nazareth and others. How all of these groups of critics have been involved
in a long and continuous debate since independence (and before), and how
a critical radical school has been formed as a result of this debate shall now
be discussed. The debate started in the early 1960s with Fanon's *The
Wretched of the Earth*, a classic for progressive Third World thinking. In Africa south of the Sahara it had been anticipated by the the great novel of
Sembène Ousmane, *God's Bits of Wood*, a masterpiece of realism cum modernism, manifesting solidarity with the oppressed and a remarkable use of
traditional techniques combined with modernistic modes of writing.

Had criticism in Africa followed Abiola Irele's demand we would have
had a basis for a radical aesthetics already in the early 1960s. But African
critics obviously were more concerned with Africaneity, specificity, literariness. There are exceptions, of course, but the advice of these critics has
not been heeded. We can single out Lewis Nkosi's *Home and Exile*, Ngugi
wa Thiong'o's *Homecoming*, Peter Nazareth's *Literature and Society in Modern
Africa* (later republished as *An African View of Literature*), Amilcar Cabral's
Return to the Source, and essays by Grant Kamenju and Omafume F. Onoge.
Part of the debate was the rectifying view of Negritude, representing a clear
bifurcation between vacuous formalism (the main stream Negritudinists)
and the more commited Negritudinists such as David Diop, who according
to Lewis Nkosi was 'from the beginning the most radical, the most aggre-
sively direct and frankly internationalist in his concerns, who also thought
it necessary to caution against a poetry which was merely commited to the
'revival of the great African myths".'[46] But in the meantime Negritude is
seen for what it really has been: non-progressive. New perspectives on the
embattled concept of Negritude have given way to new concepts which are
of a politically more relevant nature and which do not hide the disappointment in Negritude's social mission (which virtually was absent) while not

denying the formalist achievement of the 'movement'. The objective facts of the situation have become clear since the work of Irele, Nkosi and others. With a better grasp on the objective facts of Negritude, a revision is now taking place with regard to the entire development of post-independence literature in Africa. The second most important debate in this attempt to correct mythic concepts is the so-called Transition debate which involved an essay by Chinweizu, Onwuchekwa Jemie and Ihechukwu Madubuike, collective effort, 'Towards the Decolonization of African Literature', which was printed in the journal *Okike* and then reprinted in the Soyinka journal *Transition* with Soyinka's own riposte over-rhetorically entitled 'Neo- Tarzanism: The Poetics of Pseudo-Tradition'. This crossing of swords of two opposing views of tradition versus commitment, modernism versus populism, while fought largely with the weapons of rhetoric instead of the weapons of criticism, historically is a major debate in the development of a truly radical aesthetics in Africa. Although frequently naive in both their assumptions, provokers and respondent opened the doors to a more fruitful debate which is still on-going and which can be, it seems to me, more fruitful if some of the problems discussed here are taken into consideration. Chinweizu's essay 'Towards the Decolonization of African Literature' was an early, albeit angry attempt to caution against formalism/modernism and its dangerous implications for African literature and criticism. It was by no means Marxist in orientation and was unaware of the considerably more sturdy and contemporary essay by Onoge. While observing characteristics in the works of the Ibadan/Nsukka poets ('obscurantist cesspool', 'plethora of imported imagery', 'addiction to archaisms') the three critics' metaphors betray a rhetorical animosity which requires further analysis since their statements are not far from pamphleteering. Their model of an ethnically based traditionalism (Okot p'Bitek's *Song of Lawino* is cited in this context) could lead, and indeed has led, to the same formalism that Brecht had attacked already in Lukács. Wole Soyinka, then, has treated this simplified quasi-Marxist position in his *Transition* article under the provocative title 'Neo-Tarzanism'. While it appeared to be easy game for Soyinka to dismantle the unsound position of the Troika critics, he did so largely with a new set of metaphors; and with metaphors none of the issues relevant to literature can be solved, least of all the fundamental issue of formalism and Marxism, they can only be deferred. Against his will Soyinka opened up doors for new attacks against him which so far have only demonstrated that his position is at least as unsound as the position of the 'neo-Tarzanists'.

This recent debate strikes me as a continuation of the Lukács-Brecht debate of the 1930s. Lukács attacked Brecht as a formalist/modernist who avoided the proper tradition (i.e. critical realism of the nineteenth century), while Brecht felt justified to call Lukács' model-building formalistic. Brecht, however, avoided the metaphors and the anger which characterize the present debate. The more recent debate between the Troika critics and Wole Soyinka aptly shows that a wrong authenticity based on the ethnic imperative must lead to another formalist dead end. Both Soyinka and the Troika critics work with wrong notions of tradition and with the absence of sound class analysis. None of them has looked at the Marxist tradition. With due respect for the search of a national literature (as an educative tool) it will be patently impossible to arrive at a separate (alias African) aesthetics. With aesthetics as with realism more is at stake than art. In searching for an aesthetics which would be viable for the future, Brecht set an example without giving up completely what had been gained by modernism. So has Neruda in Chile, Cardenal in Nicaragua, Sembène Ousmane in Senegal, and Ngugi wa Thiong'o in Kenya. So has Amiri Baraka/LeRoi Jones in the United States, who at one time was at least as opposed to Euro-American concepts of literature as Soyinka and quickly turned away from Beat literature and post-Eliotic modernism. A comparative study of Amiri Baraka and Wole Soyinka could answer many of the questions presently confronting the African literary scene. Such a study is by no means intended here. Suffice it to say that both writers are heavily indebted to modernism. It has been said that Baraka at one point 'constructs his poetry on, and out of, the ruins of his Eliotic shell'[49]. Both writers work in all three genres, drama, poetry, and the novel (the latter in both cases with lesser success). Both at one point objected to Marxism while thinking of themselves as being politically engaged. Amiri Baraka became an Afro-American nationalist and joined Islam, Soyinka became an Ogunist-traditionalist. While Soyinka remained rather static in his development, however, Baraka has been able to analyse his black constituency as merely siding with the class he is opposed to. He has been able to see that the answers to the problems he faced have very little to do with ethnicity. He has painfully learned to turn away from nationalism and even from Islam and has turned to the study of Marxism-Leninism-Maoism. Similar to Brecht but independent of him, he has arrived at what he has called 'populist modernism', and apparent oxymoronic coinage which upon analysis provides the answer to many literary critical problems of our period. Without any awareness of Brecht, he states in the introduction of his recent collection of political poems, *Hard Facts* (1975):

> . . . We aim at an art that serves the great majority of people, the working masses of people . . . we should try to make a poetry, an art that speaks to, after 1st learning from, those same dynamic working masses. We learn from the omnieyed, multinational mass, the scattered, raw, unsystematized, and even refined, and reorganize, reintensify, dynamize, make gigantic and give back what we have learned . . . To take the popular and combine it with the advanced. Not to compromise, but to synthesize. To raise and to popularize . . . The question of the audience is key, is central to the work. 'For Whom' is the problem as Mao Tse Tung sounded it. For whom does one write, the audience standing there as you compose, to whom, for whom, it is directed.[50]

And when asked about how important the racial perspective is to him – in an interview with Werner Sollers – he could say:

> How important is nationality to perception. Obviously, it adds something to it. It fixes it in a particular matrix. Ultimately, it is just a contributing factor, certainly not the principal factor, by no means.

The question of national oppression of Black people is an important aspect, certainly of everything I have ever done. But now, I see the national question as part of the stranglehold that this particular system has on all life, all nationalities, the majority of working people. Now I can take a view that is not so subjective or chauvinistic. Finally it is a question of how people live, survive, develop. And I see that through a revolutionary process. But the question of Black liberation, what is that related to? You talked about Andy Young as Clay. We've come so far, in that sense. What's good about naming Young, and I hope Carter names a lot – I hope he names Gibson, Labor leaders, Barbara Jordan – because what that means is that it cuts away the illusion. In a little while, we are going to see that it's not going to change a thing. The masses of people are still going to suffer from it. But it cuts away the illusion from race. People will see that it's the whole *method* of doing things, whether it's got Black faces in it or white faces in it, that has to be altered, destroyed. Something else has to come in its place.

Q. But as long as there are no 'Black faces' in office, this is hard to recognize?

A. Right. That's why Andy Young makes the system measurably stronger. But dialectically, he weakens it. Stronger, because they can then say, look, here is a man who was a civil rights leader, who fought in the streets, and is now 'in charge of the United Nations', of all our policies dealing with South Africa. On the other hand, he weakens it because the illusion is destroyed that the system would change if Blacks were only in it.[51]

Aesthetics, as Baraka has learned, is something which goes beyond nationalism and interpretation of individual works. So is realism. So are modernism and populism. In a final analysis it is an ideological problem and not a literary problem. Brecht offers us an appropriate anecdote of his own experience with workers that illustrates this point:

> I shall never forget how a worker looked at me when I replied to his suggestion that I should add something else to a chorus about the Soviet Union (it has to go in – otherwise what's the point?), that it would destroy the artistic form. He put his head on one side and smiled. A whole area of aesthetics collapsed because of his polite smile.[52]

The collapse of precisely this kind of aesthetics can be felt in African writers such as Ngugi, Sembène Ousmane, Alex La Guma. They are Africa's true 'populist modernists'. The increasing difficulty and search for a personal solution of Soyinka and others must slow down a development which is pertinent to the African (and not only African) situation. The serious consideration of the African populist-modernist tradition in the light of the Marxist literary tradition will permit the critic to sharpen 'the weapons of criticism'.[53] 'We have,' someone suggested, 'in modernism a shift from life

15

to art.' The modernist, wherever his geographical location, is 'often concerned with mystical or occult experience'. We have, then, in post-modernism, a shift from art to life (with still an overemphasis on aesthetics, more on the production than on the final product). But we seem to have in 'populist modernism' not so much a rejection of the two main forms of modernism but the incorporation of both, combined with 'critical' (Lukácsian) and 'socialist' (i.e. Brechtian) realism. This gives our new populist modernism a clearly defined teleology: to change the status quo, to improve, to abolish classes, to end exploitation, imperialism, colonialism and neo-colonialism. 'Modernism, i.e. the old kind, in a word, has a profound connection with the transition of the epoch of imperialism.'[54] Modernism is closely connected with reactionary politics.[55] The perception of modernism in Africa is closely linked to neo-colonialism. One cannot be against imperialism and write in the tradition of T. S. Eliot and Ezra Pound. The issue, a Marxist modernist critic has suggested, is 'the problem of establishing the right tone'.[56] But the right tone can only be established with the right ideology. Africaneity alone will not do the job although the debate frequently continues on this ground.

The Transition debate did not end with Soyinka's riposte nor with Soyinka's defense of Ogunism and the Fourth Stage in *Myth, Literature and the African World*. It is an ongoing debate for which the basic framework has merely been charted, largely in the wordy, polemical but bush-clearing attempts by Chinweizu, Onwuchekwa Jemie and Ihechukwu Madubuike. What Soyinka has termed Troika critics and neo-Tarzanism cannot be brushed aside as easily as in 1974. The 1980 publication of the Troika critics' counter-attack on the best known and most influential of the Eurocentric critics and their African followers as well as of writers such as Soyinka and what they call the 'Hopkins disease' (another term for modernism) deserves our attention. The book provides one of the best analyses of African orature linked with the best demolition job of Eurocentric critics of African literature. But its basic aim is Africaneity. While neither Marx nor any later Marxist is referred to (largely due to the intended and irritating Africaneity which is looked for) radical works such as Ngugi's *Petals of Blood* or *Writers in Politics* remain unmentioned. But the book has a polemical honesty rare in recent discussions of literature:

> We hope that the positions we have taken will provoke efforts, whether out of agreement or flat disagreement, to investigate African literature and its traditions, and to formulate critical canons and procedures adequate for our times. Let controversy rage; may it stimulate creative discussion.[57]

Chinweizu's 'Africocentric liberationist perspective' is a harsh attack on modernism and Soyinka. Modernism is seen as leading to the same dead end as Lukács had suggested. But the view of tradition has sharply changed. Soyinka who attacked their traditionalism turns out to be a pseudo-traditionalist in a way that Lukács' attack of formalism made him, in the eyes of Brecht, a formalist. Soyinka is seen as the 'pointman and demolition expert' in the British campaign to slow down and lead astray any active nationalist consciousness in the literatures of their African colonies and neo-colonies.[58]

While Chinweizu's criticism appears at first to be more radical than Brecht's in its demands, it finally turns out to be quite conservative and brings back the wrong notion of Africaneity into the debate. A more balanced view of African literary developments can be found in Lewis Nkosi's appropriately titled *Tasks and Masks* which clearly sees the priorities for African literature as the title indicates (tasks = change, masks = form, mimesis). Without claiming to be a Marxist, Nkosi is aware of recent developments in Marxist literary scholarship citing Althusser and Macherey, although he may be wrong in calling Lukács the arch-priest of 'socialist realism'. He never refers to Brecht directly and is less enthusiastic about Ngugi's *Petals of Blood* as one would expect from a critic so keen in resetting the priorities from masks to tasks, from mythopoeia and the exotic to commitment and change. Nkosi nevertheless corrects our view of Negritude, gives us a convincing summary of South African literature rooted in commitment and protest, and generally points out the direction for a class-oriented progressive criticism. Often this is not theoretically stated but implicit as in his description of the South African D. M. Zwelonke's novel *Robben Island*:

> Zwelonke shows us how extreme anguish can be turned into viable art in which aesthetic effect has no autonomous claim on our response separate from the claims of truth.[59]

And concerning the continuous centerpiece of the debate, Wole Soyinka, Lewis Nkosi, who is full of praise for Soyinka's dramatic strength, comes very close to a Marxist analysis when he dialectically formulates the issue at hand:

> This undoubtedly is Soyinka's greatest strength as a writer; his relentless attack on the tragic abuse of power by the present ruling élites in Africa; but important as this criticism is, it is not mounted from any radical standpoint; on the contrary, its symbiotic alliance with the present sources of power becomes clearer with each reading of Soyinka's fiction and other important works. For Soyinka never questions the whole social and economic edifice upon which rests the power of the present ruling classes; he complains only of the misuse of that power. His attack on the ruling élites is not based on any demand for radical transformation of African society; indeed, his social criticism is attached to the same modes of thought as those Soyinka attacks. What Soyinka wishes to see is a replacement of a group of vulgar philistines with a more polished, more discriminating group of young pretenders.[60]

Underneath such statements by Nkosi is a very clear basis for an African aesthetics, a Brechtian basis: facts, history, class-consciousness, radical transformation of African society, the question of for whom?/against whom? This claim for factuality and objectivity, this urgent sense of the real tasks of literature are what bind all the new Marxist scholars of literature in Africa together. They all write against what Nkosi has termed 'the kola-nut school of writing' with its 'inevitable apparatuses of African fetish priests and "tribal" gods'.[61] A number of young critics of the so-called Ibadan-Ife Group continue this new quest for ethics, facts, and internationalism. Since the mid-1970s, in particular since the Ibadan symposium in 1977, a new critical voice is finally heard in Africa. Darah, Onoge, Jeyifo and others all share in the collective formation of this new African criticism. They are the new Brechtians, class-oriented, change demanding, socially conscious. Theirs is a criticism that tries to speak to, after first learning from the dynamic working masses, a criticism which embraces combative realism without giving up what can be learned from modernism, a criticism which discovers the causal complexes of African society and which unmasks the prevailing view of things as the view of those in power who are the functionaries of superpowers. Workshops on radical perspectives on African literature and society continue. In the future it will become increasingly difficult to brush the new Marxist critics away with the metaphor of 'radical chic-ism'. Their criticism has come of age. Their poetics is a truly internationalist Third World poetics. It opposes bourgeois universalism. And it sees nationalism and ethnicity as what they are: transitions on the way to the aesthetics of the future: ethics. The Fourth Debate shall help to make this transition a reality.

Notes

1 Ezekiel Mphalele, 'The Function of Literature at the Present Time: The Ethnic Imperative', *Transition* 45, 9 (1974), pp. 47–53.

2 See in particular Wole Soyinka, 'The Fourth Stage (Through the Mysteries of Ogun to the Origin of Yoruba Tragedy)' in *Myth, Literature and the African World*, Cambridge University Press, 1976.

3 Subtitle of G. C. M. Mutiso's *Socio-Political Thought in African Literature*, Macmillan, London, 1974. Mutiso opens his study with a reference to this concept: 'Literally, *weusi* means blackness. Many in Africa have yearned for a black ideal as the antithesis to colonial bondage.' p. ix.

4 Wole Soyinka, *Ogun Abibimañ*, Rex Collings, Ibadan, London, 1976. According to Soyinka the Akan word *abibimañ* means 'The Black Nation; the land of the Black Peoples; the Black World; that which pertains to, the matter, the affair of, Black Peoples.' p. 23.

5 Chinweizu, Onwuchekwa Jemie and Ihechukwu Madubuike, *Towards the Decolonization of African Literature*, Vol. I, African Fiction and Poetry and their Critics, Fourth Dimension Publishing Co., Enugu, Nigeria, 1980, p. 145. In the following to be cited as Chinweizu, *Decolonization*.

6 See Robert Pring-Mill's introduction to Ernesto Cardenal, *Zero Hour and other Documentary Poems*, New Directions, New York, 1980, p. ix.

7 See Walter Benjamin, *Das Kunstwerk im Zeitalter seiner technischen Reproduzierbarkeit*, Suhrkamp, Frankfurt, 1963. The English text can be found in Walter Benjamin, *Illuminations* (ed. Hannah Arendt), Harcourt, Brace and World, New York, 1955.

8 Stefan Morawski, *Inquiries into the Fundamentals of Aesthetics*, MIT Press, Cambridge, Massachusetts, 1974.

9 Lee Baxandall, Stefan Morawski (eds), *Marx and Engels on Literature and Art*, Telos Press, St. Louis/Milwaukee, 1973, p. 71. In the following cited as MELA.

10 See Dennis Duerden, 'Art and Technological Progress', *Transition* 45. Relevant for this point is, obviously, Ernst Fischer, *The Necessity of Art, A Marxist Approach*, Penguin, New York, 1963.

11 Lewis Nkosi, *Tasks and Masks: Themes and Styles of African Literature*, Longman, London, 1981, p. 181.

12 Grant Kamenju, 'Black Aesthetics and Pan-African Emancipation', in Andrew Gurr and Pio Zirimu (eds), *Black Aesthetics*. Papers from a colloquium held at the University of Nairobi, June 1971, East African Literature Bureau, Nairobi, Kampala, Dar es Salaam, 1973, p. 177.

13 D. S. Izevbaye, 'The State of Criticism in African Literature', in *African Literature Today*, No. 7, Focus on Criticism, edited by Eldred Durosimi Jones, Heinemann, London, 1975, p. 16.

14 D. S. Izevbaye, 'Criticism and Literature in Africa', in Christopher Heywood, *Perspectives on African Literature*, Heinemann, London, 1971, p. 25. Unfortunately, Izevbaye singles out the Akan tradition of criticism, i.e. criticism which was largely practised by the producers of literature themselves. A modernist notion of criticism similar to this one has been presented by Ezra Pound. Needless to say, this paper does not agree with the position that only the writer has a right to criticize writers.

15 A few works in the ever increasing Pound criticism have analyzed Pound's connection between a modernist aesthetics and fascism: (1) Eva Hesse, *Ezra Pound. Von Sinn und Wahnsinn*, Kindlers Literarische Portraits, München, 1978; (2) Georg M. Gugelberger, 'Ideologische Bemerkungen zum Mediavalismus bei Pound', *Mittelalter Rezeption II* (ed. Ulrich Müller), Göppinger Arbeiten zur Germanistik, 1983; (3) William M. Chase, *The Political Identities of Ezra Pound and T. S. Eliot*, Stanford University Press, Stanford, 1973.

16 Walter Benjamin *Illuminations*, p. 244. A major study on modernism and fascism is Fredric Jameson, *Fables of Aggression: Wyndham Lewis, the Modernist as Fascist*, University of California Press, Berkeley and Los Angeles, 1979.

17 Abiola Irele, 'The Criticism of Modern African Literature', in Heywood, *Perspectives*, p. 15.

18 Tony Bennett, *Formalism and Marxism*, Methuen & Co. Ltd., London, 1979, p. 104.

19 Terry Eagleton, *Marxism and Literary Criticism*, University of California Press, Berkeley and Los Angeles, 1976, p. vii.

20 Jacques Derrida as quoted in Michael Ryan, *Marxism and Deconstruction: A Critical Articulation*, Johns Hopkins University Press, Baltimore and London, 1982, p. xv.

21 Wole Soyinka used this Tom Wolfe misnomer in his key-note address to the plenary session of the twenty-second African Studies Association Meeting, Los Angeles, October 1979.

22 *MELA*, p. 115.

23 *Ibid.*, p. 99.

24 *Ibid.*, p. 114.

25 Leon Trotsky, *Literature and Revolution*, University of Michigan Press, Ann Arbor, 1960, p. 178.

26 Some major essays on the Brecht-Lukács debate are: (1) Klaus Völker, 'Brecht und Lukács: Analyse einer Meinungsverschiedenheit',*Kursbuch* 7, 1966, pp. 80–101; (2) Werner Mittenzwei, 'Marxismus und Realismus'. 'Die Brecht-Lukács Debatte', *Das Argument* 46, March 1968, pp. 12–43; (3) the translation of Mittenzwei's article in Gaylord C. Le Roy and Ursula Beitz (eds), *Preserve and Create: Essays in Marxist Literary Criticism*, Humanities Press, New York, pp. 199–230; (4) Eugene Lunn, 'Marxism and Art in the Era of Stalin and Hitler: A comparison of Brecht and Lukács', *New German Critique* 3, 1974, pp. 12–44.

27 The English essay under its new title, 'Idea and Form in Literature' can be found in Georg Lukács' *Marxism and Human Liberation*, Dell, New York, 1973.

28 Georg Lukács, *Realism in Our Time: Literature and the Class Struggle*, Harper & Row, New York, 1964, p. 95.

29 *Ibid., p. 78.*

30 Quoted in Henri Arvon, *Marxist Esthetics*, Cornell University Press, Ithaca, New York, 1973, p. 108.

31 Ngugi wa Thiong'o, *Writers in Politics*, Heinemann, London, Ibadan, Nairobi, 1981, p. 97.

32 *Aesthetics and Politics: Debates Between Ernst Bloch, Georg Lukács, Bertolt Brecht, Walter Benjamin, Theodor Adorno*, New Left Books, London, 1977, p. 71.

33 *Ibid.*, p. 69.
34 Fredric Jameson, 'Reflection in Conclusion', *Aesthetics and Politics*, p. 204.
35 *Aesthetics and Politics*, p. 71.
36 *Ibid.*
37 *Ibid.*, p. 74.
38 *Ibid.*, p. 81.
39 *Ibid.*, p. 82.
40 *Ibid.*, p. 82 and p. 81.
41 Aside from the known essays by Benjamin and Adorno on Kafka, the following works are indicative of an increasing Marxist concern for Kafka: Lee Baxandall, 'Kafka as Radical' and Kenneth Hughes, 'The Marxist Debate, 1963' both in Angel Flores (ed.) *The Kafka Debate: New Perspectives for our Time*, Gordon Press, New York, 1977. Also Kenneth Hughes (ed.), *Franz Kafka: An Anthology of Marxist Criticism*, University of New England Press, Hanover, New Hamshire, 1982, and Armand Nivelle, 'Kafka und die marxistische Literaturgeschichte', in *Beiträge zur Vergleichenden Literaturgeschichte*, Festschrift für Kurt Wais zum 65, Geburtstag, Max Niemeyer, Tübingen 1972, pp. 331–54.
42 Michael Ryan, *Marxism and Deconstruction*, p. xvi.
43 Fredric Jameson in *Aesthetics and Politics*, p. 119.
44 Ayi Kwei Armah, 'Larsony: Fiction as Criticism of Fiction', *First World* 1, 2, 1977, pp. 50–5. This essay is extensively cited in Chinweizu, *Decolonization*.
45 In Chinweizu's *Decolonization* we read: 'we are *bolekaja* critics' defined as 'Come down let's fight!–a term applied in Western Nigeria to passenger lorries ('mammy wagons') from the outrageous behavior of their touts.'Chinweizu *et al.* see themselves consciously as such touts, 'administering a timely and healthy dose of much needed public ridicule to the reams of pompous nonsense which has been floating out of the stale, sterile, stifling covens of academia and smothering the sprouting vitality of Africa's literary landscape.' p. xiv.
46 Lewis Nkosi, *Tasks and Masks*, p. 138.
47 First in *Okike* 6, 1974, pp. 11–27, then reprinted by Soyinka with his riposte in *Transition* 48, 1975, under the titles 'Towards the Decolonization of African Literature', and 'Neo-Tarzanism: The Poetics of Pseudo-Traditionalism' respectively. Another defense of Ogunism is Donatus Nwoga, 'Obscurity and Commitment in Modern African Poetry', *African Literature Today* 6, 1974, pp. 26–45.
48 Omafume F. Onoge, 'The Crisis of Consciousness in Modern African Literature: A Survey', *Canadian Journal of African Studies* 8, 2, 1974, and reprinted in this collection of essays.
49 Werner Sollors, *Amiri Baraka/LeRoi Jones: The Quest for a 'Populist Modernism'*, Columbia University Press, New York, 1978, p. 39.
50 *Selected Poetry of Amiri Baraka/Leroi Jones*, William Morrow, New York, 1979, p. 236.
51 Sollors, *Amiri Baraka*, pp. 258–9.
52 *Aesthetics and Politics*, p. 84.
53 Title of Norman Rudich, *Weapons of Criticism: Marxism in America and the Literary Tradition*, Ramparts Press, Palo Alto, California, 1976. Obviously the concept is Marx's who used it in his 'Towards the Critique of Hegel's Philosophy of Law', where we read the following frequently cited lines: 'The weapons of criticism obviously cannot replace the criticism of weapons. Material force must be overthrown by material force. But theory also becomes a material force once it has gripped the masses.'
54 The last three quotations are from Gaylord LeRoy and Ursula Beitz, 'The Marxist Approach to Modernism', *Journal of Modern Literature* III, 5, July 1974, p. 1158.
55 See William M. Chase, 'The Political Identities of Ezra Pound and T. S. Eliot', and Tom Gibbons, 'Modernism and Reactionary Politics', *Journal of Modern Literature* III, 5, July 1974.
56 Gaylord LeRoy, Ursula Beitz, 'The Marxist Approach to Modernism', p. 1158.
57 Chinweizu, *Decolonization*, p. xiii.
58 *Ibid.*, p. 208.
59 Nkosi, *Tasks and Masks*, p. 103.
60 *Ibid.*, p. 68.
61 *Ibid.*, p. 173.

CHAPTER TWO

THE CRISIS OF CONSCIOUSNESS IN MODERN AFRICAN LITERATURE:
A survey (1974)

Omafume F. Onoge

INTRODUCTION

> What is Africa to me
> Copper sun or scarlet sea
> Jungle star or jungle track
> Strong black men or regal black
> Women from whose loins I sprang
> When birds of Eden sang?
> One three centuries removed
> From the scenes his father told
> Spring grove, cinnamon tree
> What is Africa to me?

Countee Cullen, *Heritage*[1]

Decades after the sensitive Afro-American poet, Countee Cullen, posed this question about the meaning and significance of the African heritage, the answer still remains unsettled in African literature. African writers and critics still have not provided us with a consensual view about the ways in which the African experience is to be conceptualized retrospectively or prospectively. On the contrary, there is a host of diverse opinions often marked by contradictory thrusts to justify our title, *the crisis of consciousness*.

African writers and critics are themselves aware of this crisis. For, ever since the definitional debate about what constitutes African literature was shelved, albeit unresolved, the perspective which should govern the relationship between the writer and his African experience has become the dominant theme in conference discussions of the literature. The number of anthologies published on this subject is increasing rapidly.[2] Usually, African writers have phrased the problem under the conceptual rubric of 'role', 'responsibility' or 'commitment' of the writer to his society. While critics, African and foreign, have generally posed it in terms of the validity of the *sociological* character of the contents of the bulk of the literature.

Although we suggest a crisis, the situation is not one of unrelieved

21

chaos. The differing opinions, both contradictory and complementary, also fall into certain classifiable patterns. It is the mapping of these broad patterns, orientations or consciousness that is the central subject of this paper. Moreover, it is the conscious reflections of the writers, contained in their *theoretical* statements about the norms that should inform their relationship with society, rather than their novels, plays and poems, that will constitute our primary data source in this paper.

The patterns of orientations which we shall outline have undoubtedly received *some* of their determination from the individual psychologies of the writers. However, a large part of their *consciousness has* been a result of sociological conditioning. By this we mean that the socio-political visions of the artists have been set in motion by dialectical developments within the political economy of Africa, as well as between Africa and the world. (What this means is that in the near future, if not now, it should be possible to account coherently for the *growth* of our writers' consciousness from a dialectical framework. A few decades hence, the cumulative growth of consciousness, via dialectical shifts, should become quite clear. The appearance of random innovation or mutation of idea, which tends to dominate the current scene, should be shown to be just *appearance*.)

THE SOCIOLOGICAL BACKGROUND

In fact, we cannot ignore these sociological forces, if we have to maintain any modicum of fidelity to the historic origins of modern African literature. For modern African literature was born in a hostile milieu. A milieu of colonial conquest where a virulent capitalism *on the march* had begun to deform, in fundamental ways, pre-colonial African social relationships and values associated with the 'village mode of production'.[3] Following closely on the heels of the slave trade, colonialism completed the alienation of the African in ways much graver than that endured by the European proletariat. We were reduced, as Fanon was to sum up this experience, to *The Wretched of the Earth*.

To rationalize this holocaust, European 'men of culture' assured their bourgeois classes, in a torrent of 'creative' literature, that the holocaust was a necessary 'mission of civilization'. It was chronicled as a heroic effort by Europe to humanize the 'benighted' African. They assured their imperial colleagues that there was no anthropological parity, no common psychic unity, between the African and the European. On the contrary, the African was the savage *id*, the 'dark negation' of European egos and superegos. In their *The Africa That Never Was*, an important study of four centuries of British imaginative writing on Africa, the two anthropologists, Jablow and Hammond, concluded with this paragraph:

> Four centuries of writing about Africa have produced a literature which describes not Africa but the British response to it. The literature persistently recounts the fantasy of the Englishman in confrontation with Africa. As in a morality play, the British and the Africans are the exemplars of civilization and savagery, respectively. In the Victorian version civilization equalled the positive good and savagery

its abhorrent negation. Modern writers often reverse the equation as an expression of their uncertainties.

Whether confident or doubtful, the writers describe Africa in the same conventions. The image of Africa remains the negative reflection, the shadow, of the British self-image.[4]

There was never a doubt in the minds of those who were later to launch modern African literature with the proclamation of Negritude[5] that European literature on the colonial theme was a classic case of art committed to the service of imperialism. Later schools of African writers recognized this truth as well. For example, Chinua Achebe, a non-Negritude *realist* writer, was himself inspired by this truth in his encounter with Joyce Cary's travesty, *Mister Johnson*. In a televised interview with Lewis Nkosi and Wole Soyinka in 1964, Achebe stated that he decided to become a writer in order to correct the distortions of the African past which Joyce Cary's works had epitomized.[6] In another essay, Achebe stated this motivation in the following memorable terms

> I would be quite satisfied if my novels (especially the ones I set in the past) did no more than teach my readers that their past – with all its imperfections – was not one long night of savagery from which the first Europeans acting on God's behalf delivered them. Perhaps what I write is applied art as distinct from pure. But who cares? Art is important but so is education of the kind I have in mind. And I don't see that the two need be mutually exclusive.[7]

To repeat ourselves, the point we have tried to underscore in the foregoing is that modern African literature was conditioned sociologically by the colonial milieu. The artists were fully aware of this fact. From the very beginning, the literature could not but be *reactive*. It was a literature using the 'weapons of words' for the *légitime défense*[8] of the African heritage. The consciousness which dominated this reaction was one of African *affirmation*.

THE AFFIRMATIVE CONSCIOUSNESS

The affirmative consciousness which typified Negritude, contained two tendencies right from the inception of the movement. These two tendencies which, initially, were merely divergent, are today quite opposed. They are the *revolutionary affirmation* associated with Césaire, and the *mystical affirmation* associated with Senghor. It is the failure to factor out these two separate strands that is mostly responsible for the monolithic conception of Negritude. A consequence of this is an undifferentiating acceptance or rejection of the Negritude movement by commentators since Sartre celebrated it in his *Orphée Noir*. For example, the movement in its entirety has been hailed either as the 'intellectual origins of the African revolution' (Kesteloot) or indicted as irrelevant 'escapist narcissism' (Soyinka and others).[9]

Revolutionary affirmation

When Césaire coined the concept of Negritude in his proclamation, *Return to My Native Land*, in 1939, the dialectic triad which informed his vision could be summarized as follows: *thesis* (sovereignty, harmony and glory of pre-colonial Africa), *antithesis* (colonial alienation, political, economic and cultural oppression because of colonialism), *synthesis* (acceptance of pre-colonial heritage, removal of colonialism). Denying any further legitimacy to the prevailing ideological charters of colonial constrictions and cultural arrogance, Césaire declared:

> Heia for those who have never invented
>   anything
> those who never explored anything
> those who never tamed anything
> those who give themselves up to the essence
>   of all things
> ignorant of surfaces but struck by the movement
>   of all things
> free of the desire to tame but familiar with
>   the play of the world
> truly the eldest sons of the world
> open to all the breadths of the world
> fraternal territory of all breadths
> undrained bed of the waters of the world
> flesh of the flesh of the world pumping with
>   the very movement of the world.[10]

This celebration of the colonial stereotypes of African 'uninventiveness' was not an invitation to a primal dance. It was in fact a signal to open revolt for he had prefaced the *Heias* with the warning:

> my negritude is not a stone,
> nor deafness flung out against the clamour
>   of the day
> my negritude is not a white speck of dead water
> on the dead eye of the earth
> my negritude is neither tower nor cathedral.[11]

As the artist-critic, Eseoghene Barret, has observed, Césaire here uses the 'tone of social declamation to establish a positive attitude towards the life of the black man. In speaking of what Negritude is not, he cleverly suggests deep anger against the culture that rejects his own historic humanity.'[12]

The horrors of colonialism were not restricted to the cultural domain. Colonialism visited concrete disabilities on the black man. The first sections of the poem are in fact devoted to a concrete social census of the ravages of colonialism:

> At the end of the small hours delicately
>   sprouting handles
> for the market: the West Indies, hungry, hail-marked
> with smallpox, blown to bits by alcohol, the

West Indies
shipwrecked in the mud of this bay, wickedly
    shipwrecked
wrecked in the dust of this town.

this disowning town and
its wake of leprosies, consumption, famines:
    its wake of
fears crouching in the ravines, hoisted in the
    trees, dug
out of the soil, rudderless in the sky, piled
    together. This
disowning town and its fumaroles of anguish.

neither the teacher in his classroom
nor the priest at catechism can get a single
    word from
this half-asleep nigger child . . .
for his voice has lost its mind in the marshes
    of hunger
and there is nothing, nothing to be got out of
    the little food-for-nothing
nothing but a hunger which can no longer climb
    the tackle of his voice
a heavy, flabby hunger
a hunger buried in the deepest heart of the
    Hunger of the famished Morne.[13]

The triumph of colonialism is temporary. Its proclaimed victories simultaneously carry their very negation:

Listen to the white world
appallingly weary from its immense effort
the crack of its joints rebelling under the
    hardness of the stars
listen to the proclaimed victories which trumpet
    their defeats
listen to their grandiose alibis (stumbling so
    lamely)
Pity for our conquerors, all-knowing and naive![14]

Césaire's post-colonial prospective dream is offered in the form of a prayer, a ritual invocation of a community of kinsmen pursuing, in peace, creative agrarian tasks of moulding, sowing and harvesting. He volunteers himself to usher in this haven:

All that I would wish is
to answer the universal hunger
the universal thirst

to prescribe at last this unique race free
to produce from its tight intimacies the
    succulence of fruit.[15]

In a 1967 interview with the Haitian poet, René Depestre, Césaire appraised the *Return* – as 'a plunge into the depths. It was a plunge into Africa for me.'[16] Appraising the Negritude movement as a whole, he described it as a 'resistance to the politics of assimilation'[17] and the prevailing European devaluation of the African heritage.

The anti-colonial protest of the *Return* is in no doubt. In the colonial epoch, which, in the inter-war years, still had the illusion of eternity, the act of converting the grand taboo (the African past) into a *positive* heritage, implied an assault on the established order. But the terms on which the assault was to be launched still lacked rigour in the *Return*. After all it was Césaire's first book and he had written it at the early age of twenty six. Moreover, it was a novel plunge without a coherent precedent. Thus, it retained the flavour of a 'plunge into Africa' without any precise descriptions of that Africa. Instead we find assertions, undemonstrated, of an African ethos marked by an openness 'to all the breadths of the world/fraternal territory of all breadths'. Quite apart from the controversial query about the validity of this openness, there remains the more serious question of why this readiness for indiscriminate absorption should be celebrated. Perhaps, in the thirties, openness had to be asserted in the face of European ethnocentrism!

Another example of what we consider the lack of rigour in the mode of the anti-colonial assault is shown in the partial definition of Negritude. After we are told that it is neither inanimate 'nor tower nor cathedral', we get an ambiguous statement of what it is:

it plunges into the red flesh of the soil
it plunges into the blazing flesh of the sky
my negritude riddles with holes the dense
    affliction of its worthy patience.[18]

Question: Will it plunge into the concrete struggle riddling with holes the colonizers?

However, Césaire's revolutionary intentions *vis-à-vis* colonialism are revealed without camouflage in his later theoretical works. Combat by emigration into a pastoral and metaphysical past is completely absent. His activist political temperament – he was a communist – comes across without deflection.

In the *Discourse on Colonialism*, a document which reveals his enormous familiarity with the ethnographic literature of the time, no anthropological report, no matter how liberal, which evades the colonial presence, and engages, instead, in *idealist* interpretations of African culture, receives approval. Thus Césaire saw the intrinsic dishonesty of Reverend Placide Tempels' celebrated discovery of the 'vital forces' of Bantu philosophy. The theme of 'vital forces' which was later to form the cornerstone of Senghor's outlook and other studies of African philosophy, was, for Césaire, another instance of anthropology in the service of imperialism:

> From the Rev. Tempels, missionary and Belgian, his *Bantu Philosophy*, as slimy and fetid as one could wish, but discovered very opportunely, as Hinduism was discovered by others, in order to counteract the 'communistic materialism' which, it seems, threatens to turn Negroes into 'moral vagabonds.'[19]

> Since Bantu thought is ontological, the Bantu only ask for satisfaction of an ontological nature. Decent wages! Comfortable housing! Food! These Bantu are pure spirits . . .[20]

What Césaire demanded from Africanist social scientists, were analyses grounded in *historical materialism*, revealing the exploitive nature of capitalist imperialism and not metaphysical 'conjuring tricks' that were potential opiates crippling the will to revolt. Thus he charged that the 'paternalist' circle of the Tempels, Mannonis, the Gourous were *enemies*, who should henceforth be answerable to the 'violence of revolutionary action'.[21]

We are therefore not surprised by the conclusions Césaire reached in a later essay where he spoke directly to the responsibility of the artist.[22] In this essay, Césaire discussed the artist's function in relation to the anti-colonial struggle. The colonial order, he reminded his audience, represents a breach in the historical continuum of the colonized. The colonizer, in his quest to monopolize all memory, relegates the past of the colonized to the passive realm of *pre-history*, and his intellectual creations to the category of folklore. Henceforth, the colonizer is the sole *creator* while the colonized is confined to the passive role of *consumer*.

In this context the very existence of an African artist represents a threat to the colonial hierarchy. For by his very birth, the artist is recognized as upsetting the creator–consumer partition. This is why black artists like René Maran and Rabearivelo were immediate targets of colonial repression. In consonance with these direct political implications of being a black artist, an anti-colonial consciousness should be informed by the twin realisation: (a) decolonization is not automatic. It is achieved only through mass struggle; the artists' 'legitimacy resides in our wholehearted participation in our peoples' struggle for freedom.'[23] (b) There are *true* and *false* decolonizations. Therefore, 'it is the mission of the black man of culture to prepare good decolonization'[24] – a decolonization without the exploitative *aftermath* of neo-colonialism.

It is this revolutionary affirmative consciousness that we can creditably attribute to Césaire's conception of Negritude. He was not without followers. In the body of African literature in French, usually labelled as Negritude, we can see hints that at certain phases of their artistic careers, the withering satire of Mongo Beti and Ferdinand Oyono, the revolutionary advocacy and optimism of David Diop, *were* in the tradition of Césaire.

Mystical affirmation

The mystical variant of what we have called the 'affirmative consciousness' is quite appropriately associated with Senghor. On the face of it, the Senghorean definition of Negritude as 'the sum total of the values of the civilization of the African world,'[25] is no different from Césaire's definition in the *Return*. Both proffer the same explanation for the origin of the movement as a resistance against the assimilationist programmes of the colonial establishment.

However, before we justify our classification of Senghorean Negritude, perhaps we should place in the forefront our theoretical understanding of the designation of 'mystical'. We rest on Ernst Fischer:

> Mystification and myth-making in the late bourgeois world offer a way of evading social decisions with a reasonably clear conscience. Social conditions and the actual phenomena and conflicts of our times are transposed into timeless unreality, into an eternal, mythical, changeless 'original state of being.' The specific nature of an historical moment is falsified into a general idea of 'being.' The socially conditioned world is presented as a cosmically unconditional one.[26]

In so far as he advocated a return to the African roots, Senghor, like Césaire, implied a rejection of the surrounding colonial reality. The invocation of the past contained the implication of a quest for the reenactment of our pre-colonial sovereignty. However, unlike Césaire, Senghor's Negritude has never strayed beyond the particular *identity* concerns of the culturally 'uprooted' black *petit bourgeois* class that was emerging in the '30s. Senghor offers no insights consistently related to the needs of collective revolution among the African masses for whom problems of psychological identity were irrelevant.

With Senghor, the taming of the revolutionary potential of Negritude becomes complete. Given his preoccupation with the politics of identity, his theory of colonialism is strictly *cultural*. The colonial situation is diagnosed *essentially* as a cultural encounter between Africa and Europe. Senghor, as far as we know, has nowhere advanced a *systematic* critique of the colonial order in terms of economic exploitation. To be sure, he did have occasion to state colonial alienation in the following:

> The proletariat of the nineteenth century was estranged from humanity. The colonized people of the twentieth century, coloured peoples, are estranged even more seriously. To economic alienations, others are added: political, social, and cultural.[27]

But it turns out that this is merely to highlight the *cultural* alienation and to set the justification for his advocacy of an 'African socialism' realisable by fiat rather than through class struggle.

Thus, in Senghor's perception of colonialism, we are left with the impression that all would have been well had the colonialists acknowledged the validity of African values. He did in fact justify this impression by his enthusiastic acceptance of the idealist ethnological speculations of the French anthropologists. Lévy-Bruhl and Tempels, who were for Césaire implacable enemies, were for Senghor valid sources for African cultural reconstruction. Vital forces, religious preoccupations, innate rhythms, congenital emotionality, a-logicality and a non-analytic participation with the physical environment in a perennial orgy of tom toms become the ingredients of Senghor's view of a pre-colonial African essence. This *unhistoric* essence of a data bank of ancestral symbols is his antithesis to the assimilationist colonial reality.[28]

Senghor's poetry is a tireless orchestration of these imputed undynamic primordialities. Thus for example, we find that whereas, for Césaire, it was the genocidal violence of the colonizers that impressed him about the Congo, for Senghor it was the primeval essence of the River Congo. In spite of the pressing heritage of King Leopold's bestiality, Senghor found time for the startling gaiety of 'Oho! Congo Oho!'[29] and the projection of an ultra-romantic past which does not intersect with the brutal colonial reality.

Given the reality of the violent changes consequent upon colonialism, the tenor of Senghor's retrospective explorations is an *undignified* retreat. In fact, in Mbella Sonne Dipoko's view, Senghor and other Negritude romantics have got the 'people's dream of happiness all wrong'. We must quote Dipoko's interesting insight at some length:

> For the masses, happiness was, as it still is, a *prospective* dream. Better conditions of living, higher purchasing power, personal freedom, a share of all the good things of modern life, from industrial products to learning; in short, a longing for better days to come. The prestige which educated Africans have among their people shows how forward-looking the common man is . . .[30] (*emphasis mine*)

When we come to a discussion of Senghor's contemporary views on the responsibility of the African artist, the initial concession of an implied anti-colonialism in the affirmation of cultural nostalgia must now be withdrawn. This is because it does seem that, once the validity of the African heritage had been affirmed, the identity quandary – the status of being a 'cultural half-caste'[31] – is transformed from its original problematic nature into a beneficial and necessary advantage. This transformation of the very *raison d'être* of Negritude, Senghor accomplishes by analogical reference to the *acculturation* theory of civilizations:

> I think all the great civilizations were civilizations that resulted from an interbreeding, objectively speaking – Indian civilization, Greek civilization, French civilization, etc., etc. In my opinion, and objectively, this interbreeding is necessary. It is a result of the contact of civilizations.[32]

Under this law of necessary contact, there are no longer any grounds for the critique of colonialism that has managed to shed the assumptions of cultural arrogance. Thus on the eve of independence, Senghor redefined French imperialism in the following material terms:

> On the economic level France can get along without Black Africa, but she cannot get along without it on the political or cultural plane. France is not Holland. She is a great lady who needs to spread her

radiance over a large family. Reduced to her European dimensions, she would fail in her mission to the world, which is to defend Man: she would lose her soul and *raison d'être*.[33]

Under this law of necessary contact, we must perforce thank France, Britain and the other imperialists for giving birth to the 'cultural half-castes' who, with their double vision, can now play the cultural diplomatic[34] role of building the *Civilization of the Universal!*

Interlude

THE VULTURES

In those days
When civilization kicked us in the face
When holy water slapped our cringing brows
The vultures built in the shadow of their talons
The bloodstained monument of tutelage
In those days
There was painful laughter on the metallic hell of the roads
And the monotonous rhythm of the paternoster
Drowned the howling on the plantations
O the bitter memories of extorted kisses
Of promises broken at the point of a gun
Of foreigners who did not seem human
Who knew all the books but did not know love
But we whose hands fertilize the womb of the earth
In spite of your songs of pride
In spite of the desolate villages of torn Africa
Hope was preserved in us as in a fortress
And from the mines of Swaziland to the factories of Europe
Spring will be reborn under our bright steps.[35]

David Diop

POST NEGRITUDE SITUATION

Negritude has served as the benchmark from which contemporary controversies about the consciousness of the African writer have been debated. Historically, moreover, the vast body of African literature which constituted the immediate data for this on-going debate was produced under a different political climate. It was a literature of transition produced either on the eve of formal independence or during the on-going quest for economic development in the new African states. Predictably, the changed political circumstances carried with it the potential for new aesthetic forms and literary attitudes. This, in fact, has been the case. The literary world of contemporary Africa is marked by the *co-existence* of different types of socio-political consciousness. It is this variety of post-Negritude consciousness that we shall now sketch. Foreign critics as well as Africans have participated and continue to participate in these debates. And, as we have pointed out, there has been a tendency of each of the new schools to refer back to one of the two variants of negritude consciousness.

The writer's role (foreign prescriptions)

In general, foreign critics of a bourgeois persuasion have advocated a literature uncontaminated by a concern for the political problematics of our colonial history. Indeed, in the very first conference on African literature held in Kampala in 1962, an English critic recommended the repudiation of the tradition of Negritude commitment because it was preoccupied with 'public gesture rather than with private and particular observation'. He objected to the concern for the 'situation of the Negro' and advocated, in its stead, 'particular, exploratory statements about the situation of the individual writer at a particular moment in space and time'. The revolutionary poetry of David Diop gave him the opportunity of pressing home the aesthetics of bourgeois individualism:

> The agonies described here were real enough under primitive colonialism . . . But they were not experienced by David Diop *himself*. His passion is genuine enough, but is a *vicarious* passion. He is not leading us into the heart of an immediate situation, but lecturing us from the *public* platform.[36] (*emphasis mine*)

Fortunately, the conference account reports that his speech was greeted with 'irritated protests from the floor'.

In general, however, there is a certain inconsistency, if not dishonesty, in the attitudes of many foreign bourgeois critics. For it often turns out that they are not fundamentally averse to a commitment of a purely cultural anthropological nature. What they reject is a *political* commitment that inveighs against the colonialism of the West. It is therefore not unusual to find these neo-Platonic lovers of a 'pure art' informed solely by the 'private,' 'particular' standpoint, assuming the magisterial role of 'cultural psychoanalyst'. With this new Freudian mantle, they intend to 'restore the confidence to the victim (the African writer) of cultural anxiety' to enable him to report on his culture without ego guilt. Madame Lilyan Kesteloot deserves to be quoted more extensively:

> Once a critic has noticed this inconsistency ('cultural anxiety') he should try to get in touch with the writer concerned, either directly or by inducing him to tell the *truth* as he sees it (even at the risk of giving Europeans a shock) and to describe the problems that disturb him in their full complexity. For instance, one can urge a writer to attack abuses of the dowry system or of polygamy, not the institutions themselves, which have sound roots in African civilization.[37] (Abbia, p. 40; first parenthesis mine)

Hurray for cultural liberalism!

In the less liberal hands of a Dorothy Blair, whose concern is to introduce an anaemic corpus of African literature into her Witwatersrand curriculum, anti-colonial politics is out. The quest for anthropological exotica becomes a hysterical mandate. In her view, an artist for whom the

> expression of his African solidarity is the principal and dominating function of his talent runs the risk of creating such mediocrities of literature ... I shall also say that publishing firms such as *Présence Africaine* who publish such childish stuff in the name of 'protest', in the name of *négritude*, do great harm to the cause of African literature.[38]

In the manner of the museum curator, Dorothy Blair would substitute works that probe

> the metaphysics, the ethics, the philosophy of the black continent with its animism and its telluric sentiment. ... From this results an authentic exoticism ...[39]

Moreover, 'another sort of exoticism and local colour, equally authentic,' which she would encourage is the literature that probes the 'marriage of two cultures'. Reduced to *acculturation*, the colonial formula here becomes 'the picture of the African coming to grips with the problems of his daily life'.[40] Not, it should be emphasized, the portrait of the African coming to grips with the harrowing collective oppression and suppression which define the colonial encounter.

We note, albeit in passing, that the most celebrated of Western critics, the triumvirate of Gerald Moore, Janheinz Jahn and Ulli Beier, are not exempt from the advocacy of bourgeois individualism. A perceptive Russian critic, Y. L. Galperina, has recently pointed out the subtle *ban* on social themes of an anti-imperialist nature in works of these three critics.[41]

These responses of active foreign critics are part of the reality in which the African writer today reflects upon his work. A more fundamental part of the reality, however, derives from the political situation in the new African states. African independence, thus far, has been a record of tragedies. Tragedies in which the African leadership has played a delirious part. Political repression, assassinations and coups, and the pauperisation of the masses. Indeed as Okot p'Bitek phrased it: 'The sharks of Uhuru have eaten their own children.'[42] African independence has thus far meant a transition to neo-colonialism and the consolidation of capitalism. As we have already suggested, the chaotic process of neo-colonialism is mirrored in the contemporary superstructure. Among African writers, three patterns of theoretical apprehension of the disillusioning reality are discernible. We have called them 'art for art's sake', 'critical realism' and 'socialist realism'. (Once again we are leaning heavily on Ernst Fischer's characterization of these concepts in his *The Necessity For Art*.) Our classification is distilled from the many statements made by African writers and critics on the issue of *commitment*.

Art for art's sake
Some African writers, albeit still in the minority, hold the view that the

artist's responsibility is strictly to the perfection of the form of his craft. For, to use Lewis Nkosi's apt phrasing, the artist is a citizen of a 'special kind of republic, the republic of letters'.[43] The artist *qua* artist is committed only to this exclusive élite republic. Any social commitments or duties he assumes, he assumes as a 'man' not as a writer. This position, which is also close to that of John Pepper Clark, argues that social considerations should have no place in the valuation of a writer's works.

Quite often, this subtle distinction between 'man' and 'artist' (even if debatable) is lost sight of by others in the art for art's sake tradition. Often it degenerates into an *extreme* immaculate and exceptionalist conception which exempts the artist from any social duties whatsoever, in any capacity. John Nagenda exudes this extreme glorification of the 'elect' personality of the artist against the common mass:

> I want to suggest that dealing with the individual in society is the primary consideration; as far as I am concerned, my part in society is not necessarily to make the society better than I found it. If I can help to make the world a better place than I found it, that is a good bonus, but essentially all I care about as an individual, as a writer, as this thing that is sitting at this table, is that I have an individual capacity, an individual possibility, to live my life in this world before I die. And anything, whether it be to stop other people being shot or whether it be something less than that, anything that stands in the way of myself having this experience of what is around me I must consider to be a buffer between myself and the spontaneous enjoyment of life. And if it came to a point at which all the rest of the world was being murdered and I could escape to a little cave and still manage to find a private 'explosion', I would do that, and to hell with the rest of the world! Therefore, in conclusion, I want to say that, whether we react to situations outside ourselves or not, finally our only responsibility is to ourselves. For myself, my own work must stem from this understanding and be judged by it.[44]

Another strand of the art for art perspective acknowledges without regrets the sociological conditioning of the colonial milieu which marked the birth of the literature. However, the proponents of this variant go on to insist that in the contemporary 'post-colonial' milieu, the justification for social concerns no longer exists. If the literature is to 'mature', they argue, it must move from the 'public' to the 'private' domain of the artist. This aesthetic mode, which shares affinity with that favoured by bourgeois foreign critics, has been neatly articulated by Dan Izevbaye, the sensitive Nigerian critic:

> With this new emphasis in criticism, that is the suppression of the social reference of literature as a significant influence in criticism, it may be easier for critics to pay greater attention to the literary work itself. But the influence of the referential element on African criticism has not really been an intrusion. The social factor was important only because the literature itself was largely sociological. As the literature becomes less preoccupied with social or national problems and more

concerned with the problems of men as individuals in an African society, the critical reference will be *human beings* rather than society, and the considerations which influence critical judgment will be *human and literary* rather than *social* ones[45] (*emphasis mine*).

It does not seem to us that the African advocates of art for art's sake have grounded their position in any theory of opposition to the banalities and commercialism of the neo-colonial situation. It is not the case of an extrication of artistic *beauty* – despite the romantic implications of the term – from the ugliness of the new nations. On the contrary, it appears that African writers simply adopted art for art's sake as *the* correct theory of art regardless of epoch.

There is the possibility, however, that the theory was a response to the great *press* from foreign publishers 'hovering like vultures to snatch this and that'[46] from any writer with an *African* label. The purely commercial intent of the *African* label had led publishers to promote work which, in the eyes of some African writers, was in danger of *depressing* aesthetic standards. This, undoubtedly, is one of the reasons why some African writers wish to be known solely as *writers*, without any ethnic modifier. Perhaps it is in this framework that we should appraise the *poésie pure*, and literary contempt for the non-poet, adopted by the later Christopher Okigbo.

However, if we ignore the foregoing caveat and accept our initial interpretation as tentatively correct, we see here an illustration of the *uninventiveness* of the African bourgeoisie presaged by comrade Fanon in *The Wretched of The Earth*. Fanon had argued that the African bourgeoisie, because of the circumstances of its emergence, would identify only with the decadent *consumption* stage of its Western counterpart. The African bourgeoisie would miss the revolutionary *productive* characteristics which marked the rise of its Western counterpart from the ashes of feudal Europe. Consequently, it would adopt the liberal philosophical outlook of the decadent phase of the Western bourgeoisie as a universally valid outlook. The Western bourgeoisie's particular *truths* would be accepted as the *eternal* truths.[47]

We are not here scapegoating the African writers. The condition is in fact general to the vast majority of the writers' class colleagues in the contemporary intellectual establishment in Africa. In our universities today, the dominant ethos is one of immaculate isolation from the pressing problems of our societies. Under the rubric of academic freedom, *pure* rather than *applied* research is rewarded. On the few occasions when attempts are made to situate university scholarship in social relevance, the applications do not stray beyond simple *reformist* parameters. The paralytic condition of the social sciences in Africa bear testimony. In these sciences application is limited to *adapting* the individual to social, economic and political subservience under the domination of foreign monopoly capital. There is no attempt to *subvert* the present neo-colonial order in the anticipation of a non-capitalist future.

Thus, under these conditions, it is no surprise that some artists, like the majority of their class colleagues, would advocate the isolation of art, in total congruence with the division of labour of the capitalist market.

CRITICAL REALISM

The *critical realist* approach to the African experience is today the most typical of African writers. These writers are dismayed, in the words of Wole Soyinka, by the 'lack of vital relevance between the literary concerns of writers and the pattern of reality'[48] that currently oppresses citizens in the new African nations. They advocate a literature that is *engaged* with the contemporary reality in a critical way.

In general they reject the positing of an unhistoric African essence and are impatient with the celebration of the past. When they present the African past, the intention is neither to seek a retreat nor to romanticize. On the contrary, its virtues and weaknesses are presented, without however, compromising the dignity of Africans as persons. Achebe's trilogy and Soyinka's *Dance of the Forests* are illustrative.

Again, if we may quote Soyinka, what the critical realists demand is that our writers should eschew the attitude of mere celebrants or 'mere chroniclers' and realize that 'part of [their] essential purpose in society is to write with a very definite vision'.[49] Typically, the justification of the normative prescription of the artist as *conscience* to society, is anchored on the functional integration of the *traditional* African artist to his society. The model of the traditonal artist is often interpreted in two slightly different ways. Achebe tends to stress his integral role, while Soyinka lays emphasis on his critical role. In either case, of course, the model serves as an argument against the disembodied conception of art of the art for art's sake school.

Although the critical realists are united in seeking to maintain role continuity with their 'traditional' counterparts, there is no agreement on the nature of the 'very definite vision' which should inform their contemporary works. Precisely because of their undialectical conception of the artist in traditional society, critical realism in Africa *criticizes* from a variety of standpoints. Typically, after we have been impressed by the truth of their criticism, we are left with the question: *What next?*

Their conclusions either show an indifference to prospective statements or imply a host of philosophical positions ranging from liberal reformism, nihilism to cosmic pessimism. Satire is the favoured method, and typically all social classes are satirized equally. *A Man of the People* is a case in point. In the hands of a more pessimistic thinker, the preoccupation with satire and irony tends to retreat into an individualist aesthetic involution. Sometimes, the powerlessness of an individual actor to interrupt the oppressiveness of the political process is enlarged as a symptom of the 'collapse of humanity'.[50] Perhaps a more valid interpretation is that a certain amount of convoluted expression, indirection and innuendo is a necessary survival kit for the *individual* protester who has been targeted as such by a repressive political establishment.

Much to the irritation of some of the artists, critical realist works are lavishly praised by foreign bourgeois critics. Foreign bourgeois critics see these works as letting the West 'off the hook', so to speak. The liberal faction sees these works as evidence of the universality and endemic quality of oppression, while the reactionary wing sees them as a confirmation of

African infantilism. In any case, the popularity of these works is in no doubt. It is instructive, for example, to contrast the hostile reactions to René Maran's *Batouala* and Mongo Beti's *The Poor Christ of Bomba* on the one hand and the lavish praise heaped by French critics on Yambo Ouologuem's *Le Devoir de Violence* on the other.[51]

Foreign praise is extraneous to the central motivation of many of the critical realists. They are really more concerned with engaging the critical attention of their fellow citizens. This is precisely why they have tended to eschew the safe cultural anthropological literature for the immediately political. This choice is fraught with concrete dangers for the artist. Often the excessive external praise is used by the internal political establishment to compromise the artist. The establishment can attempt a distortion of the issues by saying: See, he is loved by our colonial enemies! However, in instances where the literature has been technically accessible, the gravity of the surrounding reality has assured its ready reception by the reading public in Africa. The successes of *A Man of the People* in Nigeria, and *Song of Lawino* in East Africa, are good illustrations. But this is precisely why the question of 'What next?' remains a pressing political one. A few African writers, at least in their theoretical statements, have begun to focus on this question. This leads us into the discussion of the *emergent* 'socialist realist' consciousness in the ranks of African writers.

SOCIALIST REALISM

This nascent consciousness which we have designated by Maxim Gorky's coinage, 'socialist realism', incorporates and surpasses critical realism. For in addition to the criticizing of the surrounding reality which marks the critical realist approach, 'socialist realism' implies the 'artist's or writer's fundamental agreement with the aims of the working class and the emerging socialist world'.[52]

The socialist realist artist – or intellectual for that matter – shows the world as changeable. And because of his historical materialist outlook, his prospective vision is a positive statement on behalf of the revolutionary aspirations of the exploited classes. Thus it is not enough for the artist to dissociate himself from the decadent environment by the adoption of a self-distancing, contemptuous, satirical or reformist attitude. Fischer elaborates the point:

> True socialist realism is therefore also a critical realism, *enriched* by the artist's fundamental acceptance of society and a *positive* social perspective. The artist's personality is no longer engaged in a romantic protest against the world that surrounds him[53] ... (*emphasis mine*)

Among African writers, Ngugi wa Thiong'o and Sembène Ousmane have consciously adopted this standpoint in their recent theoretical statements. (An artistic demonstration of this class perspective was already present in Sembène Ousmane's early novel, *God's Bits of Wood*.) In principle, they do not dismiss *ab initio* the concentration on the rehabilitation of the past which marked the early literature. This attention was a necessary step for the restoration of the African's self-confidence – a self-confidence which was itself a prerequisite for fighting colonialism. What was wrong was a retrospective fixation. The artist

> forgot that his society was no longer peasant, with egalitarian values. Conflicts between the emergent, élitist middle class and the masses were developing, their seeds being, of course, in our colonial past. And when he woke up to his task, a little surprised that events in post-independent Africa could take the turn they had taken, he only tried to be a *liberal referee*, an interpreter, standing on the fence between the new men of power and the people.[54]

Ngugi's definition of the people is unambiguous. By the people he means the 80 per cent 'who are living below the bread-line standard'.[55] His prescription on the responsibility of the African artist is equally unambiguous. It deserves to be quoted at length:

> I believe that the African Masses will build a place to feel at home. For they are not alone. In Asia, in Latin America, in Black America, the people are fighting the same battle. I believe the African novelist, the African writer, can help in this struggle. But he cannot do this if he insists on a liberal posture. He must be committed on the side of the majority ... whose silent and violent clamour for change is rocking the continent. By diving into himself, deep into the collective consciousness of our people, he can seek the root, the trend, in the revolutionary struggle. He has already done something in restoring the African character to his history, to his past. But in a capitalist society, the past has a romantic glamour: gazing at it ... is often a means of escaping the present. It is only in a socialist context that a look at yesterday can be meaningful in illuminating today and tomorrow.[56]

We encounter the same ideological thrust in a recent interview which Sembène Ousmane gave on the subject of films.

> Sembène: I'm going to make a film on the birth of a black
>   bourgeoisie, a Senegalese big businessman.
> Weaver: Briefly, why?
> Sembène: Because we're witnessing the birth of an aborted
>   child and some of these circumstances are very
>   dangerous – too dangerous because they are
>   manipulated from the outside, Europe, and I want
>   to show how they're being manipulated. . .how the
>   people must kill them.[57]

Several facts emerge from the foregoing exerpts. *First*, unlike the critical realists who merely testify to the condition of social crisis, the socialist realists offer a precise diagnosis. They *name* the existing reality – capitalism. It is from this vantage point that the bribery, violence, poverty and the rigging of elections which critical realists have attested to, is to be understood. There are classes. A capitalist social formation, like all class societies, is inherently based on the exploitation of the majority by the privileged few. In addition, the extreme depersonalization, and the erection of money as the solvent of all values, which critical realists tirelessly document, are a special condition of capitalist society.

A socialist realist perspective accepts that these problems can be overcome only by the *liquidation* of the capitalist state. Critical realist literature on Africa often leaves us with the implication that our crisis would be overcome if only the right men – and decent men – manned the state apparatus. If only the prime minister were an intellectual! If only the minister of health had a medical training! If only our leaders were God-fearing! If only the judiciary were free from politics! If only . . . From a socialist realist viewpoint these are irrelevant, reformist moral effluvia. For example, an honest, 'apolitical' judge in capitalist Nigeria can only honestly enforce bourgeois rights to private property. 'Justice' becomes the right of the labourer to his shack and the right of the business tycoon to his mansion. The right of the labourer to the smoky *Scania* bus co-existing with the right of the tycoon to his *Mercedes*.

A *second* fact that emerges is that socialist realist writers trace this development of exploiting capitalist relationships to its colonial roots. They understand the essence of the colonial epoch in Africa to be the incorporation of our continent into the capitalist social order. Although cultural repression did occur, they do not mistake this for the primary motivation of the colonizers. The motivation was economic. This awareness allows the socialist realists to anticipate correctly that an internal African revolution will also imply structural disengagement from the capitalist structures of Europe. We must insist on this linkage of African capitalism to our colonial experience in view of the fact that many critical realists today glory in the fact that they have abandoned the colonial theme. This amnesia may please bourgeois critics. From an African perspective, however, it is a false conception of our autonomy. It distorts our knowledge of the obstacles that need to be overcome. A clear recognition of the colonial roots of our problems does not, as some liberals maintain, mean that we ignore the internal oppressors. On the contrary, the recognition of the comprador status of the internal oppressors means that revolutionaries do not underestimate the enemy.

A *third* fact which emerges from the Ngugi-Ousmane passages is a clear definition of the writer's *constituency*. They do not, in the first instance, seek to address themselves to some abstract humanity. Rather it is the 80 per cent of our people who live below the breadline that they advocate as the focus. This is why, for example, the peasants and proletarians in *God's Bits of Wood* are never ridiculed.

A *fourth* and related implication is that the socialist realists are optimistic. They have confidence that their constituency, the masses, are the agents for change. And against the faceless passivity which is credited to the masses in the bulk of contemporary African novels, they recognize in the peasant rebellions, tenants' associations and labour strikes, the unabated clamour for change.

A *fifth* and final implication is the necessity for a pan-African and, indeed, a proletarian-internationalist outlook. Fortunately, there is already a transition to this perspective in the theoretical outlook of two of our leading artists – Achebe and Soyinka.[58] In a recent interview with Biodun Jeyifo, Soyinka, after taking pains to dissociate himself from 'orthodox Marxists', stated:

> I happen to believe and accept implicitly what goes under the broad umbrella of socialist ideology, a secular socialist ideology, believing this to be the logical principle of communal organization and true human equality. What this means for me are varied. They include: the eradication of the very policy of wealth accumulation at the expense of any sector of society; eradication of the mere possibility of tyrannization by one class of society over another; the eradication of class distinction within society where class implies a category of privilege or superiority or advantage. The other logical processes can be assumed; state ownership of all land and production means; equal education, opportunities, etc.[59]

Socialist realism in Africa; problems

Although we are, in the long run, optimistic, the development of socialist realist consciousness in the creative imagination of African writers will not be automatic. Its growth can only come from the result of an increasingly fierce class struggle in the domains of ideology and political economy of the new nations. The multiplicity of contradictions in contemporary Africa poses, at the moment, a host of ideological and institutional hurdles in the way of the development of socialist consciousness in the entire intellectual domain.

There is first the urgency of Leon Trotsky's observation in *Literature and Revolution* about the dialectical contingency of socialist literature on the concrete realisation of a socialist revolution. In this respect, the empirical situation in Africa leaves much to be desired. It is today the case that the African continent is the most reactionary among the political zones customarily referred to as the Third World. As a single unit, the revolutionary momentum in Africa, even of the limited anti-colonial thrust, is tame in comparison with Asia. Morover, the attempts at the liquidation of neo-colonialism in a socialist direction, within specific African states, continue to meet a range of setbacks. The specific concoction of an 'African socialism' excepted by fiat from the necessity of class struggle, constitutes, in its own right, a major ideological bottleneck. A glaring consequence of this is the ironic unanimity between certain segments of the critical intelligentsia and the political establishment, in the justification of their opposed aims by the invocation of an unhistoric African essence.

The absence of socialism in Africa means a realistic tailoring of our expectations. Following Trotsky's observation, we can more realistically expect the development of a 'revolutionary realism' with the possibility that the imagined changed reality will contain imprecisions about the character of socialist societies that are to be born in Africa.

Revolutionary artists will have to contend with the heritage of colonial mentality and the liberal outlook which dominate the educational institutions in many African societies. It is in these institutions that the theoretical orientation of the writer's readers is shaped. And it is the case that capitalism is taught as the *natural* social system to which humanity can aspire. The inherited capitalist social order has been *literally* sacralized by our historians and social scientists as 'modernization'. Although we cannot pursue the matter here, it is a supreme irony that African historiography, which is today the most developed discipline in our universities, has managed to deny the *historicity* of capitalism in Africa. Those who seek to break with the tradition – like Walter Rodney – are dismissed as ideologues. Left intellectuals are under pressure in our universities. Their academic abilities are doubted, their works dismissed as value-laden propaganda.

The level of ideological depravity is attested to by the fact that long after the Achebes, Soyinkas, Pepper Clarks, Ngugis were available on our shelves, African secondary students were still being made to read the biographies of imperialists like Churchill as exemplary literary texts! The universities are not exempt. Until fairly recently, as Ngugi's account on the University of Nairobi shows, the mere suggestion to Africanize the content of literature departments, was considered a threatening 'revolutionary deviation'![60] Under these circumstances, the potentially revolutionary writer cannot automatically expect positive reinforcements that could aid his own development of consciousness from the educated audience.

Yet to break with this audience, as he must, in order to adopt the *people* as his constituency, poses communication problems which have no easy solution at the moment. For the African case, it is not just the colonial tongue which isolates the writer from the people. There is also the question of mass illiteracy even in our own languages!

A final obstacle on the path to the development of a revolutionary literature has to do with the institutional structure which oversees the manufacture and dissemination of our artistic works. We refer here to the sociology of the publishing process. The relationship between the publishing industry and Africa is today one of the most vivid dramatizations of our neo-colonial status. It is still the case that African writers are accredited abroad. It is after their external accreditation that they are imported to us as models. This has been true since the time Amos Tutuola wrote *The Palm-wine Drinkard*. In essence, we do not know what ideas have been edited from the literature in the process of its external manufacture. Perhaps the very paucity of revolutionary content in our literature is due to the unwillingness of capitalist publishing houses to publish such literature.

Given the understandable ambition of writers to get published, young writers who are still struggling to establish a name may therefore be forced to tone down their militancy and come to terms with the safe *telluric* metaphysical concerns of Macmillan. We know for example that some of our colleagues in the social sciences have had their scholarly works rejected purely on the grounds of their anti-imperialist implications. In general, at the moment, the alternative to capitulation is silence. It is any wonder, then, that the bulk of our literature appears to be wrapped up in dialogue with Europe rather than with fellow Africans?

We have neither concocted, nor exaggerated this problem. Leading

African writers and critics have themselves diagnosed it in an even more severe idiom. The *vulture* is a favourite metaphor. Let us cite two examples:

> In fact, sometimes I wonder if such a thing as an African writer exists, because he might be a creation essentially of Europe. . . . .the publishers hovering like vultures to snatch this and that . . .[61]

George Awoonor-Williams

> The curiosity of the outside world far exceeded its critical faculties and publishers hovered like benevolent vultures over the still-born foetus of the African Muse. At a given signal they tore off bits and pieces, fanned up with powerful wings delusions of significance in commonness and banality. The average published writer in the first few years of the postcolonial era was the most celebrated skin of inconsequence to obscure the true flesh of the African dilemma.[62]

Wole Soyinka

In line with Dan Izevbaye's observation on 'the importance of criticism in the formation of a literary tradition',[63] some African critics like Eldred Jones, and writers like Achebe, have now established journals of their own resources in order to help break the external monopolization of literary criticism.[64] The same developments are true of East and Central Africa.

The lack of national institutional mechanisms for disseminating our creative work is even more graphically illustrated with regard to painting, sculpture and film. With regard to the first two, we are thrown back to the so-called 'age of discovery'. Just as the Livingstones and Mungo Parks 'discovered' our rivers and mountains in an earlier epoch, contemporary 'Oshogbo art' has to be 'discovered' by Ulli Beier and Suzanne Wenger! In Nigeria our painters and sculptors are 'discovered' and presented to us by the British Council, U. S. I. S., and the German cultural centers. Our colonial psychoses have prevented us from erecting auditoria where our cultural products can be appreciated. Suppose a Nigerian painter or sculptor wanted to depict the horrors of the slave trade and colonialism rather than fairies, gnomes and *orisas*. Could he show them at the British Council? With the cinematic art, we already have hints of the formidable difficulties which the African artist will encounter. In Nigeria, the production of *Kongi's Harvest* was the occasion for such education. Ironically, it was this film, which had trivialized radical political concerns with imperialism and neocolonialism, that ran into a concrete demonstration of the *correctness* of the neo-colonial argument. For as it turned out, this film could not be shown in the existing cinema houses. The Lebanese merchant class which owns these theatres refused to distribute the film. Despite the tame political ideology of *Kongi's Harvest*, this parasitical merchant class recognized the very fact of its *African* authorship as a threat to the future of their cheap cowboy films. They wanted to prevent the formation of the habit of the demand for African films among their Nigerian audience. Nonetheless, they crowned their insolence by rushing through for mass distribution a degenerate film, *Son of Africa*, manufactured by them in Lebanon.[65] And so we saw *Kongi's Harvest* in boxing halls!

Socialist realism in Africa, prospects

The future is not entirely bleak. In the midst of the ideological and institutional obstacles, there are counter opportunities in favor of a revolutionary and socialist consciousness. At the level of social movements, it is a significant fact that the current liberation movements in Guinea-Bissau and Southern Africa have escaped the chloroforming mantle of constitutionalism which mummified the first flush of independence in the early sixties. Unlike yesterday, the anti-colonial struggle of today is being waged with arms and under advanced socialist revolutionary theories. As these struggles continue to extend their victories, the sacrifices and visions are bound to be reflected in intellectual and aesthetic consciousness. It is perhaps not fortuitous that Sembène Ousmane and Ngugi wa Thiong'o, who today are the leading advocates of socialist realism, had earlier based their major creative works on concrete anti-colonial movements led by the peasants and proletarians of Senegal and Kenya.[66]

Secondly, we are fortunate that the bourgeois epoch in Africa does not have the historic advantages of its European counterpart. In Africa, the bourgeois epoch was born with signs of mortality writ large on its veins. Unlike Europe, the African bourgeoisie has had to contend right from its inception with the counter consciousness of the peasants and proletarians. Even if they are still largely 'paper rights', it is nonetheless significant that the bourgeoisie had to recognize the rights of workers to organize as trade unions in the national constitutions. The African bourgeoisie arrives at a time when it cannot exploit child labour and indulge in the excesses of its nineteen century European counterpart with an infinite ideological assurance. When the Union Jacks were lowered, the peasants and labourers who had made this possible were already there demanding their freedoms.

It is from this perspective that the Nigerian Marxist political economist, Comrade Ola Oni,[67] interprets the current political instabilities of the new African states. According to him, these instabilities are occasion for hope rather than despair. Against the prevailing clichés, Comrade Oni insists that the intra-élite squabbles which result in the foundering *coups*, are at bottom a result of the perceived discontent of the masses. It is the rumblings from below which deny ultimate stability to the neo-colonial body-politic. Therefore, if we may appropriate Chou En-lai's metaphor, the African bourgeoisie, fragmented, 'runs, hither and thither like ants on a frying pan'[68] vying with one another in reformist adventures. The political seat is becoming a blazing inferno. The ruling class cannot count on the ideological docility of the masses which made divine kingship possible in an earlier epoch. Again, to use the example of Nigeria, the historicity of so-called 'natural rulers' is demonstrated from time to time with the beheadings of dictatorial Obas and chiefs. Under these conditions, the possibility of the revolutionary overthrow of the African bourgeois state can now be confidently entertained. It is only the *timing* of its occurrence that remains contingent.

There is also the factor of the changed international climate. The hegemony of the capitalist-imperialist system has been shattered. Despite their contradictions, the socialist alternative is now an empirical reality. We are privileged witnesses of the revolutionary tenacity of the Vietnamese peoples. The African revolutionary today has overcome the encirclement and isolation which were imposed on his Mau Mau predecessor. It is significant that the theoretical syntheses which guide the armed struggles in Guinea-Bissau and Southern Africa show a critical familiarity with the revolutionary theories of their counterparts in Asia and Latin America. As Ngugi wa Thiong'o rightly observed, the African masses are no longer alone. 'In Asia, in Latin America, in Black America, the people are fighting the same battle'.

Even if we were to restrict ourselves to the domain of the artistic tradition itself, there are, in the contemporary situation, opportunities for the development of a socialist consciousness. The retreat from the romantic, retrospective vision of the early literature and the predominance of the critical realist approach constitutes a necessary link to the transition to a socialist consciousness. It is significant that although the conclusions of the vast body of the critical realist literature show ideological confusions, few of them can be dismissed as artistic opiates. They typically have shied away from the easy happy endings of the fairy-tale motif. We have therefore a rich background of genuine artistic integrity in which the philosophical quandary of the artist is bared without camouflage. The problem of *anticipation* – 'tremors of the future', after the merciless critique of the present – will become increasingly soluble, as African writers shed the fantasy of their transcendent, supra-class assumptions and recognize the class basis of the struggle in contemporary Africa.

In this respect, they are in a more favorable position for developing a clarity of vision than their counterparts in diaspora. The race-class problematic, whose concrete salience for Africans in diaspora complicates the burdens of the struggle in the Americas, is necessarily abstract on the homeland. For here we find colonial and capitalist cannibalism vividly mediated by a black comprador. In our anti-imperialist struggle, the politics of class collaboration with the 'lumpen-bourgeoisie' is vividly untenable. Thus, we can speculate with some confidence that had the later Richard Wright lived long enough to write a blueprint for African literature in our contemporary epoch, the uneasy tension between race and class which runs as an undercurrent in his 1937 *Blueprint For Negro Literature*[69] would have been overcome.

Contemporary African artists have a maximum opportunity for developing ideological clarity. Years ago, Mao Tse-Tung in the midst of an analogous revolutionary situation, reminded Chinese writers and intellectuals that 'ideas do not fall from heaven, nor do we receive them as a gift of God while we sleep'.[70] The source of ideas could not be accounted for by a pagan invocation of a mysterious muse. On the contrary, ideas – artistic ideas included – are the products of social praxis. In class societies, ideas take on a class stamp – together with all the dynamic contradictions of the class struggle.

In tackling the invasion of bourgeois aesthetic theories about an abstract love of mankind and an invariant human nature, Mao Tse-Tung had this to say:

there is only human nature in the concrete, no human nature in the abstract. In a class society there is only human nature that bears the stamp of a class, but no human nature transcending classes. We uphold the human nature of the proletariat and of the great masses of the people, while the landlord and bourgeois classes uphold the nature of their own classes as if – though they do not say so outright – it were the only kind of human nature.[71]

Therefore, Mao argued, the central problem facing revolutionary artists is the 'For whom?' question. From the standpoint of the revolutionary, the political criterion of excellent art is art which serves the struggle of the people against their oppressors. A recognition of this political criterion does not imply any dogmatic legislation as to artistic forms. Each artist according to his talent and theme will experiment with forms until he achieves a unity of form and content in his work. Indeed, precisely because of the political function of art in class societies, the revolutionary artist has an urgent duty to achieve the technical excellence that would facilitate the communication of his ideas. For he realizes with Mao that

Works of art, however politically progressive, are powerless if they lack artistic quality. Therefore we are equally opposed to works with wrong political approaches and to the tendency towards so called 'poster and slogan style' which is correct only in political approach but lacks artistic power.[72]

While we accept the relevance of Mao's ideas to our artistic situation in Africa, this caveat is even more in order. Although we already have some previews of the character of socialist art in some of the works of Sembène Ousmane, it would be foolhardy to prescribe technical forms. Given our peculiar cultural and linguistic problems, the artist who wishes truly to communicate with the 80 per cent who live below the breadline will have to create truly revolutionary artistic vehicles. However, in the light of the record of his past achievements, the African writer stands a better chance of effecting the communications breakthrough than the majority of his class colleagues in the intellectual establishment.[73]

The African writer has already surpassed the majority of his class colleagues in telling us where we came from and where we are at the present. If he is to complete the task by telling us where we are going, he must be prepared to commit *class suicide*. To raise the people's consciousness, he must himself defect from his petit-bourgeois class and enrich his own consciousness from the experiences of the people's struggles. Realizing, of course, that a developed consciousness, though a necessary prerequisite, is not the total answer. As Nkrumah pointed out, the African revolution now has a *material* dimension.[74]

CONCLUSION

However, in keeping with the theme of this paper, and the way we began, we choose to underscore this final point by quoting from one of the new poets among Africans in diaspora. Our poet is Don Lee. Here is what he wrote:

I ain't seen no poems stop a .38,
I ain't seen no stanzas break a honkie's head.
I ain't seen no metaphors stop a tank,
I ain't seen no words kill
& if the word was mightier than the sword
pushkin wouldn't be fertilizing russian soil
& until my similes can protect me from a night stick
i guess i'll keep my razor
& buy me some more bullets.[75]

Notes

1 Countee Cullen, *On These I Stand: An Anthology of Selected Poems*, Harper, New York, 1947.

2 Some recent examples are Per Wastberg (ed.), *The Writer in Modern Africa*, Africana Publishing Corporation, New York, 1969; Dennis Duerden & Cosmo Pieterse (eds.), *African Writers Talking*, Africana Publishers, New York, 1972; and *Palaver, Interviews with Five African Writers*, African and Afro-American Research Institute, Austin, Texas, 1972.

3 This is a concept introduced by the Marxist economist, Samir Amin, in one of his sensitive exploratory studies of the social formations of pre-colonial Africa. See for example his 'Class Struggle in Africa,' published under the anonymous signature of XXX, in *Revolution*, vol. 1, no. 9, 1964.

4 Dorothy Hammond and Alta Jablow, *The Africa that Never Was: Four Centuries of British Writing About Africa.*, Twayne Publishers, Inc., New York, 1970, p. 197.

5 The designation of the Negritude movement as *the* beginning of the 'modern' literature is strictly for our convenience. In fact, modern African *written* literature is much older than that. For a sense of this impressive antiquity of the literature, see Janheinz Jahn, *A History of Neo-African Literature*, Faber and Faber Ltd., London, 1968, and especially, Lalage Bown, 'The Development of African Prose-Writing in English: A Perspective', in Christopher Heywood (ed.), *Perspectives on African Literature*, Heinemann, London, 1971. It should also be remembered that we have excluded from discussion modern artists using the traditional oral form.

6 Excerpts from this interview were published in a special issue of *Africa Report*, July, 1964.

7 Chinua Achebe, 'The Novelist as Teacher', *New Statesman*, January, 1965.

8 This was the name of a black radical journal in Paris on the eve of the invention of the term 'Negritude'. Lilyan Kesteloot's *Intellectual Origins of the African Revolution*, Black Orpheus Press, Washington, D. C., 1972, is our source. On page 30 she writes: 'In 1932 a group of West Indians started again with a small inflammatory brochure, *Légitime défense* (Legitimate defense), which was prohibited immediately'.

9 Lilyan Kesteloot's celebration is obvious in her book, *op. cit.* Soyinka's most recent critique of Negritude is contained in his 'The Writer in a Modern African State', in Per Wastberg (ed.), *op. cit.* For an excellent, and thorough-going Marxist critique, see Stanislas Adotevi's paper, 'The Strategy of Culture', in *The Black Scholar*, 1, 1, 1969.

10 Aimé Césaire, *Return To My Native Land*, (translated by John Berger and Anna Bostock), Penguin Books, London, 1969, p. 75.

11 *Ibid.*, p. 75.

12 Eseoghene L. Barret, 'Negritude: The Duality of Concept and Execution in the Development of a Creative Black Reality', unpublished lecture, 1972.

13 Aimé Césaire, *Op. cit.* pp. 37, 39 and 41 respectively.

14 *Ibid.*, p. 76
15 *Ibid.*, p. 78.
16 Aimé Césaire, *Discourse on Colonialism*, Monthly Review Press, New York, 1972, p. 68.
17 *Ibid.*, p. 72
18 Aimé Césaire, *Return to My Native Land, op. cit.*, p. 75
19 Aimé Césaire, *Discourse, op. cit.*, p. 34
20 *Ibid.*, p. 38–39.
21 *Ibid.*, pp. 33–34. This is a passage of pure revolutionary energy.
22 Aimé Césaire, 'The Responsibility of the Artist,' in Wilfred Cartey and Martin Kilson (eds.), *The African Reader: Independent Africa*, Vintage Books, Random House, New York, 1970, pp. 153–61.
23 *Ibid.*, p. 160.
24 *Ibid.*, p. 156.
25 Léopold Sedar Senghor, 'Negritude', in John Reed and Clive Wake (eds. and trans.), *Senghor Prose and Poetry*, Oxford University Press, London, 1965, p. 99.
26 Ernst Fischer, *The Necessity of Art*, (trans. by Anna Bostock, Penguin Books, London, 1963. (1970 reprint), pp. 95–6.
27 Léopold Sedar Senghor, *Nationhood and the African Road to Socialism*, Présence Africaine, Paris, 1961, p. 21.
28 Consider for example Senghor's theoretical essays in Reed and Wake (eds.), *op. cit.* See also Senghor, The Foundations of *'Africanéité'* or *'Négritude' 'Arabité'*, Présence Africaine, Paris, 1967.
29 This poem, 'Congo', teeming with crocodiles, manatees, etc., originally published in his collection *Ethiopiques*, is available on pp. 139–41 of Reed and Wake (eds.), *op. cit.*
30 Mbella Sonne Dipoko, *'Cultural Diplomacy In African Writing'*, in Per Wastberg (ed.), *op. cit.*, p. 63.
31 L. S. Senghor, 'We Are All Cultural Half-Castes', in Reed and Wake (eds.), *op. cit.*, pp. 74–5.
32 *Ibid.*, p. 75.
33 L. S. Senghor, *Nationhood, op. cit.*, p. 35.
34 The definition of Negritude as cultural diplomacy was first advanced by Mbella Sonne Dipoko, *op cit.*
35 David Diop, 'The Vultures', in Alan Bold (ed.) *The Penguin Book of Socialist Verse*, Penguin Books Ltd., London, 1970, p. 440.
36 Cited from Bernard Fonlon's 'The Kampala Conference', in Albert H. Berrian and Richard A. Long (eds.), *Negritude: Essays and Studies*, Hampton Institute Press, Hampton, Virginia, 1967, p. 106.
37 Lilyan Lagneau-Kesteloot, 'Problems of the Literary Critic in Africa', *Abbia*, p. 40. Kesteloot advocates playing 'cultural psycho-analyst'.
38 Dorothy Blair, 'African Literature in University Education', in Gerald Moore (ed.), *African Literature and the Universities*, Ibadan University Press, 1965, p. 78.
39 *Ibid.*, p. 79
40 *Ibid.*
41 Y. L. Galperina, 'Under the Sign of Ogun. The Young Writers of Nigeria, 1960–1965', in *Africa in Soviet Studies*, 1969 Annual, pp. 162–83.
42 Okot p'Bitek uses this metaphor in his *Song of Prisoner*, The Third Press, New York, 1971.
43 Lewis Nkosi, 'Individualism and Social Commitment', in Per Wastberg (ed.) *op. cit.*, p. 48.
44 John Nagenda, in Per Wastberg (ed.), *op. cit.*, p. 54. He made these remarks in his discussion of Lewis Nkosi's paper above.
45 Dan S. Izevbaye, 'Criticism and Literature in Africa', in Christopher Heywood (ed.), *op. cit.*, p. 30.
46 George Awoonor-Williams, in Per Wastberg (ed.), *op. cit.*, p. 31. Awoonor-Williams made these remarks during his discussion of Soyinka's paper, 'The Writer in a Modern African State'.
47 It is obvious that the original formulation of this tendency belongs to Marx. See *The German Ideology*.

48   Wole Soyinka, 'The Writer in a Modern African State', in Per Wastberg (ed.), *op. cit.*, p. 14.

49   Wole Soyinka made these remarks in his discussion of Lewis Nkosi's paper, *op. cit.*, in Per Wastberg (ed.), *op. cit.*, p. 58.

50   This theme is very salient in Wole Soyinka's philosophical outlook. Professor Eldred Jones is, to my mind, the most profound analyst of Soyinka's world view. See for example his two essays: 'Progress and Civilization in the Work of Wole Soyinka', in Christopher Heywood (ed.), *op. cit.*, pp. 129–37, and 'The Essential Soyinka', in Bruce King (ed.), *Introduction to Nigerian Literature*, University of Lagos, Evans Brothers Ltd., 1971, pp. 113–34.

The 'convoluted' style of much of Soyinka's writing has been mentioned by many critics. I think though that it was Lewis Nkosi who first coined this expression in reference to Soyinka. However, in our view, Soyinka's obscure style may be politically inspired. We offer as tentative evidence the total clarity of his language in his *Before the Blackout*, which was immensely popular with the Nigerian audience. The point we are making here is that at the time he wrote *Before the Blackout*, there was strong evidence that Nigerians were clamoring for political change. In those circumstances, the critical artist was no longer a political isolate. He could afford to speak to his audience directly in the public idiom.

51   We are told that French literary critics abandoned the canon of *L'art pour l'art* in favor of political justification of the French colonial presence in Africa when René Maran and Mongo Beti's works were published. Yet until they recently levelled the hypocritical charge of plagiarism at Yambo Ouologuem, his work was celebrated as a piece of 'stunning realism'. This is a work which unfortunately mystified the class approach to let French colonialization off the hook.

52   Ernst Fischer, *op. cit.*, p. 108.

53   *Ibid.*, p. 113.

54   Ngugi wa Thiong'o (James Ngugi), 'The African Writer and His Past', in Christopher Heywood (ed.), *op. cit.*, p. 8. A slightly modified version of this paper is also available in Ngugi's *Homecoming*, Heinemann, London, 1972.

55   This concrete designation of the writer's constituency is part of Ngugi wa Thiong'o's critical remarks in which he rejected John Nagenda's individualism and Soyinka's 'metaphysical' universalism during the conference discussions recorded in Per Wastberg (ed.), *op. cit.*, The full passage appears on pp. 25–6.

56   Ngugi wa Thiong'o, 'The Writer and His Past', in *Homecoming*, *op. cit.*, p. 46.

57   Harold Weaver, 'Interview with Sembène Ousmane', in *Issue*, 11, no. 4. Winter 1972, p. 64.

58   Several of Achebe's recent public lectures underscore this socialist vision. For Soyinka, the transition is clear from the footnote below.

59   'Wole Soyinka: an interview with Biodun Jeyifo' in *Transition*, 42, 1973, p. 62.

60   See Ngugi wa Thiong'o's instructive experience in 'On the Abolition of the English Department', in *Homecoming*, *op. cit.*, pp. 145–50.

61   George Awoonor-Williams' remarks appear on page 31 of Per Wastberg (ed.), *op. cit.*

62   *Ibid.*, p. 17.

63   Dan S. Izevbaye, *op. cit.*, p. 25.

64   See for example Eldred Jones, *African Literature Today* and Achebe's *Okike*. Let us legitimize our grave concern for this external monopolization of the journals of literary criticism by citing at length the remarks of an African authority on these matters, Professor Eldred Jones:

> As soon as we start thinking about African Literature in English or French for that matter, we soon realize that the readership is not mainly African. The publishers who decide what shall or shall not be published mostly live and work outside the environment which produced the literature. The majority of the critics also live outside the home of these works. Thus the standing of African writers has largely been determined outside Africa. This has led to assessments which almost frighten many intelligent African readers, among whom the standing of Tutuola, for instance, must be rather lower than the excessive praise heaped on him outside Africa would seem

to indicate. Of course, non-Africans are fully entitled to participate in the criticism of literature of Africa, and they should and will make their views known. But when the main critical voices are non-African there is a danger that the writers may come to emphasize the values which they think their foreign readership demands. This could lead to an expatriate literature produced by Africans, and to false artistic values . . . excerpted from his 'Academic Problems and Critical Techniques', in Gerald Moore (ed.), *op. cit.*, pp. 89–90.)

For our part, however, we think the major consequence of this monopoly, is the dulling of the potential revolutionary outlook of our writers and intelligentsia.

65   The distribution difficulties which plagued *Kongi's Harvest* in Nigeria were an eye opener for all of us. A Nigerian art-critic called '*Son of Africa*' 'Son and Daughters of Lebanon'!

66   Sembène Ousmane based his *God's Bits of Wood* on an actual railway workers' strike of October 10, 1947–March 19, 1948, on the Dakar–Niger railway line. Ngugi based his *Weep not Child*, and *A Grain of Wheat* on the anti-colonial Mau Mau movement.

67   Comrade Ola Oni, president of *The Nigerian Academy of Arts, Sciences and Technology*, is one of the few Marxist political economists and leading theoreticians of the socialist struggle in Nigeria. His insights on which I have leaned here stem from his theoretical exploration of the nature of the *crisis* of neo-colonial formations.

68   This is an expression attributed to Chou En-Lai on the day the Peoples Republic of China won enthusiastic admission into the U. N. despite the objections of the imperialist powers.

69   Richard Wright, 'Blue Print for Negro Literature', *New Challenge*, 1937. Also now available in *Amistad* no. 2, 1972, and in Addison Gayle, Jr. (ed.), *The Black Aesthetic*, Doubleday, New York, 1971.
      The uneasy tension between the racial and class perspectives which bothered radical Afro-American writers of Richard Wright's generation, continues to feature in contemporary discussions of the 'black aesthetic' in America. The dominant tendency in these discussions is to devalue the salience of class for the black revolution. While this issue is still in need of more sophisticated analysis, we nonetheless maintain that the African writer on the homeland cannot now retreat from a class perspective on the crisis of our neo-colonial regimes by the indiscriminate invocation of a supra-class *Africaneity.*

70   Mao Tse-Tung 'Where Do Correct Ideas Come From' (May 1963), *Selected Readings of Mao Tse-Tung.*

71   Mao Tse-Tung, 'Talks at the Yenan Forum on Art and Literature' (May 23, 1942), in Anne Freemantle (ed.), *Mao Tse-Tung: An Anthology of His Writings*, A Mentor Book, The New American Library, 1962, p. 259.

72   *Ibid.*, p. 259.

73   This issue has begun to receive the attention of some African writers. An early concern is indicated by Achebe's paper, 'English and the African Writer', *Transition*, 4, no. 18, 1965. A more recent one is contained in Soyinka's interview with Biodun Jeyifo, *op. cit.* In the interview Soyinka appears to suggest a 'continental language' that will secularize the esoteric language, the possession of which, is one of the current bases for the manipulation of the masses by the African bourgeoisie. Others have moved beyond suggestions to some form of direct action to solve the linguistic problem. Aimé Césaire appears to have abandoned the isolation of the poetic form for a more accessible medium of prose-drama. On this see E. A. Hurley's perceptive study, 'A Theatre of Frustration–The Theatre of Aimé Césaire', in *Black Images*, 2, no. 1, Spring, 1973. The boldest step thus far has, of course, been taken by Sembène Ousmane, who has begun to concentrate on films rather than novels. Films are absolutely crucial. In Nigeria, we suggest that it may become necessary for radical playwrights to write in pidgin English (with a standardized orthography) and to adopt the practice of so-called 'guerrilla theatre' in staging their plays in the streets and market places. We in Nigeria do in fact have a rich precedence for this.

Missionaries, Aladura prophets, magicians and medicine hawkers perform daily in our streets and markets. For how long will our radical writers permit these peddlers of mysticism to preempt our public arena? If our artists are serious, they must break with the bourgeois tradition of exclusive air-conditioned theatres.

74 See for example Kwame Nkrumah, *Handbook of Revolutionary Warfare*, International Publishers, New York, 1972, and *The Class Struggle in Africa*, International Publishers, New York, 1970.

75 Don Lee, 'Two Poems' (from 'Sketches from a Black-Nappy-Headed Poet'), available in Stephen Henderson, *Understanding the New Black Poetry*, William Morrow & Company, Inc., New York, 1973, p. 332.

CHAPTER THREE

TOWARDS A MARXIST SOCIOLOGY OF AFRICAN LITERATURE

Omafume F. Onoge

COLONIAL POLITICS AND AFRICAN CULTURE

> In the world today all culture, all literature and art belong to definite classes and are geared to definite political lines. There is in fact no such thing as art for art's sake, art that stands above classes or art that is detached from or independent of politics[1]
>
> Mao Tse-Tung, *Talks at the Yenan Forum*

Political interests have been the crucial factors in the appraisal of African culture since the colonial period. At no time was the domain of African culture conceived of as a neutral field for the unfettered play of objective study. The only significant division has always been one of 'whose political interest?' The politics of oppression versus the politics of liberation. This political partisanship which is now obscured in 'post-independence' African culture and literary studies was boldly visible in the cultural policies of colonial regimes.

As is now common knowledge, the colonizer did not stop at the conquest of the pre-capitalist relations of production. The cultural superstructure was also a major target of assault in order to bring about a new collective consciousness and individual psychological habits favourable to the advance of the violent installation of the capitalist economy. This cultural assault is what today is summed up by the expression, 'cultural imperialism'. In the days of colonial self-assurance, the process of cultural imperialism often entailed a ban on traditional productions and performances of sculpture, dances and songs on the ostensible grounds that they were pagan pollutions in the christian colonial theocracies. 'Coming-out' ceremonies of age-groups – important occasions for dramatic performances of democratic transfer of political power from one generation to another – were banned in societies such as Banyakyusa and the Agikuyu, because of the fear that they could escalate into realistic dramas of anti-colonial politics. The cultural imperialist process went beyond mere acts of vandalism. The vandalism, we must always remember, had as its goal the creation of a personality type, whose essential attribute would be the lack of self-affirmation. A personality that would define *itself* by an ascribed 'constitutional depravity' and thus accept the new world of the King Léopolds as

50

an essential passage to salvation. Fanon, as always, grasped this subtle process of consciousness-transformation in these words:

> Native society in not simply described as a society lacking in values. It is not enough for the colonist to affirm that those values have disappeared from, or still better never existed in, the colonial world. The native is declared insensible to ethics; he represents not only the absence of values but also the negation of values. *He is . . . the enemy of values, . . .* the absolute evil.[2]

And as Fanon noted, the christian missionary and his religion functioned as the special ideological DDT to destroy the 'native parasites'.

This violent psychological conversion was not without its successes. Until fairly recently, the new personality with its negative consciousness affected the educated African's relationship to the traditional arts. There was a time when many educated Africans required a major act of intellectualization to ascribe aesthetic value to our traditional arts. I recall the dismay of an American professor of art history who complained, in the early sixties, that his African students recoiled from his exhibitions of African masks with a 'missionary complex.' This negative response to the traditional arts has also been featured in recent African fiction. In Chinua Achebe's *No Longer at Ease*, for example, there is a scene where Obi's father reacts strongly against the performance of traditional welcome songs on the grounds of their 'heathenist' content.

The emergence of African literature written in the colonizer's tongue did not escape this encounter with colonial politics. In Southern Africa, Thomas Mofolo's first novel was refused publication by the Morija press until he turned to themes reflecting the official manicheism of colonial society. That is, only works in which Mofolo created characters whose moments of insight and maturity coincided with their recognition of the 'superiority' of Christian ethics, were published. René Maran, we were told, was placed in considerable difficulties with colonial officials and French literary critics, because of his naturalistic depiction of the material deprivation which French colonialism visited on Africans, in his novel, *Batouala*. Indeed, 'by their mere presence', African writers in the middle period of colonialism, 'created a scandal'. Let us reproduce Aimé Césaire more fully:

> Under a colonial society there is not merely a hierarchy of *master and servant*. There is also, implicit, a hierarchy of *creator and consumer*.
>
> The creator of cultural values, under good colonization, is the colonizer. And the consumer is the colonized. And everything goes well so long as nothing happens to disturb the hierarchy. There is one law of comfort in every colonization. 'Si prega di non disturbare.' Please do not disturb.[3]

This situation is still very much with us today in parts of the continent. Today, as we in Nigeria dance away our temporary oil harvest in Festac, there are many African writers who still constitute a scandal in South Africa by their presence. Their works exist under an automatic ban. In fact, for some of them, the simple physical act of transferring thought to paper, is defined as veritable treason.

In light of the above, the current boom in African literature is traceable, in its broad aspects, to the concrete gains of anti-colonial struggles and changes in the international political scene. The new literature, not only suffered political obstacles at its birth, but was also conditioned by this very politics. As we have argued elsewhere,[4] the general thrust of the new petty-bourgeois African literature has been anti-imperialist because African writers saw their motivation in anti-colonial political terms. The forerunners of the Negritude movement in Paris conceived of their literary journal, *Légitime défense*, as a vehicle for a literature using the 'weapons of words' against colonialism. And three decades later in West Africa, Chinua Achebe restated this political motivation in his conception of the novelist as teacher:

> I would be quite satisfied if my novels (especially the ones I set in the past) did no more than teach my readers that their past – with all its imperfections – was not one long night of savagery from which the first Europeans acting on God's behalf delivered them. Perhaps what I write is applied art as distinct from pure. But who cares? Art is important but so is education of the kind I have in mind. And I don't see that the two need be mutually exclusive.[5]

Achebe's statement will serve as our point of departure for a more direct confrontation with the subject of this paper. Consider the statement once more. Its apologetic tone is unmistakeable. In one of our earlier submissions on this subject, we argued that this 'apologetic tone in Achebe's justification of the applied or functional purpose of his works is a reflection of the unsettled nature of the criteria by which modern African literature should be appraised'.[6] We have not revised our judgement. The dominant mode of academic criticism of contemporary African literature and culture is unable to judge the literature in any satisfactory way. The dominant mode is bourgeois. Most of its errors and inconsistencies stem from both theoretical handicaps of a bourgeois outlook and its lack of fidelity to the *political* circumstances of the evolution of African literature. Our purpose in subsequent sections is to indicate the nature of this confusion in current bourgeois African literary studies and why a Marxist sociological criticism is advocated.

This bourgeois domination of the field does not imply a consensus of approach within the ranks. The empirical situation is one of sharp controversy. A recent issue of *African Literature Today* devoted specially to *criticism*, shows that the language of the polemics has been quite robust and often intemperate. The considerable output of this school shows many different nuances. It is by a process of analysis that we have arrived at the conclusion that their differences are mere variations within a single bourgeois conception of literature and society.

The central issue around which bourgeois critics have polemicized with one another concerns the status of sociological factors in the evaluation of African literature. In the theoretical pronouncements there is a noisy division between those who insist on a formalist appraisal of literary techniques and those who emphasise the sociological understanding of the idea–content of literature. Given the marked socio-political content of the literary works themselves, the polarization reduces ultimately to *a-political* versus *political* criticism. The advocates of a non-sociological criticism actually are the African variety of the familiar theorists of the disembodied conception of 'art-for-art's sake'.

Art for art's sake critics

It is the intervention of this kind of criticism that forced Achebe into his self-doubt. 'Perhaps what I write is applied art as distinct from pure.' The Nigerian critic Dan S. Izevbaye is the most sophisticated advocate of art for art's sake criticism. In 1971, he acknowledged without apparent regret the sociological conditioning of the colonial milieu which informed the birth of literature, but hoped that a literature with a 'suppressed social reference' would develop, so that non-sociological criticism could in fact advance:

> With this new emphasis in criticism, that is the suppression of the social reference of literature as a significant influence in criticism, it may be easier for critics to pay greater attention to the literary work itself. But the influence of the referential element on African criticism has not really been an intrusion. The social factor was important only because the literature itself was largely sociological. As the literature becomes less preoccupied with the social or national problems and more concerned with the problems of men as individuals in an African society, the critical reference will be human beings rather than society, and the considerations which influence critical judgement will be human and literary rather than social ones.[7]

In his most recent survey of *The State of Criticism in African Literature* (1975) there is a stronger tone of lament that the suppression of the social reference has still not dominated literary scholarship. In the process his earlier theoretical errors of a false counterposing of abstract 'human beings' against society, remain intact. The immaculate conception of a transcendent literature remains unrevised. Instead of seeing the predominance of sociological criticism of African literature as a signal of the intrinsic *sociality* of literature, he blames this critical tendency on the 'present intellectual climate which encourages the critical faculty' towards the 'sociological imagination'.[8] And in a further ambiguous sentence, which is nonetheless ideologically revealing, he states that 'the political option implied in this preference for sociological significance over moral values may be related to the precedence which political liberation takes over religious piety in Africa'.[9] Thus, Izevbaye's art-for-art's sake advocacy is really for a depoliticized literary universe inhabited by abstract human beings with the abstract moral values of an abstract religious pietism. A literary universe which, our prosaic logic compels us to add, must be created by astral writers and equally astral critics!

If with Izevbaye, we end up with an astral animism, with Eustace Palmer, the search for the ideal literature of pure form, leads us to a fundamental linguistic perversion. For a critic who never tires of searching for 'signs of technical competence' in his recent book-length study of African novels, he displays remarkable linguistic incompetence. Consider the following usage of 'decolonization' in this passage:

> The decolonization of African literature is already in progress. Novelists are becoming less preoccupied with cultural and sociological matters, and more concerned about exposing the corruption and incompetence which are so wide-spread in African political and government circles.[10]

In this search for 'decolonized' literature in which the ordinary meaning of 'sociological matters' is newly restricted to social issues of an anti-colonial salience, Eustace Palmer virtually *misreads* all the novels he has considered in his book. To take a ready example, his enthusiasm for Western civilization, makes him transform the content of Mongo Beti's *Mission to Kala*, into its very opposite:

> *Mission to Kala* is neither an attack on education nor on Western civilization; rather, it is a brilliant satire directed against all those half-baked young men who feel that a partial exposure to Western ways makes them superior to their countrymen who still live the tribal life. Mongo Beti subjects Jean Marie's personal weaknesses – his condescension, arrogance, and stupidity – to rigorous criticism by means of his comic act.[11]

The foregoing excerpts, brief as they are, sufficiently indicate the ideological motivation of the art for art's sake advocates. Their true concern is to proscribe literature of an anti-imperialist content. It is this preoccupation that leads them to misconceptions about the meaning of the term 'sociological.' In their practical criticism, of course, they are unable to concentrate solely on technical stylistic matters. In fact, with a critic like Palmer, the much-vaunted formalistic criticism does not go beyond the labelling of an author's style as 'ironic' or 'satirical.'

Criticism of this type very often consists of documenting the technical affinity between an African writer and a writer in Euro-America. However, this documentation, this tracing of an author's artistic ancestry, is not pursued with the knowledge that artistic forms are themselves historical products. The fact that Euro-American models, which are often held as the atemporal, immutable yardsticks with which the African writer's achievement is judged, were usually consequences of conscious literary manifestos by writers consciously reacting to the political issues of their times is ignored. For example, when the symbolism or surrealism of this or that writer is praised, there is no awareness of the ideological purposes for which these literary movements were created in the milieu of capitalist-industrial Europe. Whether or not such ideological purposes are at cross-purposes with contemporary African reality is never broached.

Interlude

> The bourgeoisie has stripped of its halo every occupation hitherto honoured and looked up to with reverent awe. It has converted the physician, the lawyer, the priest, the poet, the man of science, into its paid wage labourers.

Marx and Engels, The Communist Manifesto

Bourgeois sociological criticism

In light of the foregoing, it is not surprising that most bourgeois criticism of African literature is predominantly of the sociological kind. But even here the theoretical premise does not rise above the *obvious truth* that 'literature deals with life'. Thus, whereas we encounter abstract 'human beings' without political and cultural vitality among the purists, here we are faced with the conception of a literature that flows from an undifferentiated life. It derives from a conception of society that is undifferentiated by class. If the 'mellifluous universalism' (Kwame Nkrumah's phrase) of art for art's sake is tempered by a recognition of concrete particularity, then it is only the particularity of culture. Within each culture there are no class cleavages. All is consensus. The favoured image of a society or culture is the organismic one.

The theory of art and literature implicit in this sociological criticism is naturally the rigid mimetic one. Art and literature reflect the whole cultural organism – the 'collective mind' of the whole society. Literature does not struggle against society. Its reflective attribute is invested always with the integrative flavour characteristic of the homeostatic functions which functionalist social anthropology ascribed to any and all institutions. In fact, in their contest with the art for art's sake theorists, they cite the findings of social anthropologists of the functionality of traditional African arts for the sustenance of religious values, socialization, social control and the like.

In recent debates with art for art's sake advocates, protagonists of the sociological school frequently cited, for support, Abiola Irele's 1971 justification of the sociological approach as:

> . . . attempts to correlate the work to the social background to see how the author's intention and attitude issue out of the wider social context of his art in the first place and, more important still, to get to an understanding of the way each writer or each group of writers captures a moment of the historical consciousness of the society. The intimate progression of the collective mind, its working, its shapes, its temper, these – and more – are determinants to which a writer's mind and sensibilities are subject, to which they are responding all the time and which, at a superficial or profound level, his work will reflect in its moods and structures.[12]

This rather undialectical conception of literature and society has led to various kinds of bourgeois sociological criticism. Bourgeois sociology of African literature is variegated: each variety has its special nuances and conclusions. However, all versions of this sociological criticism thus far, have seized on 'culture', rather than 'society' as its operational concept. This operational focus has enhanced the tendency of veering away from social-relational dynamics in the analysis of the interaction between literature and society. Culture, with its more immediate mentalistic connotations, was a sure path to various forms of literary idealism. The current in African political parlance has been to see African culture or 'tradition', not as a specific ideological rationalization of the ways our forebears at specific historical periods tackled their problem of survival, but as the eternally valid source of wisdom by which African behavior, a-temporally conceived, must be judged. This is an endemic habit of bourgeois sociological criticism. Terry Eagleton has recently shown how a progressive sociological critic of English literature, Raymond Williams, was often led to idealist conclusions, in spite of his personal radical commitment, because of the operational centrality of the concepts of culture and tradition in his early works.[13]

In the hands of the less progressive sociological critics of African material, the upshot of these fundamental concepts – African culture and African tradition – has been the institutionalization of what we may call a Festac anthropology. A 'Festac' anthropological thrust which has transmuted 'African extended family', 'African religion', 'African rhythm', 'African time' into eternal base categories for the analysis of contemporary literature. The difficulties which currently plague the new literary movement among African critics in quest of indigenous black/African aesthetics stem from this idealistic Festac anthropology. It is not surprising, that beyond the hortatory language of advocacy, the findings of the movement to date have not advanced beyond the metaphysical sensibilities of animism, spontaneous *Gemeinschaft*, rhythm, balance, and vital force, attributed to the African by the Senghorean variant of Negritude.[14]

We might add in passing, that this idealistic distortion of the African and his society is also on the rise in the new dramatic literature issuing from Nigeria. The representation of the African as being exclusively interested in 'ontological questions rather than on the "prosaic" issues of economy and politics', as well as his abdication of politics before his feudal king – negritude's 'custodian of African tradition' – has been the dominant theme of enthusiastic Nigerian petty-bourgeois theatre in the neo-fascist era of Gowon.[15]

Another kind of bourgeois sociological criticism has been the preoccupation with what we might call cultural archaeology. By this we refer to the attempt to excavate the literary texts for traditionalia, in terms of which the text is then explained. While for some this is the critical procedure, others (usually non-Africans) have absolutized the procedure into a normative requirement for good African literature. Thus the injunction that the writer should describe his 'cultural anxiety' about issues such as the 'abuses of the dowry system or of polygamy'. The writer should probe the 'telluric' sentiment of the black continent for 'an authentic exoticism'.[16] However, be it a critical procedure or normative prescription, we can do no better than quote Biodun Jeyifo, the Nigerian Marxist critic of theatre, who passed this sharp judgement on this form of petty-bourgeois sociological perspective:

> . . . (it) enthrones 'culture' and cultural facts as inexhaustible reservoirs of sociological capital. These 'natural' cultural facts are made to give either ethnic-racial-civilizational values as the determinants of the destinies of conflicted individual heroes . . . or give the use of ethno-cultural lore, idioms and motifs for the sensuous material surface of dramatic action as an undialectical validation of the social attitudes and relations which these cultural facts and traditionalia initially sustained . . .[17]

The recourse to functionalist sociology and the cultural anthropology of cultural relativity also trap critical works that seek to examine a particular corpus of African literature in dynamic perspective. The problems which beset the emphasis of bourgeois academic sociology on 'role-players', rather than role-authors, 'culture-bearers', rather than culture-creators, in the handling of structure-breaking change, exist in the literary critical tradition predicated on this sociology. The theoretical preference for *gradualist* reformist dynamics, the distortion of the colonial situation as 'culture-contact', the diagnosis of the Third World's agenda as that of 'modernization', and the projection of advanced capitalist culture as the final aspiration of true man, all of which bourgeois sociology has propagandized, are typical features of this type of criticism.

It is this essentially mellifluous utopian cultural diffusionist trajectory that informs Charles R. Larson's study of the 'emergence' of African fiction. For him the African writer's passage has been to play the 'historian of his continent's increasingly widened outlook on life, moving from a limited, virtually closed-off societal view of the village and the clan to an ever-widening world view'.[18] Since Larson never strays from within the rigid parameters of undialectical cultural anthropology, the individual-character dominated novel of this specific epoch of the bourgeois West, inadvertently becomes the true novelistic form (inadvertent because of his initial premise of cultural relativity in the determination of literature) to which the African novel is emerging.[19]

The power of a false theoretical perspective to vitiate the insights of a serious sociological critic whose personal progressive temper is not in doubt, is nowhere better revealed than in Emmanuel Obiechina's massive study *Culture, Tradition and Society in the West African Novel*. The book opens with an approving quotation of Daniel Lerner's saccharine formulation of the Third World agenda in *The Passing of Traditional Society*. Not surprisingly, the book ends with a consideration of 'culture contact and culture conflict'. This sublimination of the revolutionary project as psycho-cultural modernization, prevents Obiechina from offering a critique of the artist's apprehension of the colonial situation which produced the culture-contact in the first place. As with Larson, unfactored notions such as 'urbanization,' 'adjustment to modern social change' are used to paper over a specific critic of the writer's consciousness. Instead, Obiechina postpones the task:

> The latter themes (e.g. politics) are in themselves important and con-
> stitute a vast, promising area of their own, but it seems sound sense,
> first and foremost, to survey the terrain, to observe the physical fea-
> tures, locate the signposts and generally create an outline map as aid
> to more realistic purposeful exploration of the literature.[20]

But it is a postponement largely based on the false theoretical premise that
indigenous cultural categories constitute the dynamic basis of life in the
violent manicheism of colonial society.

THE FESTAC CONSCIOUSNESS

> If we truly seek a rebirth from the culture of colonialism to the col-
> lectivist anti-imperialist culture of the African masses, the masses
> must first have sovereignty in the decisions that affect the political
> and economic future of the nation.
>
> The Nigerian Academy of Arts, Sciences & Technology, *The Nigerian
> Peoples Manifesto, Political Programme*, Ibadan, 1974.

The Festac metaphor which we have already invoked at several junctures,
is an appropriate one for summing up the consciousness of bourgeois approaches to the study of African literature. All variants of bourgeois criticism, nationalist variants included, are implicated in this consciousness.
Like the Festac revisionisms which have become as prominent as military
coups and pseudo-economic indigenization projects, bourgeois sociological
criticism creates the illusion of a classless, cultural consensus in contemporary African societies.

Secondly, bourgeois criticism shares with Festac activists a fundamental
misunderstanding of the true purpose of colonial cultural imperialism.
Bourgeois cultural scholars imagine that cultural aggression was not necessary to colonial domination. The attempt by the colonizer to transplant his
own values is seen in the result of the colonizer's ignorance or the Christian missionary's proselytizing zeal. They fail to realize that the new capitalist economy which the colonizer introduced, logically required the
institutionalization of a bourgeois consciousness in order to facilitate the
advance of the economy. In fact, bourgeois critics as well as many of our
Festac statesmen, restrict the definition of the colonial trauma to the loss
of political sovereignty and cultural initiative. They maintain amnesia over
the decisive character of the colonial experience – which is the coerced incorporation of African societies into the exploiting capitalist social system.
It is this amnesia, which is self-serving, that makes Festac statesmen imagine that the periodic revival of 'traditional' dances in the urban sports stadia
of our African capitalist societies, would stem the erosion of our pre-colonial
heritage. When bourgeois literary critics devalue anti-colonial literature a
priori, they are in the throes of this amnesia.

Since this literary criticism is even more backward than the actual
literature which it 'criticizes', it is unable to evaluate literary content in any
rigorous manner. Confronted with two novels inspired by the same social

theme, bourgeois literary criticism is unable to tell us in any scientific way, which treatment is more valid. If we may invoke Plekhanov, this criticism has been largely unable to discriminate between false and true ideas.[21] Instead, criticism of content stagnates on the mere descriptive reproduction of manifest material.

In so far as criticism is held to have an impact on the development of literature, the effect of bourgeois criticism of African literature can only impede, rather than inspire it towards revolutionary heights. The defects of bourgeois criticism are not solely a question of the handicaps of theoretical outlook in every instance. In a world where the N.L.F., PAIGC, FRELIMO and MPLA exist as concrete realities, the persistence of a bourgeois outlook must stem also from the material class interest of the literary critic. The 'educational' role which bourgeois critics have ascribed to their activity has, in several instances, become a mask for a self-promoting careerist industry. For example, when in a study of Soyinka's plays, a Nigerian critic can talk of 'alleged corruption', 'alleged election rigging' during the blatantly obvious man-of-the-people politics of pre-war Nigeria, we are forced to agree with Biodun Jeyifo's conclusions that criticism has become a 'parasitic, opportunistic vocation of salaried, petty-bourgeois intellectual hustlers.'[22]

Interlude

> Revolutionary literature and art should create a variety of characters out of real life and help the masses to propel history forward. For example, there is suffering from hunger, cold and oppression on the one hand, and exploitation and oppression of man by man on the other. These facts exist everywhere and people look upon them as commonplace. Writers and artists concentrate such everyday phenomena, typify the contradictions and struggles within them and produce works which awaken the masses, fire them with enthusiasm and impel them to unite and struggle to transform their environment.

> Mao Tse-Tung, *Talks at the Yenan Forum*

MARXISM AND AFRICAN LITERATURE, A PROSPECTUS

Unlike bourgeois criticism, Marxist criticism has never involved itself in any internal conundrums about the admissibility of sociological factors in the consideration of art and literature. Marxist criticism is necessarily sociological. This sociological nature, as Lunacharsky[23] once argued, is what immediately distinguishes it from all other types of literary criticism. However, its sociology is rooted in the materialist understanding of cultural consciousness given by Marx:

> The mode of production of the material means of life determines, in general, the social, political and intellectual processes of life. It is not the consciousness of human beings which determines their existence, it is their social existence which determines their consciousness.[24]

59

Marxist critics have always insisted that in class societies, this contingent relationship of intellectual production and consciousness on material economic relationships is mediated by the class structure, by way of class interests and class psychology. In class societies, culture, art and literature take on a class character. Literature in such circumstances is fully implicated in the class struggle. It can either evince a consciousness that seems to conserve the society in behalf of privileged interests or exude a revolutionary consciousness congruent with the objective interests of the oppressed class which is engaged in the struggle to change the social status quo.

The charge by bourgeois critics (often heard at conferences on African literature) that Marxist critics devalue art and literature is, of course, unfounded. A host of Marxist critics, Plekhanov, Hauser, Caudwell, Fischer and Thomson, to name a few, have in fact demonstrated the importance of art in the very evolution of human culture. *The Necessity of Art* is indeed the revealing title of Fischer's contribution. It is bourgeois critics who, having concocted a variety of non-historical pagan muses as the sources of literature and art, have in fact robbed artistic productions of any vitality in the activities of *real* men to liberate themselves from social exploitation and prostration before nature.

Given this revolutionary understanding of the dialectical relationship between literature and social struggle, Marxist critics do not conceive of literary criticism as an abstract academic activity with abstract justifications. Marxist critics are necessarily class partisan. They do not camouflage this partisanship. Marxist critics also recognize that the very analytical categories which constitute the vocabulary of literary scholarship are themselves historical products. These vocabularies and theories, like their counterparts in other domains of scholarship, must at all times be subjected to a radical sociology of knowledge – a sociology of knowledge which includes an assessment of the objective material interests of the class creators of the ideas. Marxist critics are always concerned, in the final analysis, with the assessment of artistic visions in terms of their practical relevance to the struggle for ever more democratic forms of social existence.

Consequently, Marxist criticism also goes beyond a formal and content analysis of artistic works, to a consideration of the very institutional processes of art creation and art-criticism. Marxist critics are concerned to struggle for a democratization of the structures of artistic production and criticism. They are concerned to free the artistic process from structural fetters. This has become very pressing in our late capitalist period where art and literature have value, only as commodities. The Marxist critics' dream is for a community where all can be artists and art-appreciators.

Finally, we must repeat (because of the state of decadence of contemporary African sociology) that a Marxist sociological perspective is not to be confused with the bourgeois sociology or anthropology which sees men as passive 'role-players' and 'norm-bearers'. For a Marxist sociology, men are not just stage performers, they are also fundamentally playwrights and authors. Roles and norms are not scripted by a *deus ex machina*. On the contrary, it is always within the possibility of *real* men living in *real* societies to alter the scripts.

TOWARDS A MARXIST SOCIOLOGY OF AFRICAN LITERATURE

The achievements of Marxist critics such as Lukács and Goldmann in the field of European scholarship are no longer contested. Therefore, my final remarks will be devoted to a prospectus of the possibilities of a Marxist criticism of African literature. Perhaps we should begin by drawing attention to what the emergent Marxist mode of African literary criticism has in fact achieved.

African Marxist criticism has thus far concentrated on the ideological critique of the literature. This critique of the social-world outlook of African writers as represented in their concrete texts, is founded on a firm sociology of the exploiting capitalist essence of the colonial social order. This critique of the history of the new literature reveals that it is the colonial social order that constituted its concrete parameters. Marxist criticism is therefore predicated on the practical necessity of anti-colonial revolution which is anti-imperialist and prospectively socialist. The class constituency of this criticism is unabashedly the proletarian-peasant. From this standpoint, Marxist critics have been able to indicate whether or not the conceptual representations and evocative images which infuse the social universe imagined in a writer's poem, story or play, are progressive, reactionary or reformist. They do not, like bourgeois critics, reach these judgements by an abstract a-historical universalism. On the contrary, their materialist premise and their dialectical method has led Marxist critics to show that African literary movements such as Negritude were in the historical situation of their emergence, progressive tendencies. Today, the development of classes and class struggle within Africa in the context of the international imperialist order has qualitatively transformed the effects of these literary ideologies into their opposite. Negritude today has an attractive reactionary purpose for many ruling circles in African states.

The problem of universalism that has plagued bourgeois criticism has generally been solved by reference to proletarian internationalism. This, for example, is one of the thrusts of the theoretical essays of Ngugi wa Thiong'o in *Homecoming*. Bourgeois African criticism lays emphasis on the analysis of 'form' as its special province of distinction in African literary studies. Yet its analysis of *form* (which is only vaguely defined) does not go beyond the itemization of technique, the tracing of Euro-American parallels and, in novelistic and dramatic literature, the judging of the appropriateness of the language of a character. But Marxist critics have also attended to this issue of formal structures. Characterization, which is crucial to literature, has been an especial focus. The Marxist concern for characterization goes beyond a mere descriptive reproduction of the surface material into a critique of the class representations. Marxist critics have not seen the *imagined* characters simply as free-floating individuals. On the contrary, the characters who populate a writer's fictional universe also belong to social classes. And it was a Marxist-oriented critic, Ngugi, who first drew attention to the fact that one of the problems of Soyinka's literature, was the unreal facelessness of his working-class characters. Since Marxists hold that the working masses are the true makers of history, the images of the masses contained in literature are crucial signals of a writer's political standpoint.

Thus, in a work like Achebe's *A Man of the People*, Nigerian critics have often pointed out the significance of the writer's silence on the 1964 General

61

Strike of the workers. Instead, workers and peasants are represented as clowns steeped in the bourgeois culture of corruption, although in real Nigerian life, they have no structural opportunities to receive bribes. These are some of the real structural weaknesses of the book. It is these, rather than its supposed 'journalism', which vitiate the artistic achievement.

However, criticism of African literature, bourgeois and Marxist, has not investigated some of the other issues which bourgeois sociological criticism elsewhere has normally thrived on. I refer here to what Terry Eagleton, in a negative context, has described as the 'means of literary production, distribution and exchange in a particular society – how books are published, the social composition of their authors and audiences, levels of literacy, the social determinants of "taste"'.[25]

In our view, these topics are important for rigorous study in Africa. First, the very sociality of literature requires that criticism go beyond the literary text to include the very structures of its manufacture. Secondly, in the special circumstances of Africa, where the entire institutional fabric of book publishing, film and record manufacture, is dominated by neo-colonial agencies, studies of their impact on what currently passes for African arts, are urgent. The reactionary ideological impact of this domination which Nkrumah pointed out long ago in his book *Neocolonialism*, was recently borne out by a letter to the Tanzanian *Daily News* during a controversy on films. This particular letter wondered why 'Kung-Fu' films, etc., popular with the Dar es Salaam audiences, were being condemned.

This kind of situation shows that when Marxist sociologists study the media and the audiences, their studies must go beyond mere empiricist fact-finding. They must be guided by the necessity to create alternative democratic structures where the masses can become creators rather than passive consumers of art. Post-Cultural Revolution China has shown this to be a practical possibility in the arts. And if African examples were needed, the traditions of *communal* artistic creation and criticism of pre-colonial and pre-class oral literatures show us what was achieved by our forebears before 'the rain began to beat' *the masses*.

Notes

1   Mao Tse-Tung 'Talks at the Yenan Forum on Literature and Art,' May, 1942, in Mao Tse-Tung *On Literature and Art*, Foreign Language Press, Peking, 1967, p. 25.
2   Frantz Fanon, *The Wretched of the Earth*, Grove Press, Inc., New York, 1968, p. 41.
3   Aimé Césaire, 'The Man of Culture and His Responsibilities', *Présence Africaine*, Nos 24–5, February–May 1959, p. 127.
4   See Omafume F. Onoge, 'The Crisis of Consciousness In Modern African Literature: A Survey', in *Canadian Journal of African Studies*, Vol. VIII, No. 2, 1974, pp. 385–410. This essay has been reprinted in this book.
5   Chinua Achebe, 'The Novelist as Teacher', in Chinua Achebe's *Morning Yet On Creation Day*, Heinemann, London, 1974.
6   Omafume F. Onoge, 'The Possibilities of a Radical Sociology of African Literature: Tentative Notes', in Donatus Nwoga, ed., *Literature and Modern West African Culture*, Ethiope Publishing Corporation, Benin, 1978, pp. 90–6.
7   Dan Izevbaye, 'Criticism and Literature in Africa', in Christopher Heywood, ed., *Perspectives on African Literature*, Heinemann, London, 1971, p. 30.
8   Dan Izevbaye, 'The State of Criticism in African Literature', in *African Literature Today* (No. 7, Focus on Criticism), 1975, p. 16.
9   *Ibid.*, p. 16.

10   Eustace Palmer, *An Introduction to the African Novel*, Heinemann, London, 1972,
     p. 129.
11   *Ibid.*, p. 154.
12   Abiola Irele, in C. Heywood, ed., *op. cit.*, p. 16.
13   See Terry Eagleton, 'Criticism and Politics: The Work of Raymond Williams',
     New Left Review, No. 95, January–February 1976, pp. 3–23.
14   See for example, Pio Zirimu and Andrew Gurr, eds., *The Black Aesthetic*, East
     African Literature Bureau, Nairobi, 1973. Several papers in this conference
     collection confirm this point. Indeed, Grant Kamenju's paper which politicized
     the topic along Fanonian lines remains isolated in this volume of idealist
     reification. The journal, *Okike*, edited by Chinua Achebe, has carried several
     essays seeking an African aesthetic. The Afro-American world of letters has also
     been involved in this search. Unfortunately, most of their efforts to seek African
     roots have been marked by a reliance on the categories of Festac anthropology.
     For example, Reverend John Mbiti's idealist *African Religions and Philosophy* is very
     popular in certain Afro-American circles.
15   For a preliminary radical critique of this theatre see, Omafume F. Onoge and
     G. G. Darah, 'The Retrospective Stage: Some Reflections on the Mythopoeic
     Tradition at Ibadan', in CH'INDABA, Vol. 3, No. 1, October/December 1977,
     pp. 52–7.
16   The quoted injunctions are from Lilyan Lagneau-Kesteloot and Dorothy Blair,
     respectively. A contextual discussion of them is contained in my 'Crisis of
     Consciousness In Modern African Literature: A Survey', *op. cit.*, pp. 396–7.
17   Biodun Jeyifo, 'Toward A Sociology of African Drama', (mimeo), Dept of English
     Staff Seminar Paper, University of Ibadan, April 27, 1976.
18   Charles R. Larson, *The Emergence of African Fiction*, Indiana University Press,
     Bloomington, 1972 (revised edition), p. 280.
19   Larson, of course, in the last paragraph of his book declaims that it would be
     'impossible to expect that there could be only one direction for African fiction',
     p. 282. However, we insist that the general thrust of his text contradicts this
     caveat. Throughout the work his conception of the Western novel – which,
     incidently is a-historical – is the contrasting yardstick for the evaluation of the
     African novel. The evolutionary forms of the Western novel in the hands of
     bourgeois and anti-bourgeois writers are ignored. (No consideration is given to the
     fact that Chinese literary history speaks of the novel form at least two centuries
     before the emergence of the 'Western' novel.)
20   Emmanuel Obiechina, *Culture, Tradition and Society in the West African Novel*,
     Cambridge University Press, 1975, pp. 265–6.
21   G. Plekhanov, *Unaddressed Letters, Art and Social Life*, Foreign Languages Publishing
     House, Moscow, 1957 (translated from the Russian by A. Fineberg).
     Note: This is a crucial point for Plekhanov in the sections of the book which deal
     with 'Art and Social Life'. Here is one of his remarks:

> I have already said that there is no such thing as a work of art which is
> entirely devoid of ideas. And I added that not every idea can serve as the
> foundation of a work of art. An artist can be really inspired only by what
> is capable of facilitating intercourse among men. The possible limits of
> such intercourse are not determined by the artist, but by the level of
> culture attained by the social entity to which he belongs. But in a society
> divided into classes, they are also determined by the mutual relations of
> these classes and, moreover, by the phase of development in which each of
> them happens to be at the time. (p. 187)

22   Biodun Jeyifo, 'Literalism and Reductionism In African Literary Criticism:
     Further Notes on Literature and Ideology', unpublished manuscript.
23   Anatoly Lunacharsky, *On Literature and Art*, Progress Publishers, Moscow, 1973
     (second revised edition).
24   Karl Marx, *Introduction To the Critique of Political Economy*.
25   Terry Eagleton, *Marxism and Literary Criticism*, Methuen & Co. Ltd., London,
     1976, p. 2.

CHAPTER FOUR

TWO AFRICAN AESTHETICS: SOYINKA VS. CABRAL

Geoffrey Hunt

> And then there is Don Quixote, who long ago paid the penalty for wrongly imagining that knight errantry was compatible with all economic forms of Society.
>
> Marx

Romanticism has often been treated exclusively in terms of one of two approaches: either as a permanent tendency of 'human nature' or purely as a historically specific cultural phenomenon. That is, either as a universal tendency in human culture or as an absolutely specific phenomenon peculiar to the first half of the nineteenth century in Europe. An alternative, which may be called the dialectical historical approach, and which has not been given due consideration, is that romanticism is neither universal nor specific in absolute senses, and both universal and specific in relative senses. What we propose is that romanticism is a cultural response to collective insecurity which to some degree, or in some form, exists in all societies in so far as such societies rest on class divisions, but that this response, as the dominant feature of culture on the artistic plane, is specific to a particular form of society, namely one under transition to capitalist economic structure and bourgeois legal-political superstructure.[1]

Romanticism is the dominant form under transition to bourgeois rule because class division is most pronounced under capitalism and the period of transition has the most profound and traumatic dislocating effects on culture, romanticism being precisely a form in consciousness of this dislocation.[2] When the transitionary period has passed and the class structure stabilized, consciousness adopts more settled and systematic responses to class division in the elaborate ideologies of capitalism: liberalism, parliamentarism, nationalism, positivism, commodity fetishism and so on. The transitionary period, however, is the period of rapid class formation, usually passing through short-lived phases of class alliances and a consequent class-ambivalence in consciousness. It is this ambivalence which is the foundation of romanticism.

If this thesis about romanticism is correct, and it is a thesis not only about the origin of the movement but about its form and even its content, then one would expect romanticism as a movement whenever there is a society in process of rapid transformation to bourgeois class structure. Some modern neo-colonial societies have recently gone, or are still going, through a process of rapid 'integration' into the world capitalist order. The more rapid the process the more rapid the new class formation and the more severe the dislocation of culture and the demand for new forms in consciousness. Nigeria is a striking example of a society which has undergone, and is still undergoing, traumatic political-economic restructuring in recent times, the process having been accelerated by the sudden dependence of the entire economic structure on the export of a single high-revenue primary commodity, oil.[3] Literature and drama in the English language have flowered in Nigeria in the interval since independence in 1960, and romanticism has been a strong trend.

The greatest representative of Nigerian literature is generally taken to be Wole Soyinka, now internationally renowned for his plays, poetry and novels. The main aims of this essay are:

1   to indicate that the category 'romanticist' is fully applicable to Wole Soyinka, a twentieth century neocolonial writer;

2   to indicate that Soyinka's neo-romanticism can be explained in the dialectical historical fashion we have outlined, in particular by means of the notions of rapid class formation, class alliance, class-ambivalence and severe cultural dislocation (Soyinka is taken as a first test case of a thesis which rests on a preliminary survey of many other instances); and,

3   to sketch the political basis and ramifications of Soyinka's neo-romanticism.

EUROPEAN ROMANTICISM AND AFRICAN NEO-ROMANTICISM

A number of critics have, of course, in one way or another, seen nineteenth century European romanticism as a specific response to the economic and political upheavals of the time, particularly in Germany and France. Arnold Hauser's thesis is perhaps the most well known.[4] Hauser asserts that: 'The fact that so many of the representatives of romanticism were of noble descent no more alters the bourgeois character of the movement than does the anti-philistinism of its cultural policy'.[5] At the same time he admits that many romanticists 'were filled with hatred and contempt for the very class to which they owed their intellectual and material existence. For romanticism was essentially a middle-class movement.. . .', but 'romanticism had an equivocal relationship to the Revolution.'[5] Hauser almost puts his finger on the true class nature of the movement, but it escapes him and he is left with an uncomfortable congeries of ideas: the romanticists were often *non*-middle-class, were *essentially* middle-class and were *anti*-middle-class.

What unifies all these points and immediately throws light on the social origin of the movement is the realization that the class basis of the movement was that of objective *class-alliance* and subjective class-ambivalence. The economic and political shocks of the period had thrown a section of the aristocracy into alliance with the upper bourgeoisie and vice-versa. The aristocracy was ready to side either with the monarchy or give up the monarchy for the new, ascendant ruling class. The same suspension of commitment occurred with the echelons of the bourgeoisie. The tendency of the group was on the whole conservative, as it feared the solidarity of the working class and peasantry, but it was forced into a progressive stance in so far as the monarchy and feudal power blocs obstructed the development of the forces of production on which the existence of the bourgeoisie rested. In Hauser's terms the alliance was essentially middle-class (bourgeois) but also non-middle-class (noble), and at the same time disdainful of the lower bourgeoisie and petty bourgeoisie. The petty bourgeoisie was that large and expanding group intermediary between the bourgeoisie proper and the working class and directly dependent upon, even parasitic upon, the bourgeoisie proper. This group was uncultured, whereas the aristocratic-bourgeois alliance was cultured and required, to legitimate its rule, an ideological-intellectual response to the neoclassicist culture of the *ancien régime*, a response which was unnecessary or impossible for the petty bourgeoisie because of its subordinate position. The alliance was dreadfully insecure and ambivalent, facing two ways at once and fearing reprisals from two other classes, one 'above' and one 'below'. The aristocratic segment was still, in the first phase, the leading element which went over to the bourgeoisie as a group of 'traditional intellectuals' in a kind of 'passive revolution'.

A typical intellectual response to a situation of class-ambivalence in a context of rapid economic transformation is escape by transference of the problem and its resolution into a mystical, other-worldly realm. This transference enable an escape from commitment and action, escape from the insecurities of shifing political alliances, escape into the certainties of the past when class alliance was unnecessary, and escape into a sphere 'free' of, or 'above', all class politics. Finally, it allows an escape from the horrors of industrialization and urbanization and the working class misery on which the new ruling class power was all too obviously founded. In the transitionary period it is not clear which class is in control, so that no particular class can identify itself as the controlling power in society. The perception of class equilibrium, of political confusion, leaves the stage open for Bonapartism and the *coup d'état*. The response of the intellectuals to this state of affairs is to relocate control in a mystified abstract realm: God, the Ego, the State, the Individual, Tradition, Nature.

The thesis of class-ambivalence in a bourgeois-revolutionary setting might also have the advantage of offering an explanation of the *development* and diversificatiton of the romantic movement. Its passage from a supposed liberalism to conservatism in Germany, from conservatism to liberalism in France and England is to be explained perhaps by shifts in class alliance and an overall shift from class alliance to single-class preponderance; and the demise of romanticism could be accounted for in the eventual stability of single-class hegemony. As Hauser recognizes at one point,

> Formerly the middle-class writers adapted themselves to the conservatism of the aristrocrats, whereas now even the aristocratic Chateaubriand and Lamartine go over to the opposition.[6]

It might seem that the existence of the so-called 'revolutionary romantics' undermines our thesis. One might immediately recall 'Red Shelley',[7] Byron's martyrdom, Hugo's dictum that 'Romanticism is liberalism in literature', and Mazzini's radical politics. In fact, Lord Byron ever remained an aristocratic anarchist, Hugo's political vacillations between monarchy and democracy are dizzying and it is doubtful whether Shelley, heir to a baronetcy who attended Eton and Oxford, ever transcended 'reactionary socialism'.[8] As regards Mazzini, Gramsci saw how the *Partito d'Azione*, founded by Mazzini in 1853, was deeply ambivalent:

> the so-called Action Party did not base itself specifically on any historical class, and the oscillations which its leading organs underwent were resolved, in the last analysis, according to the interests of the moderates.[9]

On the whole the romantic conservatives represent the bourgeois-aristocrats (Chateaubriand) and the romantic revolutionaries represent the aristocratic-bourgeoisie (Hugo).

Although neo-colonial countries like Nigeria are not undergoing bourgeois revolutions in the same way that the western European nations did, nevertheless many of them are certainly undergoing a process of rapid economic and political transformation in which a new and ambivalent class is created based on an alliance with the foreign bourgeoisie, and involving the absorption of bourgeois values and the destruction of rigid, hierarchical values centered on status.

The ruling class in a neo-colony of Nigeria's type is what has been variously named a comprador bourgeoisie, a pseudo-bourgeoisie or a national bourgeoisie. The essential characteristic of this class is that it does not own or control capitalist means of production but acts as a commercial and sub-managerial intermediary between the foreign bourgeoisie and the local population of workers, peasants and tenant farmers. This class is dependent on the foreign bourgeoisie, its ally against the local working class and peasantry, but at the same time bases its legitimacy on the notion of 'national independence' and objectively develops interests which come gradually into conflict with those of the foreign bourgeoisie. Members of the comprador bourgeoisie are class-ambivalent in a deep, structural manner. This is obviously sustained by the twin necessity of denouncing foreign 'interference' and control as well as foreign values at the same time as having to woo the foreign bourgeoisie in order to ensure its continuing survival; and extolling traditional values while at the same time being detached from the peasantry and traditional life.

Frantz Fanon and Amilcar Cabral give us a clue to the psychology of the neocolonial intellectual in pointing to his sudden detachment from his indigenous society coupled with his, often racist, rejection by the colonizer. Most importantly, he belongs to a class which does not possess the crucial forces directing the life and development of his society, forces which thus appear alien and out of control.[10] In our view the work of Wole Soyinka is one of the highest cultural expressions of this neo-colonial class-ambivalence. It is a modern variant of romanticism.

It would clearly be tautologous if romanticism were defined in terms of certain general features of Soyinka's work only to show that his work is indeed romanticist. Instead, we can begin inductively from the examination of the features of the European movement of the early nineteenth century in order to arrive at a general designation, and use this designation to classify other cultural movements. This would still suffer from the deficiencies and risks of superficial empiricism, however, unless the general phenomenon so designated were theorized, that is, given an explanatory framework in terms of certain concealed but essential entities and processes. These are to be sought in the political-economic dynamics of societies, although we have not attempted this here except in the most preliminary fashion. However, the general literary designation of romanticism which we accept, with some historical guidelines from Hauser, is that of René Wellek.[11]

We can certainly disregard Soyinka's professed abstinence from any 'literary ideology' for he is undoubtedly a romanticist and in fact displays, with new content, and no doubt without conscious influence, all the general features of the European romanticists.[12] These features are:

1   mystical holism; the direct spiritual intuition of an absolute unity and harmony of society, nature and the individual soul. An emphasis on imagination and emotion tending to irrationalism. This mystical unity is evoked by means of word-painting.

2   A tendency to look to tradition and a more meaningful past; preoccupation with myth and a cult of the 'Volk'; an unlocated dissatisfaction with the present, and a sense of homelessness.

3   A suspicious and sceptical assessment of science and technology and a complementary emphasis on religious revival.

4   Extreme individualism; preoccupation with personal freedom and its negation in death. We now intend to examine Soyinka's work in the light of these general features.

MYSTICAL HOLISM

Mystical holism we take to be the view that all experience, all aspects of reality, are related in some deep cosmic unity which is only made apparent by mystical intuition or an emotive leap of the imagination, as Soyinka puts it, beyond 'this technologically remediable world'.[13] Where Wordsworth spoke of 'affinities, In objects where no brotherhood exists, To passive minds.....The great social principle of life, Coercing all things into sympathy.. . .', Soyinka speaks of the 'cosmic totalism' of African thought involving 'the harmonisation of human functions, external phenomena and supernatural suppositions within individual consciousness. . .'[14] Sekoni, the medium of Soyinka's philosophy in his novel *The Interpreters*, stammers out,

> In the dome of the cosmos, there is complete unity of life. Life is like the godhead, the plurality of its manifestations is only an illusion. The godhead is one. So is life, or death; both are contained in the single dome of existence.[15]

Where the European romanticists discovered their holism in an appreciation of Nature in contrast with the mechanical, materialistic and vulgar 'passive minds' of the industrial centres, Soyinka's 'totalism' is the preserve of traditional Africa threatened by a vulgar Western world inhabited by unperceptive Europeans blinded by a 'compartmentalizing habit of thought'.[16] For Soyinka, European period styles are a product of this compartmentalizing habit rather than a result of social changes, a view which is 'the purest example of the romantic view' according to Hauser.[17] Even when Soyinka recognizes that Ancient Greece manifested similar totalistic and unifying philosophies his romanticism precludes the possibility of explaining similarities and changes in culture over space and time. It could not occur to him to begin by comparing the level of petty commodity production, class structure and the politics of the warring kingdoms of pre-Socratic Greece with those of pre-colonial Yorubaland.

For Soyinka, death is the definitive means by which cosmic unity is reasserted and rediscovered. The noble, all-redeeming death, typical of European romanticism, is a constant theme of Soyinka's plays, such as *The Strong Breed, The Road, Death and the King's Horseman*, because in Soyinka's philosophy death is the bridge between the physical and the divine aspects of this universe, and it is through a ritual death that the unity of the two aspects is collectively achieved.

Soyinka's mystical holism is expressed through the usual romanticist medium of highly emotive and poetic language. Poetry is Soyinka's principal mode of expression even when writing drama or prose. The European romantic universe of mountains, lakes, forests, harvests, rain, rivers and moonlight occurs in Soyinka's writing too, complemented by the traditional village setting of baobab, goats, cowries, palm oil, yam, honey, palm wine, calabashes and plantain bound together with a mystical language embracing the 'mythopoeic', the 'abyss of transition', the 'cosmic', the 'cthonic', 'essence-ideal', 'dome of existence', and so on. His poetry is suffused with romantic emotive words verging on sentimentalism: sighs, weeps, loves, longs for, fears, dies, dares, despairs, yearns, etc. As Marx said of Chateaubriand's writing, here is 'multicoloured iridescence, word painting, the theatrical, the sublime'.[18] As one might expect, the emotive, mystical form sometimes reaches a point of total obscurity:

> Who, inhesion of disparate senses, of matter
> Thought, entities and motions, who sleep-walk
> Incensed in Nirvana – a code of Passage
> And the Night – who, cloyed, a mote in homogeneous gel
> Touch the living and the dead.[19]

One should also note the significance of an obvious parallel between the neo-Hellenism of many European romanticists which, compared with the classical period, now emphasised the orgiastic, irrational side of Ancient Greek culture and Soyinka's neo-Hellenism and its similar emphasis on the Dionysiac element of the Yoruba god, Ogun. He admits in *The Fourth Stage* that 'The Phrygian god and his twin Ogun exercise irresistible fascination',[20] and he expressed this fascination most forcefully in his adaptation of *The Bacchae* of Euripides.[21] In the 'Introduction' to this play he rejects

George Thomson's suggestion that in the Orphic brotherhoods 'men whom the class struggle had humbled and oppressed fed on the illusion of a lost equality.'[22] For Soyinka the religious belief is a real social force: 'As a social force, its powers were incalculable.'[23] However, mystical religion, like romanticism, is reconciliation or escape by transference and even Soyinka recognizes that the members of the exploited class in Ancient Greece 'are not yet strong enough to cast themselves in the role of protagonists of vengence or the suppressed deity. Punishment descends from the god himself.. . .'[24] Anyway, Thomson in fact admits that the illusion can under special circumstances be socially progressive, even revolutionary. But still, essentially, as Thomson writes elsewhere, in Orphism 'Robbed of their birthright, the exploited and dispossessed turn away in despair from the real world towards the hope of recovering their lost heritage in an illusionary world to come', and in normal circumstances this is hardly a militant stance.[25]

With regards to neo-colonialism, it is hardly surprising that a quest for harmony and unity should be the response of a sensitive mind buffeted in a society torn to shreds by imperialism. But to project this quest into a mystical and impregnable realm is the response of an ambivalent mind: one which tacitly recognizes that *real* unity has to be fought for and that that could only mean abandoning the very class on which one's survival, one's very self-determination, rests. The demand for mystical unity is therefore a response to the loss of a well-ordered universe, whether that of West European feudal hierarchy or that of Yoruba quasi-feudal hierarchy but it is a particular kind of response, one made from a position of deep ambivalence. Early nineteenth century Europe and late twentieth century Nigeria are both societies undergoing tremendous social dislocations, but this appears as *chaos* only from the standpoint of the group pulled in opposing directions. For the major classes in normal times history appears to be moving forward or backward, or even forward and backward in different respects, but never as directionless chaos. It is only to a perceived, irretrievable chaos that the quest for *mystical* unity is an appropriate response, indeed perhaps the only response that enables the subjects to retain sanity. Order is transferred from reality, where there seems to be no hope of regaining it, to an invulnerable mystical realm.

In *Death and the King's Horseman* the harmonious universe of the traditional Yoruba, in which the physical and the spiritual are supposedly one, is disturbed by the European district officer's interference in a ritual. Only the suicide of Olunde, the Western-educated Yoruba man, recently returned to his village from overseas, restores the cosmic equilibrium. The Western, divided self dies in order that the traditional and harmonious self may be reborn. Of course, for Soyinka it is not the real historical confrontation which has been transfered to the intellectual realm where resolution is 'immediate', but rather the opposite. He informs us, in terms of a truly Hegelian inversion,

> the Colonial Factor is an incident, a catalytic incident merely. The confrontation in the Play is largely metaphysical.[26]

TRADITION AND MYTH

The colonial experience made its impact on African societies, but the villages and culture were left for a time largely intact. Neo-colonialism, however, intrudes into the whole social space. The neo-colonial romanticist is forced to locate the mystical unity, the 'cohesive understanding of irreducible truths',[27] not so much in the village life of the present but that of the imagined past. Of course, the traditional cosmologies were in some ways 'total', and this is to be understood as the consciousness of a society in which the producer is not entirely separated from the product of his labor and thus from 'Nature', as occurs in capitalist commodity production with its attendant alienation. But not appreciating that culture or consciousness and the material basis of society constitute a historical bloc Soyinka commits a new literary version of the Quixotic error: the attempt to restore quasi-feudal relations under neo-colonial economy.

A nostalgia for the security of traditional values is to be found in *Kongi's Harvest* where the moral superiority of traditional kingship is assumed admittedly with a dose of scepticism, in opposition to Kongi's modern tyranny. The play depicts a struggle for ascendency between *oba* (traditional king) and a modern dictator. The dictator demands the first yam of the season, traditionally reserved for the *oba*. Although the *oba* finally concedes, a turn of events presents the dictator with the severed head of an old man on a platter in place of the fresh yam. The power of tradition is vindicated, and the sacrilegious attempt to disturb the just order of the universe fails.[28]

In *The Swamp Dwellers* the blind begger still trusts the fertility of the soil to sustain him despite the setbacks of natural disaster and against the despair of those who leave the traditional way of life on the land for the wastes of the modern city.[29] And the Third World critic, Peter Nazareth, has pointed out how Soyinka's play *The Lion and the Jewel* (completed 1957),

> has a reactionary message. For what is the play really saying? That the old ways of life, with chieftaincy, polygamy, etc., etc., are to be accepted because they are African and natural and that Westernisation is to be rejected. Yet the Westernisation represented.... is pseudo-Westernisation.[30]

In *The Interpreters* Egbo's choice of the civil service is correctly presented as 'inevitable', but as certainly cowardly and morally wrong, faced with the alternative of restoring damaged traditions by accepting a kingship which is his by hereditary right. To leave the village for the city is to go astray, as with the European romanticists. Sitting in a canoe on the river (a symbol of 'transition', that is, psychological transference) near his village Egbo is still undecided:

> But there remained the question of a choice still and he had made none, none at least that he was directly conscious of.
> 'All right, let's go.'
> 'Which way, man? You haven't said.'

Perhaps he had hoped they would simply move and take the burden of choice from him, but it was like Bandele to insist although motiveless. So, leaving it at that Egbo simply said,
'With the tide.'
Kola grinned. 'Like apostates?'[31]

And thus the imperialist tide sweeps away traditional life, and with it the very possibility of Egbo's choice.

One might recall that Soyinka once made the sound declaration that 'The African writer needs an urgent release from the fascination of the past.'[32] This was made in a much heralded 'radical' speech given in 1967, and then promptly discarded by Soyinka himself. One of his most recent productions, *Death and the King's Horseman* (published 1975), has a message almost identical with that of *The Lion and the Jewel* of nearly two decades earlier. In the present case the suicide of Olunde, first son of *Elesin Oba*, is the medium of the message, whereas in the earlier play it was the attractive Sidi's preference for the traditional chief rather than the young 'educated' man who is made to look ridiculous by Soyinka.[33]

The security, order and harmony of the past stand in stark contrast with the uncertainties, chaos and homelessness of the present. But another dimension is added to Soyinka's artistic universe by his translation of the contrast of past and present into a universal principle of construction-destruction. In *A Dance of the Forests*, says Nazareth, Soyinka,

> was showing what could go wrong because of the failures and weaknesses of human nature, not because of the political forces at work. There is no mention in this play of imperialism.[34]

Of course, there is no reason why Soyinka should explicitly 'mention' imperialism, but still one would expect a realistic philosophy of art to make social dynamics intrinsic to the form and content of a work, and in Soyinka's play imperialism is present only in so far as it is translated into the mystical. The chaotic present is simply identified with an 'eternal' aspect of the 'human condition', the negative aspect. The Yoruba god, Ogun, symbolizes the universal principle of past–present, construction–destruction; he 'represents this duality of man; the creative, destructive aspect. And I think this is the reality of society, the reality of man' says Soyinka.[35] Human history continually repeats itself, and it follows that progress is just an illusion. The point for Soyinka appears to be that while in the past there was the means of reconciliation with this human 'Destiny', in the present the 'tragic understanding' has declined, man has lost the ability to cross 'the abyss of transition', to cope spiritually with his lot.[36]

This is the message that also comes over, for example, in *Madmen and Specialists*, which is imbued with the fatalistic idea that war and suffering are inescapable, but spiritually remediable, features of the human condition. There is nothing specific in the play in point of space or time to enable us to identify causes and seek solutions. All rings of nihilism and hopelessness, and the incoherent speech of the 'Blindman' recalls the speech of 'Lucky' led by the blind Pozzo in Samuel Beckett's nihilistic *Waiting for Godot*.[37]

Other plays such as *The Swamp Dwellers* and *The Road*[38] are very similar in general outlook; the cyclic philosophy of futility also underlies much of his poetry,[39] and even in his 'radical' 1967 speech this gloomy conservatism seeps through:

> It seems to me that the time has now come when the African writer must have the courage to determine what alone can be salvaged from the recurrent cycle of human stupidity.[40]

No doubt he finds legitimation for this cyclic philosophy in African tradition: 'Traditional thought operates, not a linear conception of time, but a cyclic reality.'[41] He has denied, unconvincingly, that he promulgates a philosophy of reconciliation, and has accused his opponents of 'literalism' in interpreting his work: 'The action is cyclic, yes, but is it claimed anywhere that society returns precisely to its original phase?' He continues,

> I insist that the ideal community is possible, which is no different from the declared end-goal of a communist state by dedicated Marxists.

A socialist declaration? No, for we do return to the 'original phase' after all: his ideal community immediately harks back to 'the "traditional" world-view of African society' and 'a recourse to myth'.[42] Once again, the reactionary romanticist not the progressive realist conception of natural and social harmony.

Traditional Yoruba mythology plays a central role in Soyinka's writing. Gods, spirits and mysterious forces appear in many of his works, such as *A Dance of the Forests* for example, often in the guise of intermediaries in 'rites of passage' between the physical and the divine planes of reality.[43] What is significant is not that such mystical entities should be introduced at all, but the role they play in Soyinka's work. So often they stand as the embodiments of abstract criteria of order, justice and goodness imposed on the real, chaotic present. In *The Fourth Stage*, an essay on drama and the Yoruba gods, Soyinka explains, 'For the Yoruba, the gods are the final measure of eternity, as humans are of earthly transience.' Tragedy arises from the severance of gods and man, and it is the role of the god, Ogun, to test the bridge between man and gods. 'Only after such testing could the harmonious Yoruba world be born. . . .'[44] Whereas the traditional pantheon of the Yoruba undoubtedly reflects the technological level, social relations and divisions of traditional society, the writing of modern literature based on this traditional universe is on quite a different level, a theological level. It is no longer a reflection of pre-colonial relations but of modern, neocolonial ones. As Hauser puts it,

> The myths of classical antiquity arose from a sympathy and genuine relationship with reality; the mythology of the romantics arises from its ruins and to some extent as a substitute for reality.[45]

Just as the European romanticists did not actually communicate with the rural 'Volk' they extolled, so does Soyinka write exclusively in an ornate

English which even the African and European bourgeoisie often find impenetrable. Soyinka's readership is largely a dispirited foreign bourgeoisie, either seeking the exotic or displaying guilt feelings for colonialism and racism. The irony that Soyinka's readership is precisely his target of attack is merely the reflection of the greater irony that his class is dependent economically on the foreign bourgeoisie which nationalism demands that it rebel against.

THE A-HISTORICAL DETACHMENT OF TRADITIONAL THOUGHT

Real, not mystical, transition demands the recognition that harmony can only be achieved on a higher level by overcoming the alienation of man from the product of his labour and the severance of knowledge from social ends, and that this in turn can only be achieved by ridding society of its class structure. The revolutionary realist confronts the present and has no interest in the past or tradition except for their significance in the repossession of the present and redirection of the future. But romanticism detaches the intellect and emotions from the ground level framework of society and hence posits a desperate but necessarily ambiguous and unstable relocation of reality in the past or 'tradition'. Romantic history is that which is not interested in the realities of the past but in expressing the author's feelings about the unpleasant present. To conceal the fact that the past way of life had its own exploitative mechanism it becomes necessary to divorce aspects of African culture from the harsh realities of the political economy from which they derive their entire sustenance and meaning.

Amilcar Cabral, revolutionary leader of the liberation movement in Guinea Bissau, affirmed that a 'return to the source' can only signify the return to Africans of the power to *produce* the means of their own welfare and hence the opportunity to recreate social and spiritual harmony at a higher level. Cabral's dynamic conception of 'tradition' is therefore diametrically opposed to the petrified, eternalized conception of Soyinka. Cabral's approach is dialectal and realistic: there is no point in the past which is not already the outcome of a dialectic of conflicting forces.[46]

Instead of treating 'traditional' thought in terms of a distinction between ideology and science, Soyinka detaches it from its social and historical bases and makes it eternal and immutable. In this way he assists in the legitimation process rather than in exposing the masking character of many of the ideas involved. Thus he succumbs to external authority, whereas Cabral's realist approach allows creativity to act on determinate conditions so challenging an arbitrary authority and re-establishing it in the people as a whole. In this way literary creativity is but the shadow of historical creativity.

In *Death and the King's Horseman* the idea of 'honour' is employed in such an abstract and a-historical fashion that the hierarchical, exploitative structure of the society in which it has its role, indeed its very existence, is obscured. It would not be too great an exaggeration to say that the whole play is about a particularly feudalist idea of 'honour' (high respect, esteem, reverence accorded to exalted worth or rank), and one which the play has the effect of defending. At the very climax of the play Iyaloja uncovers the dead Olunde and exclaims:

> There lies the honour of your household and of our race. Because he could not bear to let honour fly out the doors, he stopped it with his life.[47]

That is, under the quasi-feudalist ethic of Yorubaland there is the convenient but false identity of the royal household and the 'race' under the ideological category of 'honour'.

Soyinka is always concerened with the 'apprehension of a culture whose reference points are taken from within the culture itself.'[48] Although this is a standard warning against ethnocentricity, and even racism, we find that the Nigerian poet goes *beyond* this as a way of excluding progressive analyses. One central difficulty is that he sees no distinction between wholly participating in a traditional culture and currently understanding such a culture. Although it would result in absurdities if such a distinction were to be understood in an absolute sense, it is clear that immediately we want to understand and explain in a manner appropriate for twentieth century concerns, we must go beyond the concepts of participation in tradition. Such understanding is essential to revolutionary transformation. The effect of Professor Soyinka's rejection of 'external' concepts (it is surely too facile to reject them simply as 'alien European') is to cut off all possibility of recognizing determinants of social institutions and activities and cut off all possibility that many beliefs are ideological rationalizations. It would also rule out cross-cultural comparisons and all possibility of explaining historical change.

To take an example, Soyinka's answer to the sociological relativity of tragedy is to fight against the 'decline in tragic understanding' rather than accept what he sarcastically labels the Marxist 'principle of a revolutionary rejection of the ineffable'.[49] This is similar perhaps to the obviously conservative attitude of giving up any attempt to understand changes in the moral values of the younger generation (consider the Catholic church and contraception) and viewing these changes simply as a 'decline' in absolute moral standards.[50]

Again, one would expect a conception of death to be rooted in a particular mode of social organisation for production and its capacity and pattern for generating more or less successful ways of explaining, predicting and controlling disease, birth, life expectancy and so on. But in Soyinka's case we find that from the casual observation that most people fear death, when they think about it at all (which may not be very often), is drawn the Universal Problem of Personal Extinction, the 'one definitive human experience' says Soyinka.[51] This is then cited in 'clarification' of various rituals and beliefs, grossly different as these may be. (We will not discuss here the question of whether death is an 'experience' or an end to all experience.)

Soyinka, then, habitually detaches certain 'traditional' ideas, usually religious ones, from their socio-historical foundations. This is necessary in order to romanticize these elements, because to admit that they are in reality links in an intimate concatenation of economic production, political arrangements, art and medicine, science and technology, would be to destroy the romantic illusion with the confession that hand in hand with certain forms of religious belief, for example, go certain physical inadequacies in coping with disease, natural adversity and social conflict.

Ironically, while it is the very unitariness of the 'traditional' outlook that Soyinka finds appealing, he is forced to separate the links and 'compartmentalize' (a habit which he attributes to Europeans) so destroying the unity in order to preserve the romantic illusion. Thus we find, as a necessary consequence of his idealist detachment, the implication that technology is utterly unconnected with the ethico-religious ideas embraced by a culture, and that religious institutions are similarly unconnected with technological ideas. On the other hand, it is the same logic which requires that no real difference exists between certain elements of 'tradition' and elements of 'modernity'. That is, Soyinka needs to convince us of the eternal characteristics of traditional thought and its present day relevance. Hence, for Soyinka 'ritual' and 'theatre' are indistinguishable.

On the matter of technology Soyinka mentions that some Europeans had objected to *Song of a Goat*, a play by the Nigerian J. P. Clark, on the grounds that sexual impotence was curable so that the basis for the tragedy was implausible. On this somewhat flimsy premise Soyinka draws the following conclusion by the usual idealist path: whereas for the 'European' the universe is so constricted that technology interferes with his grasp of the independently existing spiritual universe, for the 'African' technology is or can be incorporated in a unitary vision, so that 'African metaphysics' sees no incompatibility between, for example, lightning as a stream of electrons and as the expression of the will of a Yoruba god, Shango. The former is simply an 'unnecessary and misleading' redefinition of the latter. Putting aside the Negritudinist implications for a moment, the assumption of his argument is the very opposite to what he appears to conclude: the assumption is that technology can advance while everything else remains the same, that is, technology and culture are unconnected. As usual, the fallacy is that 'tragedy' has been detached from history by Soyinka so that it is 'impervious to the accident of place and time'.[52] Elsewhere Soyinka reproaches Nigerian poet and dramatist Femi Osofisan for making the point that animism accommodates natural disaster and so negates social action for improvement, or to put it in Soyinkese: 'the Marxist view of man and history, denounces the insidious enervation of the social will by the tragic afflatus'.[53] Soyinka's response to the 'Marxist view' is:

> A little more gunpowder and, not only the natives of South America but their brothers in the North would have wiped out the white invaders.[54]

What he does not ask is what kind of social organization and associated culture and beliefs make gunpowder *possible*? To provide parody as an answer let us imagine, for instance, Australian Aborigine hunter-gatherers running after small game with boomerangs all day to hurry home to quadrophonic Stockhausen in carpeted high-rise apartments as the 4:30 work siren sounds across the desert.

On the matter of religious institutions Soyinka occasionally glimpses a connection between religion and politics, but it is always an immediate and contingent connection. For example, at one point he mentions the political motivation for Shango's apotheosis. With regard to his play, *The Bacchae*, he admits that one could give a political interpretation to the revealing of a new god, but adds that this would be to miss participation 'in the process of bringing to birth a new medium in the cosmic extension to man's physical existence'.[55] In reality, in our view, it is ultimately the contradictions of economic exploitation which give rise to the delusions of false resolution. Nowhere does Soyinka regard politics and religion as conceptually interwoven, as part of the same ideological structure.

His identification of 'ritual' and 'drama' ('theatre') is shown to be unconvincing once ritual is reconnected to its concrete social mode of existence. For Soyinka the question of,

> the supposed dividing line between ritual and theatre should not concern us much in Africa, the line being one that was largely drawn by the European analyst.[56]

Although the two activities are closely related, there is an important difference between them which is not unconnected with the different kinds of social relations of production in two historically distinct forms of society. While ritual may have its theatrical aspects and vice-versa it is vital to keep in mind that theatre is *about* reality whereas a ritual *is* reality (so perceived) and this reflects a much greater degree of alienation in the form of society to which theatre is 'natural'. Without exploring the ramifications of the Principle of Aesthetic Distance it should be clear that, for instance, a Catholic baptism might have its dramatic aspect, but is directly engaged with a spiritual reality so conceived. A crucifix or ancestral mask are not stage props.

Is *Myth, Literature and the African World* itself participation in this traditional, metaphysical universe, a microcosm of African 'totalism', or is it, as we suspect, theological? In other words, is it not a self-conscious defence of a lost security, a largely imaginary security? Soyinka's book gives the lie to his own thesis; a self-negating performance. Professor Soyinka does not, as he claims, substitute the 'European Manicheanism' of 'I think therefore I am' with the 'African totalism' of 'I am therefore I think among other things', but with the tacit dualism: 'I write books therefore I am therefore I think among other things.' Indeed, a central tension of escapist traditionalism is that of the coexistence of, on the one hand, a professed rejection of 'external' concepts of understanding in favour of participation and, on the other, a *real* detachment from the ongoing lifestyle which actually forms the foundation of traditional beliefs and practices.

SCIENCE AND NEGRITUDE

Soyinka's mystical holism leads, then, to the view that the evolution of science and technology, 'some would prefer to call it a counter-evolution' he observes, has contracted not expanded human knowledge.[57] Soyinka's mythopoeia in reaction to Western technology has its parallel in the program for a revitalized mythology advocated by Schlegel and other European romanticists as a part of the general reaction against the bourgeois scientific Enlightenment: a demand for the reinstatement of spiritual purposes in the face of the growing mechanism and determinism of the Cartesian-Newtonian revolution in thought. For Soyinka Western science constricts and compartmentalizes reality whereas 'African metaphysics' sees no contradiction between modern technology and the gods. Very often modern science merely indulges in 'wasteful and truth-defeating' redefinitions of what is already presented in mythological language.[58] This view, of course, underplays the *explanatory* role of such beliefs and overemphasises their symbolic or metaphysical one. Although the Yoruba belief in the smallpox god, Shopona, may not in logic be incompatible with the discovery that the disease is caused by a microscopic virus, the latter implies preventive vaccination while the former does not (lest it be a spiritual vaccination).

Cabral on the other hand, speaks of opposing 'without violence all prejudicial customs, the negative aspects of the beliefs and traditions of our people', of the need to 'fight fear and ignorance, to eliminate little by little the subjection to nature and natural forces which our economy has not yet mastered'. He notes that, in confronting reaction, and attempting to control social forces, it is not easy 'to fight where natural phenomena can be interpreted as a product of the will of spirits'.[59]

Soyinka reacts with vitriol to any interpretation of his work as portraying 'cultural conflict', and it is not difficult to see why: it is not the case for Soyinka that 'Western culture' and 'African culture' simply see the same things but see them differently, hence conflict. Instead, African culture sees what the European cannot. Thus despite his professed rejection of Negritude Soyinka only succeeds in presenting Negritude with a slightly different content. Instead of African 'passion' contrasted with European 'reason' we now have African 'totalism' contrasted with European 'compartmentalism'.[60] This results from his simplistic identification of 'science' with the European present and mysticism or spiritualism with the African past. In fact, the point is not, as Soyinka thinks, that there is an independently existing reality with its spiritual aspect which European culture shuts off. Instead, reality is moulded according to the structure, capacities and conflicts of a particular form of society. Capitalist economy and the quasi-feudal economy present different demands and different limitations. Hence they posit entities and processes and relations which really are different because of the very different relationships these societies have with nature and their different capacities in coping with it.

It is, of course, true that pre-colonial African cultures cannot be reduced to simplistic versions of the European capitalist ones, but this has nothing to do with abstract reasons about the perception of a spiritual reality which is *there* no matter what, but with the totally different socio-economic organization. Feudalism is not, for example, a simple form of capitalism, but is qualitatively as well as quantitatively different.

The elaboration by some European romanticists of the concept of 'Volk' into a racial myth has its direct counterpart in Soyinka's Negritude. It is bound up with a reaction to scientific and rational modes of thought which are tacitly held responsible for the breakdown of the traditional universe. Although the term 'race' is frequently used in his writings to mean his own Yoruba people, it often blurs into the more general denotation of the African people. *Myth, Literature and the African World*, for example, makes free and rather uncritical use of the adjectives 'European' and 'African' to refer to culture and art, values and 'casts of mind'. He insists that the European with his science has divided and contracted the world whereas the African apprehends the whole of reality. Everything European is 'rigid' compared with African 'protean' fluidity and syncretism.[61] He assumes a contrast between African 'cosmic totalism' and,

> what is a recognizable Western cast of mind, a compartmentalising habit of thought which periodically selects aspects of human emotion, phenomenal observations, metaphysical intuitions and even scientific deductions and turns them into separatist myths (or 'truths') sustained by a proliferating superstructure of presentation idioms, analogies and analytical modes.[62]

The simplicity of the contrast is mitigated slightly by Soyinka's admission that the assumptions of Ancient Greek (presumably European) thought, for example, have a lot in common with those of 'traditional' African thought. But for all we know, this similarity (which is exaggerated by Romantics in any case) is a charming but utterly inexplicable coincidence.

We have seen that Soyinka is largely concerned to present features of the 'self-apprehension' of the 'African world' and 'African metaphysics'. Yet nowhere in his work that I have been able to trace is there any empirical basis (or reference to any) for his assumption that the countless African cultures have common features which justify reference to *the* African culture. To lump together the hunter-gatherer Pygmies of the Cameroons, the nomadic herdsmen of Kenya, the egalitarian peasant communities of the Igbo, the hierarchical semi-feudal chieftaincies of the Yoruba, the feudal emirates of Hausaland, the neo-colonial industrial centres of Nairobi, Lagos and Accra, seems premature, to say the least. Cabral has this to say:

> A thorough analysis of cultural reality does not permit the claim that there exists continental or racial cultures. This is because, as with history, the development of culture proceeds in uneven fashion, whether at the level of a continent, a 'race', or even a society ...'[63]

This view applies equally, of course, to Europe. Cabral remarked that even in Guinea-Bissau's tiny population of just over half a million it was very important for the national liberation struggle to make a distinction between the semi-feudal Fulas and the egalitarian communalist Balantes.[64] Soyinka's generalizations from Yoruba culture may not, in reality, even extend as far as the Nigerian frontiers let alone those of the African continent.

Perhaps the best illustration of Soyinka's false European-African dichotomy is his reply to the 'European' objection to Clark's *Song of a Goat*, which we have already mentioned. Instead of regarding the objection (which hardly seems typical in any case) as evidence of the socio-historical relativity of tragedy, he concludes with unfortunate alacrity:

> It underlined yet another aspect of the essential divergence of the European cast of mind from the African: that, on the one hand, which sees the cause of human anguish as viable only within strictly temporal capsules, and on the other, whose tragic understanding transcends the causes of individual disjunction and recognises them as reflections of a far greater disharmony in the communal psyche.[65]

Here, then, the ideology of ambivalence finds another expression: although Soyinka states his rebuttal of Negritude, he is unquestionably its advocate; as Nazareth also noted of one of the dramatist's earliest works, *The Lion and the Jewel*: 'Thus, ironically, while Soyinka was supposed to be rejecting Negritude, he was unconsciously writing a Negritude play!'.[66] Between that play and *Myth, Literature and the African World* stand almost two decades. In the latter work we find a rejection of a particular version of Negritude parading as a total rejection of it. He rejects a dichotomy in terms of 'European intellect' and 'African passion' and promptly substitutes one in terms of 'European compartmentalism' and 'African totalism'. One wonders whether this is not the same concession to the 'Manichean tradition of European thought' as he accuses Senghor's Negritude of having made.[67] His aim, apparently, is to establish a neo-Negritude on the basis of *purely* African categories, on an awareness of, and rejection of 'the very foundations of Eurocentric epistemology'.[68] This is the meaning of his well known aphorism that the Tiger does not need to proclaim its Tigritude, it just pounces. A Tiger, we note, has an immutable identity rooted in genetics.

One thing that he finds faulty in the old Negritude is that 'Its reentrenchment of black values was not preceded by any profound effort to enter into this African system of values'.[69] Soyinka's neo-Negritude claims to be more profound, although this profundity would appear to have little to do with empirical enquires.

We should approach Soyinka's concept of 'race' through the concept of 'class'. 'Class' has an objective existence in the essential relations of production, even though men may not be aware of it (at least in a certain stage of history); it is primary, historical and universal. 'Race', on the other hand (when it is not being used in the strictly biological sense which is irrelevant here) is a subjective response to an objective class situation, and this applies to the most extreme cases, such as South African apartheid. And it is clear that different conceptions of 'race' follow upon differences in class structure. Just consider how a 'white' man could write,

> The wild Milesian features, looking false ingenuity, restlessness, unreason, misery, and mockery ... In his rage, and laughing savagery, he is there to undertake all work that can be done by mere strength of hand and back ... he lodges to his mind in any pig-hutch or dog-hutch ... There he abides, in his squalor and unreason, in his falsity and drunken violence ...

about *other 'white'* men, if not for the fact that he is a member of the English *ruling class* referring to Irish *workers* in the last century.[70]

In an obscure passage Soyinka attempts to reabsorb 'class' into what he considers the primary concept, 'race'. He asks:

> is the reality of African social structure – from which alone 'class' can obtain concrete definition – not a thorough fusion of individual functional relations with society, one that cannot be distinguished from a 'psychological syncretism' of self and community, from a mode of self-conceiving that is identical with that of racial belonging? The contrary is not only unprovable but is inconceivable in the traditional African view of man.[71]

This seems to be nothing more than a conflation of ideology and actual social structure (not to speak of the previously noted vagueness about the actual identity of the African community being referred to). It reminds one of those naive apologists for capitalism who deny the existence of class on the ground that the workers are happy as long as they receive a wage increase from the capitalist from time to time.

Cabral's starting point is always class, not race, although he would be the first to acknowledge that what people actually believe, even if false, is always important to revolutionary practice, for ideas are a real force. Hence, 'Contradictions between classes, even when they are only embryonic, are of far greater importance than contradictions between tribes.'[72]

INDIVIDUALISM AND SUBJECTIVISM

Gerald Moore has written that he feels that 'Soyinka does not believe in collective salvations at all: it lies in the breast of every man to find his particular god and strive continually towards unity with him.'[73] This is borne out by the heroic role that Ogun (Soyinka's chosen god, with which he often identifies himself) plays in his literature. Ogun, he says, 'is the embodiment of challenge, the Promethean instinct in man, constantly at the service of society for its self-realization. Hence his role of explorer through primordial chaos ...'[74] Ogun unleashes war in order to restore cosmic justice, a creator-artist as well as destroyer, and is the agency by which the 'abyss of transition' between man and gods is bridged; he represents 'the closest conception to the original oneness of Orisa-nla'.[75]

We should also consider Soyinka's notion of the artistic work. His ultimate justification for anything he produces is 'selective eclecticism as the right of every productive being.'[76] The word 'right' here merely imparts an aura of legitimacy to the more transparent formulation, 'I can do as I like'. But precisely what interests us is what he does like and why. He is likely to dismiss the latter question as idle speculation, for we are told that the artist chooses 'and of course we can speculate on the sociological factors involved in this choice ad infinitum.'[77] Compare with Schlegel's 'the arbitrariness of the poet does not suffer any law above itself' or Shelley's characterization of poets as 'the unacknowledged legislators of the world'. Thus Soyinka dismisses all possibility of setting artistic production in its socio-historical context and he would have us believe that his work is totally unique and inexplicably springs *de novo* from the random gyrations of the artist's gray matter.

The view of political developments which we can extract from his plays and novels is also subjectivistic. Often everything rotates around the actions of a single hero or malevolent dictator. A tendency to reduce all politics and social crises to the actions of a dictator and salvation to a hero only indicates the absence of a realist and balanced view of society and history. Even where in reality dictatorship or Bonapartism is the dominant political form one needs to be able to explain the predominance of this form rather than any other, by reference to historical conditions. In fact dictatorship or Bonapartism is very often the consequence of the very same conditions of class equilibrium which produce romanticism in the artistic realm.[78] It is precisely for that reason that the 'hero' always figures in romanticist ideology.

The play, *Kongi's Harvest*, focuses the cause of corruption and social disintegration in the figure of the dictator, Kongi, in whom Moore has detected elements of both Banda and Nkrumah.[79] The abstractness and superficiality of the category 'dictator' is immediately revealed when one recalls that Banda is the incorrigible puppet of imperialism and the South African apartheid government and Nkrumah was their defiant enemy. The recent play, *Opera Wonyosi*, is similarly superficial in its parody of the all-responsible dictator, who in this case bears the closest resemblance to (now deposed) Emperor Bokassa.[80]

The Man Died is Soyinka's most overtly political work and yet its analysis of the events surrounding the Nigerian civil war and his own imprisonment is extremely thin and personalized. Often reasoned analysis is substituted with petulant swipes at figures who are historically totally insignificant: 'animalistic regressions', 'vile heathen pig' and so on. In considering the origins of the war he does not go beyond the machinations of a Nigerian 'Mafia', presumably headed by some omnimalevolent mafioso.[81]

Romanticist individualism is a complex phenomenon to explain in social historical terms. One would have to consider the bourgeois atomisation of society through the impact of economic competition overlaid by the old values of aristocratic individual superiority and hauteur and the fact of the detachment and isolation of traditional intellectuals from society in a period of capitalist transformation. The syncretism of aristocratic hauteur and bourgeois individualism has its counterpart among the Yoruba neo-colonial élite in a fusion of the traditional 'bigmanship' inherited from the quasi-feudal past and the new commercial individualism introduced by colonial control of the economy. The neo-colonial pseudo-bourgeoisie is as susceptible to romanticist individualism as the aristocratic-upper bourgeois alliance of the early nineteenth century in Europe.

What is clear is that if the romanticist ever returns to the real world from his class-ambivalent position then he generally indulges in swashbuckling solo performances of Byronic showmanship rather than modest participation in a collective long term movement which might permanently improve the human lot. On this point we turn to a closer consideration of the political ramifications of Soyinka's aesthetics.

IDEOLOGY: TWO KINDS OF *'RETURN TO THE SOURCE'*

Cabral has written,

> But the 'return to the source' is not and cannot in itself be an *act of struggle* against foreign domination (colonialist and racist) and it no longer necessarily means a return to tradition.[82]

Many African intellectuals recognize a need to reconnect with the point at which colonialism ruptured the historical development of the continent. But the articulation of this need has taken two different forms corresponding to two alternatives of class commitment: a commitment, usually tacit, to the perpetuation of the neo-colonial agent class as a ruling class, or a commitment to the substitution of that class by completely African and worker-based power.

The writings of Soyinka contain a particularly sophisicated ideological elaboration of the class position of the neo-colonial agent class. His 'return to the source', that is, his romantic and mystical presentation of the past or 'tradition' in which culture is detached from its social and historical foundations, is an attempt to reconcile the direct experience and dim perception of the historically ambivalent role of the African neo-colonial class. This class is torn between allegiance to the bourgeoisie of the neo-colonizing powers and allegiance to millions of impoverished rural Africans, that is, contradictions presented by the political-economic role of the neo-colonial class as the agent of imperialism.

As Amilcar Cabral the revolutionary leader recognized, these contradictions can only be resolved by the rural-based revolutionary release from imperialist control and the laying of foundations for socialism. For Cabral the question of cultural reconnection or 'return to the source' is both idealist and opportunistic if detached from the question of how to release the gigantic forces of production paralysed or diverted by imperialism.

An important indication of Soyinka's politics is his inadequate conception of ideology. He has written that 'The truly creative writer who is properly uninhibited by ideological winds, chooses.'[84] His renunciation of 'literary ideologies' is made on the ground that they interfere with or restrict the artistic freedom which is his 'right'. The assumption here is that commitment or ideology is something dispensable, extraneous, contingent or external. It is imagined that one's attitude to art determines one's attitude to ideology when in reality it is one's ideology which shapes one's art. As Gramsci has noted, in criticizing Benedetto Croce's dichotomy between politics and art, the political-economic 'can become implicit in art, etc., when the (social) process is normal, not violent, when between structure and superstructure there is homogeneity . . .'[85]

While Soyinka redefines ideology as extraneous political bias, Cabral, like Marx, considers ideology to be the outdated and inappropriate form in consciousness of a specific system of productive relations ripe for restructuring. Ideology comprises all the dominant ideas, philosophical, artistic, moral, legal and religious, which have become a mental or 'spiritual' obstacle to such restructuring; just as, to take a simple example, the notion of the 'divine right of kings' was once such an obstacle to the bourgeois revolutions. Ideology, then, is not something we can escape so easily. It is inherent and internal to all our thoughts and actions. It need not 'speak itself' but 'reveals itself' in the form of word and deed.

The essence of Cabral's treatment of culture in the national liberation struggle is the apprehension of culture as ideological. The very point of the petty-bourgeois intellectuals identifying with the culture of the rural population is not mere romanticism or self-therapy but to break the ideological hold of the competing colonial, bourgeois culture on members of the indigenous petty bourgeoisie, to release them from its deceptive, hypnotic grasp and 're-Africanise' while revolutionising their minds. In this way they would begin to see the nature and mechanism of colonial exploitation and the way in which they were being used as the agents of imperialism, and so begin to organise the rural population through its own cultural medium. Cabral observes that,

> One part of the middle-class minority engaged in the preindependence movement, uses the foreign cultural norms, calling on literature and art, to express the discovery of its identity rather than express the hopes and sufferings of the masses.[86]

One should add that while this is of limited utility in the colonial context it is likely to be thoroughly reactionary in the neocolonial one because of the different political-economic role of the petty bourgeoisie.

In *Myth, Literature and the African World*, Soyinka claims that 'literary ideologies' are responsible for 'asphyxiating the creative process'. He allows the writer 'a social vision' but not a literary ideology. By the latter term he means a set of rules which lead to 'predictability, imaginative constraint, and thematic excisions' (he mentions surrealism and Negritude as examples), whereas by 'social vision' he means something which directs one to the 'extension' of experience.[87] This distinction is very convenient. It would now allow, for example, the condemnation of Marxist approaches to literature as 'ideological' without denying that literature can or should have social concerns: such a denial would plainly have been unwise. As a matter of fact, what he shuts out of the front door only comes in at the back, for having admitted 'social vision' he *has* admitted ideology, despite his own arbitrary and restricted definitions. As we have argued, he is a neoromanticist.

The emergence of a secular 'social vision' in African literature out of a reaction to the 'ideologies' of Christianity and Islam Soyinka interprets as the recreation of the 'existing mythology' of tradition.[88] Even Sembène Ousmane's socialist militancy is neutered to a Romantic conception of egalitarianism drawn from the mythical past.

Soyinka has denied that his work has recently moved towards 'ideological' statement.[89] In fact, his ideological assumptions have not changed in a quarter-century of artistic output. There is little to choose between, for example, the very early play, *The Lion and the Jewel* and the recent one, *Death and the King's Horseman*.

SOYINKA'S POLITICS

Lenin noted that after the death of great revolutionaries the bourgeoisie 'omit, obscure or distort the revolutionary side' of their ideas and they 'push to the foreground or extol what is or seems acceptable to the bourgeoisie'.[90] In this connection we should examine Wole Soyinka's treatment of the thought of Amilcar Cabral. It is perhaps the most immediately convincing indication of the politics of ambivalence, the requirements of an intellect torn between the exploited population and the foreign bourgeoisie, which ultimately expresses itself in the desire to be free of *both*. This poses an ir-reconcilable contradiction: to regain one's identity and shed the colonial mask *without* actively identifying with the exploited majority. Not only Soyinka's work but a very large part of present neo-colonial artistic production can be understood in terms of this tension; militant nationalism on the surface and an underlying conservatism.

Cabral, of course, identified unambiguously through action with the oppressed people of Guinea-Bissau, but Soyinka redigests this fact and makes it fit conservative romanticist demands. In an editorial in the journal *Transition* (editor: Wole Soyinka) a fair summary is given of the mass-based revolutionary alternative to neo-colonialism. But then an attempt is made to put a wedge between the success in Guinea-Bissau and socialism or Marxism:

> The ideology of the new society is therefore one which lives by the terminologies of contending Eurocentric systems.[91]

The editor goes on to give a quotation from Cabral which is out of context and which could be of no possible interest except that it *appears* like a denial of Marxism; this is the quotation:

> There is a preconception held by many people, even on the left, that imperialism made us enter history at the moment when it began its adventure in our countries: this preconception must be denounced. For somebody on the left, and for Marxists in particular, history obviously means the class struggle; our opinion is exactly the contrary. We consider that when imperialism arrived in Guinea it made us leave history – our history.

We get a different, and correct, understanding of Cabral's meaning when we include the sentences immediately preceding and immediately following this section, sentences which Soyinka omits and does not paraphrase. The sentence before:

> A rigorous historical approach is similarly needed when examining another problem related to this – how can the underdeveloped countries evolve towards revolution, towards socialism?

The sentence after:

We agree that history in our country is the result of class struggle, but we have our own class struggles in our own country; the moment imperialism arrived and colonialism arrived, it made us leave our history and enter another history. Obviously we agree that the class struggle has continued but it has continued in a very different way; our whole people is struggling against the ruling class of the imperialist countries. . .[92]

Clearly, Cabral is not a non-Marxist criticising Marxism, but a practising Marxist criticising a vulgar or inappropriate version of Marxism, expecially perhaps that current among some of the European Stalinist parties. He means that vulgar Marxists are wrong who think that history means a bourgeois versus proletarian struggle and that (there being traditionally no such struggle in Africa) therefore there was no history in Africa, because a Marxist analysis actually shows that there was a class struggle in Guinea-Bissau with its own dynamic *before* colonialism.

In the same issue of *Transition* an edited version of Cabral's 'National Liberation and Culture' follows the editorial. Cabral's only explicit reference to the class basis of all history is *omitted*. Here it is:

In our opinion, the mode of production whose contradictions are manifested with more or less intensity through the class struggle is the principal factor in the history of any group, the level of productive forces being the true and permanent driving power of history.[93]

Also omitted, without any indication, are *all* other important sections which emphasize the forces of production as the primary moment in historical change and their paralysis by colonialism, as well as sections manifesting Cabral's recognition of the reactionary role of indigenous culture. For example, omitted is the following crucial section, which shows that Cabral is far from Soyinka's romanticism of traditional culture:

. . . equally in some respects, culture is very much a source of obstacles and difficulties, of *erroneous conceptions about reality*, of deviation in carrying out duty, and of limitations on the tempo and efficiency of a struggle that is confronted with the political, technical and scientific requirements of war. (Emphasis mine.)[94]

One wonders whether some of these 'erroneous conceptions about reality' are not unconnected with the 'traditional' views cut off from their social structure, elaborated and romanticised by Soyinka. He writes in *Myth, Literature and the African World* that what is needed is 'to transmit through analysis of myth and ritual the self-apprehension of the African world'.[95] The primary question, of course, is who is transmitting what to whom and why?

Suffice it to note at present that for Cabral the question of a 'return to the source' 'does not and could not arise for the masses of these (rural) people. . .' He gives a preliminary psycho-social explanation of the need for this transmission: it is the élite which is doing the transmitting to itself because it is alienated, 'marginalised' and suffers from a 'frustration complex'.[96] There is nothing 'wrong' about such transmission in itself, but it can take two forms, revolutionary or opportunistic.[97] Cultural identity, for Cabral, was not merely an idealistic or subjectivistic question, nor one simply of 'psychological need' to be satisfied by government sponsored Festivals of Black and African culture or escapist literature, but of historical necessity and historical utility: mobilisation against imperialism. It therefore has a significance for Cabral very different from that which it has for Soyinka. We find that in the African petty-bourgeois class under colonialism only a tiny minority can make this complete identification while the 'silent majority is trapped in indecision'.[98] The ambivalence which reveals itself in the literature of Soyinka is a form of such indecision.

We are now in a position to understand why certain of Soyinka's works, especially his satires such as *Before the Blackout* and the recent *Opera Wonyosi* (based on Brecht's *Threepenny Opera*) have a progressive appearance.[99] For example, *Kongi's Harvest* appeared to be an attack on African dictatorship, and *A Dance of the Forests* appeared as a radical warning of corruption to come in newly independent Nigeria.[100] But a closer look reveals that these plays are almost totally devoid of all political-economic understanding (and I am thinking here of the implicit rather than the explicit).

The most explicitly political of Soyinka's works is probably his 'novel' about his prison experience during the Nigerian civil war of 1967–1970, *The Man Died*. Here we find such statements as 'the revolutionary changes to which I have become more than ever dedicated.. . .', 'For me, justice is the first condition of humanity', 'I did and still wish that the revolt in the West (of Nigeria) had achieved victory as a people's uprising'.[101] But these pronouncements are not given any flesh. Instead there is the same lack of analysis, the same perplexing ambivalence about his political position.[102] Consider the section in the novel in which he discusses an encounter with the progressives Philip Alalc and Victor Banjo.[103] He explains how the 'revolutionary ideals' of the Nigerian coup of January 15, 1966, which had the aim of putting an end to political corruption, were brushed aside by the Gowon regime, and to cause a distraction from the continuing corruption 'The Northern Mafia got together with the Lagos counterparts.. . .' and planned genocide.[104] And that is all. Virtually no mention of the mechanisms of imperialism and neo-colonialism, of past British divide-and-rule policies, of differences between colonial rule in the North and the South of Nigeria, of the operation of vast foreign monopolies, of internal differences in religion, culture, educational background and opportunities, of the creation of a rapacious comprador class in the South, of the role of the traditional ruling classes, of the causes of urbanisation and migrations, of oil and inflation, unemployment and ideology.

At this time Soyinka's conception of an alternative, of a strategy for change centred on what he refers to as the 'Third Force', which is never identified, or explained or given any clear role in the book. The following excerpt indicates the very closest to political clarity that is ever achieved; Soyinka in dialogue with Alale says:

'As for further hopes of building anything approaching a socialist state.. . .'

Alale broke out again, 'You agree that is the only chance for Nigeria?'

'There is no alternative. The army must be returned to its status as part of the proletariat. The politician-patrician mentality is already destroyed but it has begun a new life by its anonymous infiltration of a naive, purely instinctive Army. We need a Third Force which thinks in terms of a common denominator for the people.'[105]

The dotted line above is Soyinka's. It marks the greatest disappointment in the entire book: no analysis, no alternative. And then, to what extent could the Nigerian army, or any army for that matter, be considered as part of the proletariat? Is the problem really the 'politician-patrician mentality'? Despite the obvious lack of any clear vantage point Soyinka defines his experience as 'unique among the fifty million people of Nigeria'.[106]

Of course, the Nigerian poet is absolutely right in seeing the futility of the war, the void of progressive ideas in which it was waged, and that ultimately it could 'only consolidate the very values that gave rise to the war in the first place'.[107] But we are left without any intimation as to the reasons for this futility and void and what the way forward might be for the exploited majority.

COLONIALISM, NEOCOLONIALISM AND LITERATURE

The contrasts in outlook between Soyinka and Cabral on the question of culture are enmeshed in the broad historical fact that while the Nigerian poet finds himself caught up in the ambiguities and illusions of the neo-colonial situation, Cabral found himself in the much more clear-cut political situation of colonialism. The neo-colonial intellectual is often convinced (or not entirely unconvinced) that his nation is really 'independent' and he even finds the concepts of 'imperialism' and 'neo-colonialism' rather distasteful. As Cabral himself has explained, we find that neo-colonialism,

> by allowing the social dynamic to awaken (conflicts of interests between native social strata or class struggles) creates the illusion that the historical process is returning to its normal evolution[108]

He adds that the existence of a native government reinforces this illusion.

The extremity of the situation under a colonialism directed by the fascist government of Salazar and Caetano presented a clear socialist analysis to the consciousness of the most enlightened section of the petty-bourgeoisie of Mozambique, Angola and Guinea-Bissau, and the neo-colonial digression was, at least in some fundamental respects, avoided.

On the basis of superstructural criteria Cabral distinguishes between colonialism and neo-colonialism and refers to the neo-colonial agent class accurately as a 'pseudo-bourgeoisie', for this class does not actually control or own capitalist means of production. In reality the foreign capitalist class 'limits or prevents' the expansion of productive forces. But on economic criteria Cabral is able to conclude that essentially the colonial country and the neo-colonial country suffer from the same problem: 'violent usurpation of the freedom of development of the national productive forces'. National liberation, whether from colonialism or neo-colonialism, means the destruction of imperialist control.

Although Soyinka pays lip service to Cabral's ideas he overlooks what is of overwhelming and fundamental importance: that the situation in Soyinka's environment is, despite superstructural illusions, essentially *the same* as Cabral's; we have here 'two apparent forms of imperialist domination'. It is because Soyinka does not appreciate this essential identity that his view of culture and tradition and the 'return to the source' can diverge so widely from Cabral's. Soyinka's view of culture is intrinsic to the very illusion which maintains neocolonialism, doomed as the illusion may be in the long term. The 'return to the source' in Soyinka's universe is an escapist response, an attempt to recapture tradition which can only take place in the realm of pure consciousness. Meanwhile, the masses of working people in Nigeria go on as before, unable even to read the books which Soyinka writes in florid English. Theory and practice never unite. Antonio Gramsci once noted:

> The popular element 'feels' but does not always know or understand, the intellectual element 'knows' but does not always understand and in particular does not always feel.. . . One cannot make politics-history without.. . . this sentimental connection between intellectuals and people-nation.[109]

For Gramsci an element in the overcoming of this disconnection was the formation of 'organic intellectuals', engaged among the social groups who alone could bring about socialist transformation, as opposed to the 'traditional intellectuals' of the ruling class. In the African context Cabral is the supreme example of the organic intellectual, and Soyinka of the traditional intellectual; Cabral the realist and Soyinka the romanticist.

In conclusion, it should be recalled that Frantz Fanon had already put forward the view that the literature of the excolonial world, after assimilating foreign bourgeois values, passes through a cultural nationalist phase which romanticises the precolonial past. This phase is followed, he says, by a 'fighting phase', a phase of revolutionary realism, and it seems that much of neo-colonial artistic production has already entered such a phase.[110] One has only to consider the work of Sembène Ousmane of Senegal or Ngugi wa Thiong'o of Kenya and note their connection with the movement to break neo-colonial class alliance and liberate the exploited African majority.

Notes

This paper was first privately circulated at the University of Ife Nigeria in draft form in January 1978. I am grateful to Georg Gugelberger, Biodun Jeyifo and Mario Relich for their criticisms.

   1 A number of fundamental assumptions in this essay, concerning class, the
       relation of base and superstructure, the events of nineteenth century Europe and

the nature of neo-colonialism, stand without explicit support and elaboration due to brevity of space and the preliminary character of the author's theory. We concentrate here on a single illustrative case. Class we may define as the ownership relations which groups have to the means of production. Much of the class analysis here is based on a reading of Georges Lefèbvre's account of the French Revolution.

2   We are not suggesting a causal determinism here, although we reject the idea that no form of determinism is appropriate. To reject any form of determinism whatsoever, even the most subtle and 'soft', and substitute 'historical coincidence' and 'chance' as A .J. George does in his *The Development of French Romanticism*, Syracuse University Press, 1955, is to abandon all hope of formulating an adequate historical theory of romanticism.

3   On the Nigerian neo-colonial economy see Williams, G. (ed.), *Nigeria: Economy and Society*, Rex Collings, London, 1976; *The Review of African Political Economy*, No. 13, May-August, 1978, special issue on Nigeria; and Turner, T., 'Nigeria: Imperialism, Oil Technology and the Comprador State', in Nore, P. and Turner, T. (eds), *Oil and Class Struggle*, Zed Press, London, 1980.

4   See Hauser, A., *The Social History of Art*, Routledge and Kegan Paul, London, 1962, Vol.III, pages 122–213.

5   *Ibid*, pp. 166, 172.

6   *Ibid*, p. 182.

7   The title of a recent work: Foot, P., *Red Shelley*, Sidgwick and Jackson, 1981.

8   On 'reactionary socialism' see Marx and Engels, 'The Manifesto of the Communist Party', in *Selected Works*, Lawrence and Wishart, 1968, pp. 53–8. Marx denounced even the most fervent revolutionary romantics. The Jacobins he dubbed 'day dreaming terrorists' and those who made moral appeals to the bourgeoisie he called 'Utopian socialists'.

9   Hoare, Q. and Nowell Smith, G. (eds), *Selections from the Prison Notebooks of Antonio Gramsci*, Lawrence and Wishart, London, 1971, p. 57.

10   See especially Fanon, F., *The Wretched of the Earth*, Penguin, Harmondsworth, 1967.

11   Wellek, R., *Concepts of Criticism*, Yale University Press, 1963, pp. 128–221.

12   Soyinka, W., *Myth, Literature and the African World*, Cambridge University Press, 1976, pp. 61–7. Hereafter, MLAW.

13   *MLAW*, p. 49.

14   Wordsworth, W., *The Prelude*, II, lines 384 *et seq.*, and MLAW, p. 122. Incidentally, on Wordsworth's political ambivalence see Kiernan, V. G., 'Wordsworth and the People', in Craig, D. (ed.), *Marxists on Literature*, Penguin, Harmondsworth, 1975.

15   Soyinka, W., *The Interpreters*, Heinemann, 1970, (first published by Andre Deutsch, 1965). Soyinka has also spoken of 'the true African sensibility' as one in which 'the animist knowledge of the objects of ritual is one with ritualism, in which the physical has not been split from the psychic, nor can the concept exist of the separation of action from poetry. Music is not separated from the dance, nor sound from essence', *African Forum*, New York, I:4 (1966).

16   *MLAW*, p. 37.

17   *op. cit.*, p. 160.

18   Marx's letter to Engels of 30th September 1873, quoted in Lifshitz, M., *The Philosophy of Art of Karl Marx*, Pluto Press, London, 1973, p. 44.

19   From Soyinka's long poem, *Idanre*, Methuen, London. 1967, p. 62.

20   *The Fourth Stage*, reprinted in an appendix to *MLAW*, p. 158.

21   Soyinka, W., *The Bacchae*, Eyre Methuen, London 1973.

22   Thomson, G., *Aeschylus and Athens*, Lawrence and Wishart, 4th edn., 1973, p. 18.

23   *op. cit.*, p. x.

24   *Ibid*, p. ix.

25   Thomson, G., *Studies in Ancient Greek Society*, Vol. II, *The First Philosophers*, Lawrence and Wishart, London, 2nd edn., 1961, p. 238.

26   Soyinka, W., *Death and the King's Horseman*, Eyre Methuen, London, 1975, p. 7.

27   *MLAW*, p. 38.

28 Soyinka, W., *Kongi's Harvest*, Oxford University Press, London, 1967. It seems to me that Gerald Moore, in his *Wole Soyinka*, Evans Brothers, London, 1971, p. 67, is wrong to think that the play rejects 'both types of discredited leadership', the traditional and the modern. The 'farewell' passage that Moore refers to actually reasserts the traditional mystical powers of the *oba*, even when the physical powers are stripped off: 'But we cry no defilement, A new-dug path may lead, To the secret heart of being. Ogun is still a god, Even without his navel', *op. cit.*, p. 9. And at the very end of the play, when the *oba* and the dictator's 'secretary' meet by chance while fleeing Kongi's wrath, there is still the hope timidly expressed by the secretary, 'I would wish you a speedy restoration . . .', *op. cit.*, p. 90.

29 Soyinka, W., *The Swamp Dwellers*, in *Five Plays*, Oxford University Press, London, 1964.

30 Nazareth, P., *An African View of Literature*, Northwestern University Press, 1974, p. 63. See especially ch. 6: 'The Politics of Wole Soyinka'.

31 *op. cit.*, p. 14. See also pp. 11–14, 119–121.

32 'The Writer in a Modern African State', in Agetua, J., *When The Man Died*, Agetua Publications, Benin City, 1975, p. 29.

33 Soyinka, W., *The Lion and the Jewel*, Oxford University Press, London, 1963.

34 Nazareth, *op. cit.*, p. 66. Moore too says that the play 'is filled with a sense of the repetitive futility, folly and waste of human history', *op. cit.*, p. 20.

35 Agetua, *op. cit.*, p. 39.

36 'Abyss of transition' is 'explained', *MLAW*, p. 26.

37 Reproduced in Soyinka, W., *Collected Plays*, Vol. II, Oxford University Press, London, 1974, pp. 269–70.

38 Soyinka, W., *The Road*, Oxford University Press, London, 1965.

39 See comments on *Idanre and Other Poems* in Jones, E. D., *The Writing of Wole Soyinka*, Heinemann, London, 1973.

40 Agetua, *op. cit.*, p. 29.

41 *MLAW*, p. 10.

42 Soyinka, W., 'Who's Afraid of Elesin Oba?', paper presented at Conference on Radical Perspectives on African Literature and Society, University of Ibadan, Nigeria, 18–22 December 1977. p. 14

43 Note Soyinka's interest in translating from the Yoruba, D. O. Fagunwa's animistic Yoruba tale, *Ogboju Ode Ninu Igbo Irunmale*, under the title *The Forest of a Thousand Daemons*, Nelson, London, 1968.

44 *MLAW*, appendix, pp. 143–46.

45 *op. cit.*, p. 198.

46 See Cabral, A., *Return to the Source*, Monthly Review Press, 1973.

47 *op. cit.*, p. 75.

48 *MLAW*, p. viii.

49 *Ibid*, pp. 47–8.

50 *Ibid.*, pp. 32–3. When George Thomson makes some tentative suggestions in his *Aeschylus and Athens*, in explanation of the origin of ritual, he is condemned by Soyinka for having allowed his intelligence to be subverted by Marxism. When Thomson puts forward the interesting hypothesis that 'The divergence of poetry from dancing, of myth from ritual, only began with the rise of the ruling class whose culture was divorced from the labour of production' this is dismissed without any consideration as 'Marxist speculations' which are deemed to be 'outside the scope of the subject'. *MLAW*, p. 33.

51 'Who's Afraid', p. 19.

52 *MLAW*, pp. 49–50.

53 *Ibid.*, p. 47.

54 'Who's Afraid', p. 15.

55 *MLAW*, p. 13.

56 *MLAW*, p. 7.

57 *Ibid.*, p. 40.

58 *Ibid.*, p. 49.

59 Cabral, A., *Revolution in Guinea*, Stage One, London, 1969, pp. 71, 116. See also p. 129.

60 For example, *MLAW*, pp. 37–8. A reviewer who mentions the clash between the traditional and the modern in Soyinka's work is said by the Nigerian dramatist to manifest 'illiteracy' and a 'perverse mentality', 'Author's Note' to *Death and the King's Horseman*, p. 6.

61 *MLAW*, p. 121.

62 *Ibid.*, p. 37.

63 *Return*, p. 51.

64 *Revolution*, p. 46 et seq.

65 *MLAW*, p. 46.

66 Nazareth, p., *op. cit.*, p. 64.

67 *MLAW*, p. 127.

68 *Ibid.*, p. 136.

69 *Ibid.*, p. 127.

70 Thomas Carlyle quoted by Engels in his *The Condition of the Working Class in England*, Progress, Moscow, 1973, p. 130.

71 *MLAW*, p. 138.

72 *Revolution*, p. 85.

73 *op. cit.*, p. 43.

74 *MLAW*, p. 30.

75 *MLAW*, p. 31. *Orisa-nla*: roughly, God in the Yoruba Cosmology.

76 Soyinka, W., 'Neo-Tarzanism: The Poetics of Pseudo-Tradition', *Transition* (Accra), Vol. 9 (v), No. 48, April–June, 1975, p. 44.

77 'Who's Afraid', p. 18.

78 Gramsci says of Bonapartism or 'Caesarism' that 'it always expresses the particular solution in which a great personality is entrusted with the task of 'arbitration' over a historical-political situation characterized by an equilibrium of forces heading towards catasrophe', *op. cit.*, p. 219. See the entire section on this topic, pp. 219–223.

79 *op. cit.*, p. 68.

80 *Opera Wonyosi*, unpublished, first played at University of Ife, Nigeria, 16th–18th December, 1977.

81 Soyinka, W., *The Man Died*, Penguin, Harmondsworth, 1975, (Rex Collings, 1972), pp. 63, 177.

82 Cabral, A., *Return*, p. 63.

83 By a 'neo-colonial' society is meant one in which there is apparent legal and political independence but in which economy, already distorted by colonialism to produce specific raw materials, continues under the control of multinationals, with the assistance of a local élite, to the detriment of the majority. To give some concrete content to the term see, for example, Barnet, R. J. and Muller, R. E., *Global Reach: The Power of the Multinational Corporations*, Simon and Schuster, 1974, Part II. Also relevant to the theme of this essay is Mattelart, A., *Multinational Corporations and the Control of Culture*, Humanities Press, 1979.

84 Soyinka, W., 'Who's Afraid', p. 18.

85 Gramsci, A., *Quaderni del Carcere*, Einaudi, 1975, p. 1316. This passage is not in the English translation of selections.

86 *Return*, p. 68.

87 *MLAW*, pp. 61, 64.

88 *Ibid.*, p. 121.

89 'Who's Afraid', pp. 3–4.

90 Lenin, V. I., 'The State and Revolution', *Selected Works*, Vol. II, Progress, Moscow, 1970, p. 289.

91 Editorial on Guinea-Bissau, *Transition* (Accra), No. 45, Vol. 9 (ii), pp. 9–11.

92 *Revolution*, p. 56.

93 *Return*, p. 42.

94 *Ibid.*, p. 53.

95 *MLAW*, p. ix.

96 *Return*, pp. 61, 62.

97 See *Ibid.*, p. 63.

98 *Before the Blackout*, Orisun Acting Editions, Ibadan, n.d.

100   *A Dance of the Forests*, Oxford University Press, 1963.
101   *op. cit:*, pp. 12, 19 and 161 respectively.
102   Soyinka was thrown into prison at the outbreak of the war. This indicates that he was against the war, just as millions of other Nigerians were; but it was not tolerable to the military regime that Nigeria's most famous writer should say so.
103   *The Man Died*, pp. 176–83.
104   *Ibid.*, p. 177.
105   *Ibid.*, pp. 177–8.
106   *Ibid.*, p. 13.
107   *Ibid.*, p. 181.
108   This and the following brief quotations relevant to the distinction between colonialism and neo-colonialism are taken from 'The Weapon of Theory' in *Revolution*, pp. 73–90.
109   Gramsci, *Selections*, p. 418
110   *op. cit.*, pp. 78–82.

CHAPTER FIVE

TRAGEDY, HISTORY AND IDEOLOGY

Biodun Jeyifo

1

Dramatic theory and dramatic criticism have always sought to extend and enrich the mediation between the idea and form of tragedy – the 'highest' art of all – and life. In this theoretical and critical issue, 'life', itself an already over-generalized conception, confronts another conception – the idea and form of tragedy; many critics and theorists, particularly those of a materialist outlook, have thus situated this mediation in the realms of history and society. This paper is a resumption of this enquiry.

In Western theory and criticism we may identify, out of the rich, varied and multi-dimensional investigations into the nature of tragic art and its connections to history, three great *moments*: Aristotle; Hegel; Marx-Engels.[1]

Aristotle's great contribution consisted of a much needed *affirmation* and *definition*: affirmation against the powerful, influential but ultimately philistinic strictures of Plato against the art of tragedy; definition of the new realm of tragedy in the continent of drama. But speaking of tragedy *qua* history, as complete and comprehensive as his theory was, Aristotle's great deficiency was the furiously undialectical nature of his definitions. From the great classical practitioners of the tragic art Aristotle deduced the classic idea of tragedy: a spirit and a vision sublimated from life into an 'organic' form which is eternally 'true', and indifferent to the unfolding of 'life' in history. This classic idea Aristotle elaborated in the principal concepts with an unchanging essentiality: an archetypal tragic hero; and a tragic issue, equally essential, which inheres in the dramatic action. To enhance the purity of this idea, Aristotle suggested that it were much better for the playwright, in selecting a subject, to look to myth, a fantasized reality, than to history, a factual reality. In at least two subsequent periods of the resumption of the Aristotelian principles we see the congealment and sclerosis of this *idea*: in Renaissance Italy and in the mid-seventeenth to early eighteenth century France, during the hegemony of the so-called 'neo-classical' ideal.[2]

Hegel first directly opened the doors of the idea and form of tragedy to the insistent knockings of history. It must be emphasized that before Hegel there was no absence of efforts to refract the tragic form and idea through the prism of life and practice. But these efforts were in the main apologetic: if great playwrights such as Corneille and Shakespeare wrote great, moving tragedies, *against* the form and idea of the Aristotelian classic, then room must be made for enrichment, for revisions and extensions of the idea. Hegel's great contribution was to inject into the false organicism of the Aristotelian tragic idea the notion of the self-actualizing dialectic (the dialectic of consciousness, of spirit, of being and becoming).

Tragedy is the highest art, averred Hegel, because it distilled the *necessary* collisions which the World-Historical spirit, in every age and in its manifestations in racial or national communities, must go through in its self-actualisation in history. Protagonist and antagonist forces are therefore both themselves and *more* than themselves; in the objective contents of their 'volitional' collisions they reflect the contradictions which must be 'annulled', be negated for Spirit to realize itself in an age or epoch. One may thus speculate, according to Hegelian analysis, that, had the confrontation of such African leaders as Idi Amin and Julius Nyerere (to give a particularly trenchant example) resulted in a political-military contest of wills leading to the defeat of one man, the action would have symbolized, more than the confrontation of two opposing ethical and ideological outlooks, the self-actualizing activity of a spirit of history which selects contradictory human forces for its dialectical operations. If such a confrontation – always a possibility in the unstable sea of contemporary African politics – had resulted in the defeat of Nyerere and the sack of Tanzania by Amin's hordes, the Hegelian tragic issue would still have emerged intact, as shown by the following quote from Hegel himself:

> The true course of dramatic development is the annulment of *contradictions* viewed as such, in the reconciliation of the forces of human action, which alternately strive to negate each other in their conflict. Only so far is misfortune not the final issue but rather the satisfaction of spirit, as for the first time, in virtue of all that particular individuals experience, is able to appear in complete accord with reason, and our emotional attitude is tranquilized on a true ethical basis . . .[3]

Marx-Engels, in the famous conceit which everyone now knows, 'stood the dialectic on its feet', where Hegel had stood it 'on its head'. To Hegel's *dialectic of consciousness* in which great forces of tragedy merely incarnated the self-actualizing, self-totalizing activity of Spirit, Marx-Engels opposed a *consciousness of the dialectic*. True tragedy – tragedy based on historical events reflects the collisions of men and forces who are more or less conscious of the socio-historical roots of the tragic issue. More concentrated, more intense is the revolutionary historical tragedy where

> We are on historical ground and the conflict is not waged among individuals, or between individuals and the community but among social classes or forces.[4]

To sum up: between the three great *moments* of Western investigations into the connections between tragedy and history we have three *key points* along a chronological-theoretical *spectrum*. The first point is Aristotle's *idea* of tragedy. With all the enrichments and reformulations of this idea, it has remained largely intact. Its putative truth is poetic and it is indifferent to history. It is therefore held that it is far better to imagine or invent its story than to pluck it from 'banal' history. The second point is Hegel's dialectic of consciousness: whether or not tragedy uses a historical material, it reflects the dialectical activities of an immanent consciousness, a world-historical spirit which actualizes itself in history. The third point is Marx-Engels: when tragedy confronts history it is on solid ground and loses its abstract, 'artistic' purity; protagonist and antagonist forces are not agents who carry an ineluctable 'tragic flaw' which destroys them. Rather they are individuals who carry the concrete goals and aspirations of social groups, forces or classes.

Any tragedy, historical, mythical or imagined, can be placed at approximate points along this spectrum, which has now lost its chronological perspective but retains the theoretical dimension. The important point to note is that we are here dealing with the nature of tragic epistemology and that this is elaborated in the two principal structures already identified: a tragic hero (or protagonist forces) and the tragic issue in an action. Such placement, based on penetrating textual and structural analysis yields ideological and political insights crucial for consciousness raising and political praxis. This is particularly true of the historical tragedy, that impure subgenre of drama in which an exceptionally strongly articulated body of formalistic principles encounter perturbations from the real passions and struggles of real men.

2

The African theory of tragic art which demands, as a matter of ideological necessity and authentic aesthetic practice, an irreducible 'Africanness' in the form of tragedy in the contemporary African drama, cannot preclude a resumption, such as I have made above, of the Western inquiry into the connections between tragedy and history. The most compelling and persuasive of such African theories is Wole Soyinka's 'The Fourth Stage'.[5]

Whatever claims can be made for an authentic African tragic art – and in at least the area of aesthetic affectivity if not in tragic epistemology, Soyinka's essay makes a persuasive case for an 'African' tragic aesthetic – when we confront the historical tragedy in contemporary African drama a resumption of the Western enquiry is mandatory. And not just for the purposes of comparative theory and criticism. For what we routinely encounter is that no matter how strongly they call for an indigenous tragic art form, our authors smuggle into their dramas, through the back door of formalistic and ideological predilections typically conventional Western notions and practices of rendering historical events into tragedy. It is the task of this essay to uncover some of these patterns and point out certain ideological and political implications of these structures. As appropriate examples of the contemporary African historical tragedy I use Wole Soyinka's *Death and the King's Horseman*[6] and Ebrahim Hussein's *Kinjeketile*.[7]

3

Soyinka's *Death and the King's Horseman* is, to date, his only dramatization of historical material, a remarkable fact for a playwright who, by his own admission, has been largely concerned with the meaning of history and historical experience.[8] But this is remarkable only for those unfamiliar with

Soyinka's 'mythopoeic' attitude towards history, his constant penchant for transforming experience into metaphysical, trans-historical, mythic dimensions. Soyinka reveals this attitude clearly when he says in his preface to *Death and the King's Horseman*:

> The colonial factor is an incident, a catalytic incident merely. The confrontation in the play is largely metaphysical, contained in the human vehicle which is Elesin and the universe of the Yoruba mind – the world of the living, the dead and the unborn, and the numinous passage which links all: transition. *Death and the King's Horseman* can be fully realized only through an evocation of music from the abyss of transition.[9]

Moreover, of greater significance than this explicit prefatory statement is Soyinka's considerable dramaturgical departures from his historical material. The following segments of the play's action, so crucial to Soyinka's purposes as to constitute the play's basic dramaturgical supports, are entirely 'fabricated': Elesin Oba's marriage to the young maiden; the visit of H.R.H. the Prince; Olunde's sojourn and timely return from Britain;[10] and above all, the suicide of Elesin. I have cited only these crucial segments of the play's plot and action in order not to seem to be tying Soyinka to too literal a notion of historical verisimilitude. For there are many more minor details and points of departure from the historical material which unarguably belong in matters of dramatic structure, texture and tension.

It is necessary to emphasize that Soyinka is not the first major playwright to be more or less indifferent to historical exactitude in a work which deals with an historical event. The eminent authority of such practitioners of the attitude as Shakespeare, Shaw and Brecht apart, there are many important theoretical rationalizations of the attitude. Friedrich Schiller's contribution comes to mind with special relevance:

> . . . I say that tragedy is the *poetic* imitation of an action deserving of pity and therefore, tragic imitation is opposed to *historic* imitation. It would only be a historic imitation if it proposed a historic end, if its principal object were to teach that a thing has taken place and how it took place . . . It may thus be understood how much poetic truth may lose, in many cases by a strict observance of historic truth, and reciprocally, how much it may gain by even a serious alteration of truth according to history . . . It is, therefore, betraying very narrow ideas of tragic art, or rather poetry in general, to drag the tragic poet before the tribunal of history, and to require instruction from a man who by his very title is only bound to move and charm you.[11]

We shall see presently that unlike Schiller, Soyinka does not counterpose 'historical truth' to 'poetic truth'. However, an important convergence of attitudes which derives from the Aristotelian tradition must be noted: Soyinka's 'fabrications' in the plot of the play, while retaining the main outlines of the historical confrontation, all but lift the action into the realm of imagined reality. Of these 'fabrications' I want to point out for especial notice, the suicide of Elesin Oba and the sojourn of his son Olunde in Britain and his being consequently pressed into dramatic service by the playwright as the mouthpiece for the anathemas against the arrogance, the chauvinism and the egotism of European civilization. These issues have a lot to do with implicit ideological connotations of Soyinka's tragic historical issue in the play.

4

We may briefly summarize the storyline dramatized by Soyinka in *Death and the King's Horseman:*

The Alafin (King) of Oyo having died about a month previous to the action proper of the play, the important chief Elesin Oba (Commander of the King's Stables) must, as custom and tradition demand, commit ritual suicide on the night of the King's burial. Elesin Oba is more than prepared for his destiny: he embraces it in a harmonious reconciliation of personal volition and cultural and metaphysical sanctions. The system which demands his ritual suicide constitutes the organic social, moral and metaphysical rationalization of his life. Death is no negation, especially the kind of death which he will die: it is a crossing over to the world of the ancestors, one phase of the unbroken link between the world of the dead, the living and the yet to be born. As a consummation of this unbroken chain of being(s) Elesin takes a young wife on the night of his death: the product of their union – the old, ancestor-to-be and the young – will attest to that consummation . . .

However, the Oyo Kingdom is an enclave in the colonial territory of Nigeria; it is administered by a white Colonial District Officer named Pilkings. Pilkings learns of the impending suicide of Elesin and in a well-meant intervention (which, however, is not unmixed with racist disdain for 'barbaric customs') he arrests Elesin to 'protect' him from himself and his culture. The tragic reversals then unfold in a swift manner. Olunde, Elesin Oba's first son and heir who, on receiving the news of the Alafin's death, had returned home to bury his father, himself commits suicide, to save the family honour and to avert the spiritual disintegration which might arise from his father's collapse before Pilkings' intervention. Elesin is stung by the death of his son and the negation of the moral and metaphysical foundations of his existence which Olunde's suicide signifies. He therefore strangles himself in his prison cell. Pilkings is traumatized by the reversals in the effects of his actions and the other major characters of the play – Iyaloja and the Praise-Singer – lament the destruction of a people's spirit by the infliction of a rupture between their existence and the vision of life which sustains it. This is the 'threnodic essence' of the play and Soyinka's exalted lyrical reaches in the play make good his prefatory promises, as shown by the following movement in the devolution of the play's action:

> IYALOJA (moves forward and removes the covering): Your Courier Elesin, cast your eyes on the favoured companion of the King.
>
> (Rolled up in the mat, his head and feet showing at either end is the body of OLUNDE.)

There lies the honour of your household and of your race. Because he could not bear to let honour fly out of doors, he stopped it with his life. The son has proved the father Elesin, and there is nothing left in your mouth to gnash but infant gums.

PRAISE-SINGER: Elesin, we placed the reins of the world in your hands yet you watched it plunge over the edge of the bitter precipice. You sat with folded arms while evil strangers tilted the world from its course and crashed it beyond the edge of emptiness – you muttered, there is little that one can do, you left us floundering in a blind future. Your heir has taken the burden on himself. What the end will be, we are not gods to tell. But this young shoot has poured its sap into the parent stalk, and we know this is not the way of life. Our world is tumbling in the void of strangers, Elesin.[12]

5

What does one make of Soyinka's grand subject in *Death and the King's Horseman*? Barely eight years after the episode which Soyinka dramatizes and transmutes in the play, an Afro-American, Richard Wright, visited Ghana (then the Gold Coast) and seeing everywhere the absurd, pathetic products of the colonial enterprise, he made observations which seem to accord in particulars and in spirit with Soyinka's tragic issue in the play:

The gold can be replaced; the timber can grow again, but there is no power on earth that can rebuild the mental habits and restore that former vision that once gave significance to the lives of these people. Nothing can give back to them that pride in themselves, that capacity to make decisions, that organic view of existence that made them want to live on this earth and derive from that living a sweet even if sad meaning. Today the ruins of their former culture, no matter how cruel or barbaric it may seem to us, are reflected in timidity, hesitancy and bewilderment. Eroded personalities loom here for those who have psychological eyes to see.[13]

The episode which Soyinka dramatizes in *Death and the King's Horseman* took place in 1946; Richard Wright wrote the words quoted above in 1955; Soyinka wrote his play in 1975. Is Soyinka seeing, some twenty years after Richard Wright, the same vacant souls, the same bewildered victims of a fragmented world? I suppose that Soyinka himself would give both a negative and a positive response to this question. Yes: because contemporary Africa is still wracked by immense contradictions and negations, some of which are often expressed in psychological and spiritual forms. No: because Soyinka the man of the world and the self-avowed revolutionist of thought has recently and with increasing fervour observed in his writings a positive act of collective 'self-retrieval' and 'self-apprehension' in contemporary Africa. These themes find their most complete statement in his recently published collection of essays titled *Myth, Literature and the African World*.[14] By Soyinka's own lights one can therefore see in *Death and the King's Horseman* one aspect of a whole ideological programme in contemporary Africa. It presents a moment of *negativity* when the contradictions in our societies, at the level of the psychic and spiritual disjuncture, are revealed and probed. Soyinka's tragic issue in the play, the referential representativeness of his tragic hero, plus the ideological underpinnings of these structures are all to be grasped at this level of the collective psyche and spirit of a whole continent.

That a tragedy and a tragic hero can express, symbolically, the basic myths and the psychic experience of a culture, has been amply demonstrated by great examples in Western literature. One thinks particularly of *Oedipus Rex* and *Hamlet*, in an extensive field which includes, apart from the great Greek classics, others such as Shakespeare's *Macbeth* and *Lear* and Brecht's *Galileo*. How can the personal disaster or tragic destiny of one character come to express the collective destiny of a people or a race? This question has never been wholly resolved. But, to refer back to our theoretical model, it seems that we are here at a point between Aristotle and Hegel. The actions and fate of a protagonist hero assume an essentiality and a representativeness both by virtue of *his* nature and the potentiality for symbolic reverberations carried by his goals and aspirations – which are defeated in the course of the tragic action. In other words, both in his person and in the enterprise which he comes to assert and defend, a tragic hero of the kind we are discussing must embody the basic emotions and the collective will of a people.

In *Death and the King's Horseman* both Elesin Oba and the other African characters of the play, excepting the native functionaries of the colonial machine, are made to express, consciously and with considerable lyrical force, the redemptive nature of Elesin Oba's intended ritual suicide. The lyrical and rhetorical aspect must be emphasized. The play never really dramatizes either the force of Elesin Oba's personality or the inevitability of his actions. We are simply presented these matters as given structures and the playwright compels our acceptance of them by the lyrical brilliance of his dramatic language, perhaps unsurpassed by any of his other plays. In the following dialogue consider, for instance, the metaphorical language which expresses the relationship between Elesin Oba and the Praise Singer (one of the major characters of the play), a relationship that is much like that between Elesin and the other characters of the play:

> PRAISE SINGER: Elesin o! Elesin Oba! Howu! What tryst is this the cockerel goes to keep with such haste that he must leave his tail behind?
>
> ELESIN: (slows down a bit, laughing): A tryst where the cockerel needs no adornment.
>
> PRAISE SINGER: O-oh, you hear that my companions? That's the way the world goes. Because the man approaches a brand-new bride he forgets the long faithful mother of his children.
>
> ELESIN: When the horse sniffs the stable does he not strain at the bridle? The market is the long-suffering home of my spirit and the women are packing up to go. That Esu-harrassed day slipped into the

stewpot while we feasted. We ate it up with the rest of the meat. I have neglected my women.

PRAISE-SINGER: We know all that. Still it's no reason for shedding your tail on this day of all days. I know the women will cover you in damask and *alari* but when the wind blows cold from behind, that's when the fowl knows his true friends.[15]

Elesin Oba is the flamboyant, zestful cockerel and his retinue and praise-singers are his adorning and protective tail; an ingenuous, disarming image but it nevertheless expresses a relationship crucial for the action of the play. However, we are not left without a more telling, more passionate expression of the stature of our tragic hero or the essentiality of his action. The following altercation between Amusa, the police sergeant, and the market women who block his attempts to arrest Elesin and who mercilessly satirize Amusa's servitude to the white colonial administrator illustrates this point well:

AMUSA (shouting above the laughter): For the last time I warn you women to clear this road.

WOMAN: To where?

AMUSA: To that hut, I know he dey dere.

WOMAN: Who?

AMUSA: The chief who call himself Elesin Oba.

WOMAN: You ignorant man. *It is not he who calls himself Elesin Oba, it is his blood that says it. As it called out to his father before him and will to his son after him.* And that is in spite of everything your white man can do.

WOMAN: Is it not the same ocean that washes this land and the white man's land? Tell your white man he can hide our son away as long as he likes. When the time comes for him, the same ocean will bring him back.

AMUSA: The government say dat kin' ting must stop.

WOMAN: Who will stop it? You? *Tonight our husband and father will prove himself greater than the laws of strangers.* (My emphasis)[16]

In *Death and the King's Horseman* Soyinka polarizes the conflict between an African, organic and whole vision of life and an alien system of discrete laws and social polity, with tragic results for the indigenous system. In other words, it is a confrontation at the level of categorical superstructures; superstructures wrested from their economic and social foundations. Thus Soyinka can totalize the conflict such that a man like Amusa, otherwise a zealous servant of the colonial regime, is, in his mental universe, as resolutely opposed to the foreign cultural penetration (or aggression) as either Olunde or Elesin himself. This is perhaps why Soyinka is anxious, in his

prefatory notes, to tell us that 'The Colonial Factor is an incident, a cata-
lytic incident merely. The confrontation in the play is largely metaphysical . . .'

Elesin Oba's *honour* – and the honour of the race – in the play hangs
on his performance of the ritual suicide. However, as the underlined sections of the altercation between Amusa and the women quoted above indicate, the notion of honour (and integrity and dignity) for which Soyinka
in the play provides a metaphysical rationalization, rests on the patriarchal
feudalist code of the ancient Oyo kingdom, a code built on class entrench-
ment and class consolidation. The superstructures can never totally free
themselves of their material foundations. Elesin Oba is lauded, feted and
celebrated by his retinue and the women, and all this is presented by Soyinka as *naturally* due to a man on whose personal destiny rests the integrity
and maintenance of a vision of life which holds society together. But that
vision is not a natural outgrowth, like trees and leaves, not an effusion of
metaphysics but an elaborated system of human social relationships in a
precise form of society. It is useful to recall here Hegel's description of the
use in tragic writing of the notion of honour deployed by Soyinka in *Death
and the King's Horseman*:

> The difference of rank is, from the nature of the case, something
> necessary and predetermined. *If now, secular life has not yet been regen-
> erated, through the infinite comprehension of true freedom, in virtue of which the
> individual can himself choose his condition and determine his vocation, it is, on
> the one hand, and in greater or lesser degree, nature, birth, which assigns man
> to his permanent position*; on the other hand the dimensions which thus
> appear are also, through honour . . . held fast as absolute and infinite.
> (my emphasis)[17]

In the process of polarizing the conflict of *Death and the King's Horseman*
between an alien and an indigenous African world view Soyinka has suppressed the real, objective differences between conflicting groups and classes
within the indigenous system. It is illustrative of the gaps and dents in Soyinka's present ideological armour that he selected *this* particular metaphysical and philosophical order to symbolize African civilization and NOT
other more egalitarian African cosmogonic and metaphysical systems, the
erosion of which ideological and political progressives can, with greater reason, regret. A metaphysics which idealizes and effaces the conflicts and contradictions in African societies, which rationalizes the rule of the dazzling
FEW (such as Elesin) over the deceived MANY (the women, the retinue,
Amusa, etc.) is an extension, in the ideological sphere, and in the realm of
thought of class rule in the economic and political spheres. Marx has demonstrated clearly the manner in which this extension takes place:

> The ideas of the ruling class are in every epoch the ruling ideas, i.e.
> the class which is the ruling material force of society, is at the same
> time its ruling intellectual force . . . The ruling ideas are nothing more
> than the ideal expression of the dominant material relationships, the
> dominant relationships grasped as ideas . . .[18]

6

In *Kinjeketile* we are on a more solid historical ground and a more extensive field of collision. The play has a directness and a force which, on the surface, seem to make it simple and uncomplicated. We shall see that in reality *Kinjeketile's* comprehensiveness is in depth as well as breadth, in ideological subtlety and penetrative historical insight.

The play is based on the Maji-Maji rebellion led by one Kinjeketile Ngwale in the then Southern Tanganyika, 1904–1905.[19] The play was originally written and produced in Swahili; this point is not perhaps unconnected with its power and directness. The English translation was done by the author, Ebrahim Hussein, himself. Again, I think it necessary to provide a summary of the action:

The play begins with all the negative products of the German colonization of Tanganyika. There is the economic exploitation and oppression through taxation and forced, cheap labour. There is the brutality of the Germans and their minions and henchmen, the Askaris (native constabulary) and the overseers: whippings, and the rape of African women and girls. Worst of all there is the deep spiritual despair of the people, their lack of any will to resistance, and the disunity and traditional regional hostilities which keep them divided and impotent. Against this background emerges Kinjeketile. Kinjeketile is as poor as the other Africans; his life is as wretched, he does not belong to a privileged, aristocratic class. What sets him apart are his solitude and his mysticism. He sees visions and acts strangely, to the bewilderment of his neighbours. The turning point in the eventual collective destiny of Kinjeketile and the people comes when, before the very eyes of the people, Kinjeketile is 'dragged', in a state of trance, by unseen forces into the waters of the Maji river. When Kinjeketile fails to surface for a whole day, his wife and Kitunda, the man who will become his closest aide and leader of the people's army, pronounce him drowned. But some of the people believe that Kinjeketile will emerge and that this strange phenomenon is the work of Hongo, a spirit of the Maji river. Truly enough, Kinjeketile does emerge and to the rapt, spellbound attention of the people he pronounces a new dawn of unity, resistance, victory and renewal of the people's collective existence. Though still in a state of possession, Kinjeketile's instructions are detailed and his words precise. They must start the 'nywiywila', the 'whispering campaign' and spread the news of rebellion. Kitunda is appointed the general of the people's army and given instructions that he must patiently train them, while they swell their numbers and obtain arms. Crucially, for the rest of the action of the play, Kinjeketile consecrates the new spirit of the assembled people with the waters of the Maji. He pronounces that the fighting men will be protected by the water, will be invulnerable to the bullets of the Germans whom they will rout and thereafter place themselves under the protection of Seyyid Said, the Arab Sultan of Zanzibar. The people become united, their ranks swell; Kitunda raises and trains an army of the people. But an uncontrollable and dangerous fervour possesses the people: because of the promise of protection from the water, their fervour knows no bounds and ultimately, in spite of the cautions of Kinjeketile and Kitunda, they start the revolt precipitately. At this stage Kinjeketile enters into a state of despair and doubt, for in addition to the dangerous recklessness of the people, he has seen another contradiction in the prophecy he pronounced in his possessed state after emerging from the river. This is his statement that after defeating the Germans the Africans will become the children of the Arab Sultan of Zanzibar, which in effect means the replacement of one colonizer by another. In an outraged sense of betrayal and treachery from the powers that possessed him Kinjeketile repudiated his message and insists that the people must fight with realism.

For a time, the people's army is successful in its campaigns, although with predictable huge losses. But at a final confrontation during a siege on a German fortress the recklessness of the people's army exacts its crushing toll: they are crushed and the rebellion collapses. They then sink back into the depths of despair and craven defeatism and consequently denounce Kinjeketile. The final scene takes place in a German prison where an attempt to lynch Kinjeketile is barely averted. For the lives of the captured warriors, the Germans demand a recantation from Kinjeketile, a public avowal of his private repudiation of the Maji myth so that what remains of the spirit of rebellion will fizzle out. Kinjeketile refuses, against the clamours and pleadings of the prisoners, maintaining that the myth is not ultimately a lie because it has produced a historical truth: the absolute necessity for the Africans to fight and defeat the German colonizers.

7

In comparing the attitudes to history in the tragic visions of Hussein and Soyinka one encounters an initial paradox. Hussein is quite obviously closer to his historical sources and more substantial in his references. But where Soyinka understates his departures from the historical material, Hussein in fact denies that he has any real interest, outside of artistic creation, in historical reconstruction:

> However, Kinjeketile of the play – *Kinjeketile* – is not an historical evocation of the real man. Kinjeketile here is a creature of the imagination, and although the 'two men' closely resemble one another in their actions, they are not identical. I have had to mould my character to suit artistic needs, borrowing freely from the imagination when historical facts did not suit my purpose. History should not be used as the measuring stick for this play therefore, rather, its failures or successes should be gauged against rules determining a work of art.[20]

On closer inspection it seems that Hussein is really talking of *minor* artistic issues of characterization and formal composition, for he does try to portray *his* Kinjeketile along a certain archetype of tragic action: the Hamlet-like hero; the man of spirit and ideas whose capacity for action cannot match his enormous mental and emotional activity. Having released the dormant energies of the people through the myth of the Maji, Kinjeketile recognizes the inevitability of disaster, given the *conditioned* fervour and recklessness of the people. But to this terror of tragic recognition which comes *before* the denouement, he can impotently mouth his regret, with pathetic repetitousness:

> A man gives birth to a . . . word. And the word . . . grows, . . . it grows bigger and bigger. Finally, it becomes bigger than the man who gave it birth . . .[21]

In the end, however, Kinjeketile is not fundamentally a solipsist, he is not a man apart, he lives and speaks and *acts* for the people. And surprisingly we learn, too, that his author, Hussein, is not a playwright interested only in art for the sake of art as he says in words from the same introduction to the play:

> In my play, I have tried to demonstrate three things. First, I have tried to show how the Wamatumbi felt about the cruel invasion by the Germans, especially to show the master-servant relationship then pertaining. Secondly, I have tried to show briefly the political climate of that period (1890–1904). Thirdly, I have touched on the theme of economic exploitation of the Africans by the Germans, when Tanzania was being deprived of her produce and manpower . . .[22]

There is a sense in which Hussein's words here may actually be somewhat misleading, as regards his historical consciousness. For he neither merely presents an evocation of the Maji-Maji rebellion nor an itemization of historical facts. Rather, the play, by assimilating the religio-mythical traditions of the colonized 'Tanganyikans' into their politico-economic realities, demonstrates that ideology cannot be derived or elicited from a perfected metaphysical system but is created in the total life circumstances of a people and transcended in real struggle and by dialectical leaps. First, Kinjeketile used the Maji myth to unite the divided peoples and instil a spirit of resistance in them. But having done that he then secularizes the myth by grounding it on the bedrock of practical and military realities. It then remains for Kinjeketile to articulate, albeit in tragic recognition, the inevitable transcendence of the myth as an irreversible process of struggle and history:

> KINJEKETILE: Do you know what they will say tomorrow? The officer will say that we were wrong. He will tell our children that we were wrong in fighting him. He will tell that to our children, Kitunda. That to fight him is wrong! *That to fight for one's country is wrong!* And he wants me to help him by retracting all that I said. He wants me to say that the water was a lie. Do you know what that means? The moment I say that, people in the north, south, east and west will stop fighting. They will fall into hopeless despair – they will give up. I will not say that! A word has been born. Our children will tell their children about this word. Our great grandchildren will hear of it. One day the word will cease to be a dream, it will be a reality![23]

And another Tanzanian intellectual has expressed similar thoughts on the historical dynamics which Hussein dramatizes in *Kinjeketile*:

> In the end Kinjeketile's movement went down in the defeat of Maji-Maji. The future did not lie with a universalised traditional religion. But his message could be reinterpreted in secular terms. The theme of his teaching was 'unity to regain independence'. The echoes of 'Unity and Freedom' in Tanzania's coat of arms were implicit in Kinjeketile's teaching, and perhaps therein lies the legacy of the Maji ideology to Tanzanians.[24]

Finally, the utter clarity and resolute will of Kinjeketile when he chooses death rather than retract his words rules out any impulse toward an empty martyrdom or the kind of self-apotheosis we find in Flesin Oba's anticipation of his ritual suicide in *Death and the King's Horseman*. Kinjeketile's certainty of eventual victory, of the transformation of his own personal death into the triumph of the people – through struggle – can only be comprehended within that superior, secular ethical consciousness which welds the life of the individual combatant to the destiny of an embattled and battling collectivity. This consciousness Walter Benjamin has expressed in a memorable image:

> For parts of the time the conversation centred on the story, *The Next Village*. Brecht says it is a counterpart to the story of Achilles and the tortoise. One never gets to the next village if one breaks the journey down into its smallest part, not counting the incidental occurrences. Then a whole life is too short for the journey. But the fallacy lies in the word 'one'. For if the journey is broken down into parts, then the traveller is too. And if the unity is destroyed, then so is its shortness. Let life be as short as it may. That does not matter, for the one who arrives in the next village is not the one who set out on the journey, but another one.[25]

8

I have been more concerned in this essay with the subject of tragic epistemology – the 'knowledge' or understanding which tragic art can yield to us – rather than with the aesthetic-affective nature of the medium. I have thus analyzed the plays in terms of their hermeneutic structures and not in their formal, dramaturgical modes. The extensive field of theory and criticism on tragedy usually makes no separation between the epistemological and the aesthetic-affective; rather it usually fuses them. By this operation the field of investigation and speculation is open and eternal, though it must be emphasized that the issues have remained constant, from Aristotle to the present, e.g. what constitues the 'essence' of tragedy: the possibility of writing a 'true' tragedy in any particular period or for any particular culture; the contradictory or paradoxical nature of tragedy to, on the one hand, confront us sharply and hone our awareness of life and on the other, ultimately enervate or paralyze our human will, etc.[26]

It is my contention that when tragedy – the idea, the form – confronts history then we can broaden our analytical framework beyond the mainly technical and speculative vectors of discussing the art. If we get nothing else, we can uncover the playwright's, the theorist's or the critic's implicit ideological and political attitudes. I have therefore constructed what seems to me a possible model for the determinations of these issues: the Aristotle-Hegel-Marx spectrum. I advise that the reader return to my opening section before reading the following concluding remarks.

An African 'bourgeois' historical tragedy now exists in African drama and dominates the writings in this genre.[27] Its elaborated pattern and themes place it at some point between Aristotle and Hegel; near the former, in fact. The main impulse is to write according to an existent, received tragic idea, which idea dominates the historical material. Moreover, the protagonist hero in these plays are scions of bourgeois individualism and solipsism: lone tragic heroes, proposed either as great historical personages or culture heroes and avatars dominate the action; their connection to us is never dialectical; it is symbolic. This hero is always immersed in a re-cognisable, supposedly 'authenticating' African metaphysical or cosmogonic milieu; a static milieu. The oracle initiates the action of *Oedipus Rex*, the ghost of Hamlet's father, from the netherworld, sends him into the tragic fray: the supernatural or metaphysical element also serves in the bourgeois African tragedy as the external determining factor. Moreover, it also serves as the proof of 'Africanness' and the more dense and impenetrable the bet-ter. Conformism is the hallmark of this cultural and metaphysical immer-sion. *Death and the King's Horseman* is an example of this dominant school of the African historical tragedy; more than this, it is the greatest artistic realisation of the school.[28]

In Hussein's *Kinjeketile* we confront a minority tradition of which the only other example I know is Aimé Césaire's *A Season in the Congo*. Call this school the 'realist' or 'socialist' African historical tragedy if you like. Here the conception of the tragic hero, the archetypes of tragic action and the socio-cultural milieu are probed within the framework of real historical cir-cumstances and confrontations. And the confrontation is not between in-dividuals and society, but between individuals and forces which embody the irreconcilable goals and aspirations of social groups and classes or com-peting nations and alliances. Of especial interest is the treatment of the cultural, traditional milieu or metaphysical universe. The impulse is to de-mystify, to clarify, to show the dialectical operations between politics, ma-terial existence and the superstructural categories – the morality, the myths and the metaphysics of the society. There is not the need *merely* to 'auth-enticate', or celebrate the cultural milieu or reveal it as a cluster around a cultural hero.

I don't think I need emphasize here that the two patterns of the African historical tragedy discussed here return us to the lasting ideological and political query to art and drama: about whom, for whom?

AFTER WORD: FROM AMILCAR CABRAL

When the 'return to the source' goes beyond the individual and is expressed through 'groups' or 'movements' the contradiction is transformed into struggle (secret or overt), and is a prelude to the pre-independence movement or of the struggle for liberation from the foreign yoke. So, the 'return to the source' is of no historical importance unless it brings not only real movement in the struggle for independence, but also complete and absolute identification with the hopes of the mass of the people, who contest not only the foreign culture but also the foreign domination as a whole. Otherwise the 'return to the source' is nothing more than an attempt to find short-term benefits – knowingly or unknowingly a kind of political opportunism.

Return to the Source

Notes

1   I refer readers to the essay 'The Concept of Tragedy in Marx and Engels' in *Art and Society* by Adolfo Sanchez Vasquez, Monthly Review Press, New York, 1973. The model I have outlined here is my own extension of some of Vasquez's interpretations.
2   A major collection of Western dramatic theory and criticism is Bernard F. Dukore, *Dramatic Theory and Criticism: Greeks to Grotowski*, Holt, Rinehart and Winston, Inc., New York, 1974. All the quotations in this paper on theory and criticism are from this book.
3   *Ibid.*, p. 540.
4   Vasquez, *op. cit.*, p. 123.
5   In *The Morality of Art*: Essays Presented to G. Wilson Knight by his colleagues and friends, ed. D. W. Jefferson, Routledge & Kegan Paul, London, 1969.
6   *Death and the King's Horseman*, Eyre Methuen, London, 1975.
7   *Kinjeketile*, Oxford University Press, Dar-es-Salaam, 1970.
8   This is as much a prevalent critical reaction to Soyinka as his own pronouncement on history, as shown by the following from an interview with the present writer in *Transition* 42, 1973: 'It is because I believe that the forces of history may be confronted that I believe in social and political action. (On whose side was history in the last Nigerian war?)', p. 63.
9   *Death and the King's Horseman*, Author's Note.
10   It is interesting to compare, on this note Soyinka's play with Duro Ladipo's *Oba waja* (The King is Dead) on the same material. In Ladipo's play Elesin's son is called Dawodu and is away in Ghana trading, when the events take place. For an English adaptation of this play see Ulli Beier, *Three Yoruba Plays by Duro Ladipo*, Mbari Publications, Ibadan, 1964.
11   Dukore, *Dramatic Theory and Criticism*, p. 456.
12   *Death and the King's Horseman*, p. 75.
13   Richard Wright, *Black Power: A Record of Reactions in a Land of Pathos*, Harper and Brothers, New York, 1954, p. 153.
14   Wole Soyinka, *Myth, Literature and the African World*, Cambridge University Press, 1976.
15   *Death and the King's Horseman*, p. 9.
16   *Ibid.*, pp. 35–6.
17   *Dramatic Theory and Criticism*, p. 530.
18   Karl Marx, *The German Ideology*, International Publishers, New York, 1970, p. 64.
19   The source of the historical background I have used here is the excellent essay by G. C. K. Gwasa, 'Kinjeketile and the Ideology of Maji Maji', in *The Historical Study of African Religion*, ed. T. O. Ranger and Isaria Kimambo, Heinemann, London, 1972.
20   *Kinjeketile, op. cit.*, p. v.
21   *Ibid.*, p. 30.
22   *Ibid.*, pp. vi–vii.
23   *Ibid.*, p. 53.

24 Gwasa, 'Kinjeketile and the Ideology of Maji Maji', *op. cit.*, p. 215.
25 Walter Benjamin, *Understanding Brecht*, New Left Books, London, 1973, pp. 111–2.
26 For a very interesting discussion of these issues with special regard to Soyinka see
    Andrew Gurr's 'Third World Drama: Soyinka and Tragedy' in *The Journal of
    Commonwealth Literature*, Vol. X, No. 3, April 1976, pp. 45–52.
27 Other examples of this school are Ola Rotimi's *Kurunmi* and *Overamwen Nogbaisi*,
    and Seydou Badian's *The Death of Chaka*.
28 I would go so far as to state that *Death and the King's Horseman* is one of the
    superior creations in the poetic drama in English. Not all of the play is in verse,
    of course, but the conception is poetic and some of the dialogue is cast in
    Soyinka's best dramatic poetry to date. But from our present angle, the play lacks
    any real historical perspective, and from this angle it cannot begin to approach
    the author's *The Road* which is, paradoxically, not a historical tragedy. In *Death
    and the King's Horseman* Soyinka transforms history into mythical and metaphysical
    idealities whereas in *The Road*, by assimilating metaphysics and mythico-religious
    phenomena into social, economic and secular institutional life, he dramatizes the
    dialectical interplay of myth and history.

CHAPTER SIX

IMAGES OF WORKING PEOPLE IN TWO AFRICAN NOVELS:
OUOLOGUEM AND IYAYI.

Tunde Fatunde

1

This essay aims to examine the images of working people in two African novels *Violence* by Festus Iyayi of Nigeria and *Le Devoir de Violence* (*Bound to Violence*) by Yambo Ouologuem of Mali.[1]

Frantz Fanon's definition of violence is two-fold: physical harm and mental harm. This definition may be applied to neo-colonial as well as to colonial Africa.[2] Physical violence was, of course, the indispensable spine of the colonial order. It was necessary to make colonized peoples yield to the imperialist economic ambitions of the colonizing capitalists. In fact, the antagonistic relation between colonized and colonizer makes all colonial societies tend towards the police state. On the other hand, in a neo-colonial situation, the presence of physical violence is apparently attenuated and diffused. But still in this diffuse form it continues as the indispensable instrument of the local comprador bourgeoisie in its collaboration with the foreign capitalist in extracting more surplus value from African working people.

Mental violence in both the colonial and the neo-colonial situation cannot be divorced from physical violence. Religion and sexuality, for example, are parts of the superstructure moulded by the neo-colonial ruling class as effective weapons to exert mental violence on African working people. Certain class values embodied in religion and sexual relations serve to maintain the exploitative social relations of production. According to Fanon:

> The church in the colonies is the white people's church, the foreigner's church. She does not call the natives to God's ways but to the ways of the white man, of the master, of the oppressor. And as we know, in this matter many are called but few chosen.[3]

The Arab Islamic religion plays a central and oppressive role in *Le Devoir de Violence* by Ouologuem. This is in keeping with Fanon, who regards European Christian religion and Arab Islamic religion as convenient partners in the naked colonialization of African people.[4] His materialist and revolutionary position could not condemn one religion and excuse another.

Sexuality also occupies a crucial position in Fanon's theory of mental violence. In colonial and neo-colonial societies, patriarchal values predominate, and women are the victims of these values, suffering from sexual discrimination and exploitation, especially when they are working class women. Their social situation is worst when they live in feudal societies that have undergone foreign domination. Consequently, Fanon recommends that post-colonial revolutionary Africa:

> . . . must guard against the danger of perpetuating the feudal tradition which holds sacred the superiority of the masculine element over the feminine. Women will have exactly the same place as men, not in the clauses of the constitution but in the life of every day.[5]

The use of violence by the exploiting and ruling social classes calls forth the redeeming violence of the 'damned'. Fanon justifies, dialectically, the use of violence as an instrument of liberation, because the only language the colonialists understand is 'the language of pure force'.[6] Amilcar Cabral realised in practice this Fanonist theory of violence, demonstrating historically in Guinea-Bissau that a mass-based working people's violence can totally neutralize that of the exploiting ruling class. The violence of liberation is never violence for violence's sake, but a physically and spiritually redeeming counter-violence. It is difficult therefore to accept Jack Woddis' critique of Fanon's theory of liberating violence. He accuses Fanon of making 'a mystique of violence'.[7] But violence must be broadly conceived as meaning economic, political, and ideological as well as military struggle between the 'damned' and the exploiter. In liberating themselves by counter-violence from all kinds of alienating mental and physical violence imposed by the colonial and neo-colonial exploiters, the 'damned' would also be working towards the dis-alienation *of the exploiters*.[8] Fanon's concept of violence is thus dialectical.

2

The fundamental image of African working people in *Violence* and *Le Devoir de Violence* is identical: the workers are the producers of all social wealth.

In Ouologuem's novel, for over seven centuries the slaves and peasants have been forced to provide their labour power in order to guarantee and sustain the survival of the feudal Nankem Kingdom.[9] In most cases they were slaves for three different masters: the feudal aristocracy of Saif, who controls a diminishing kingdom, Arab Moslem slave dealers, and European Christian colonizers. The people are made to work in order to provide surplus-value for one local and two foreign masters at the same time. Yambo Ouologuem divides this imposed historical burden of the working people into two important epochs. For most of the seven centuries of feudal and colonial order, the working people were subjugated as mere chattel slaves. Only the last small fraction of this period is the neo-colonial epoch in which slaves had now been converted into peasants. This transformation should not, however, be considered as an emancipation, for the essential character of exploitative social relations of production remains intact.

In *Violence*, by Festus Iyayi, the working people, represented by Idemudia and others who gather at Iyaso Motor Park, are constantly looking for work. Here again, people are forced to sell their labour power to the local bourgeoisie in order to survive. In most cases they are employed merely on a daily basis, so there is no job security. Since the surplus-value created is to be shared between the local and the foreign masters, Idemudia and his comrades are grossly exploited as manual labourers in off-loading cement bags and as workers with building contractors.[10]

An implicit critique of patriarchal and sexist values is to be found in both novels. For example, Saif has a so-called divine right to mate first with the proposed wife of any of his subjects. And in *Violence* the comprador bourgeoisie uses women to gain contracts. One should note the 'proletarian' revulsion manifest by Idemudia and Adisa when they are asked, on different occasions, to satisfy the sexual needs of members of the comprador class. Saif, the feudal king of Nankem, never excludes women when he wants to sell off some of his subjects as slaves. The reason for this mixed-sex chattel slavery is simple: the reproduction of slaves can only be guaranteed by taking along both males and females. In the other novel, Adisa, the wife of Idemudia, unwillingly submits herself to sexual humiliation in order to procure the money necessary for paying her husband's hospital bill. And thus the working people have to undertake often inhuman tasks to regain crumbs of the surplus value which they themselves created. Idemudia and his comrades even have to sell some pints of their blood in order to live.

The feudal royal court of Saif has never suffered any material privation. On the contrary, it has enjoyed abundant material wealth and absorbs a large part of the surplus value in order to present itself as 'divine', 'natural', and 'normal'. Ouologuem has successfully depicted the manner in which some pre-colonial and colonial African feudal lords lived on the sweat and blood of the African working people. The social situation of the twentieth century neo-colony shown in *Violence* is strikingly similar. Obofun, a highly placed bourgeois civil servant, and his wife, Queen, squander a great deal of cash on expensive cars. They certainly do not present the image of the thrifty and hard-working bourgeoisie which is interested in saving capital in order to move from the position of hoteliers and rentiers to that of manufacturers and industrialists.[11]

The organised violence of the state is portrayed in both novels. The feudal lords of Nankem Kingdom make abundant use of the apparatus of coercion against the working people, both under Arab and European administrations. In Iyayi's work, Idemudia and his co-workers are threatened with state violence if they press on with their case for an increase in their daily wages. Queen, the business woman, feels very comfortable in her handling of the workers' demands because her personal connections with some highly placed civil servants guarantee police protection if ever a protest should arise.

The Saif ruling family of Nankem kingdom makes 'creative' use of religion. For example, Saif combines traditional religion and Islam because this is useful for subduing the working people. In the mosques and Islamic schools, Saif is presented as a divine ruler, and at the same time the presence of Arab slave traders is legitimized as a 'god-sent' partnership in the task of purifying souls.[12] With the advent of European slave-traders and colonizers, Christianity is said to have philanthropic and civilizing aims and thus helps to foist another colonial master on Africa. One is reminded that Christian benediction was given to African soldiers who were recruited to fight both the First and Second World Wars of international capitalism.[13]

Both Arab Islam and European Christianity had devastating effects on African traditional religions. Even the cultural and artistic artifacts of Nankem kingdom were stolen with the open complicity of both religions. In one case a Bishop of the Catholic Church stole accomplished artifacts under the pretence that these artistic works were pagan and must be destroyed.

3

The image of working people in *Violence* and in *Le Devoir de Violence* is the same in some respects and different in others. It is the same in so far as one immediately grasps the on-going antagonistic relation between the working people and the exploiting ruling classes. In *Le Devoir de Violence*, violence pervades the social relations of production between the feudal Islamicized ruling family of Nankem kingdom and the 'damned' under their domination. Also, one hardly perceives any sharp delineation between direct violence, religion and sexuality as instruments of the ruling class. Their synthesis and employment at times reaches the point of pathological sadism. The vivid framing of these bloody and brutal images clearly asserts the historical falsity of Senghorian Negritude, a neo-colonial ideology which presents the African past as peaceful, pastoral and devoid of class struggle. *Violence* also demonstrates both the pervasiveness of violence in an exploiting economic structure and its fusion with ideological instruments.

A fundamental difference in the framing of images by Ouologuem and Iyayi revolves around the character of the working people. In *Le Devoir de Violence* working people are presented as passive and dormant victims for over seven centuries; apparently there was not a single occasion when the people protested at their living conditions. They did not struggle to liberate themselves; rather they prayed piously and appealed to the ruling classes for their liberation. Consequently, we see occasional periods of 'liberation' of the working people by the feudal lords in Ouologuem's presentation.

In *Violence*, however, the working people are presented as individuals who believe in struggling for their liberation – as fully conscious human beings who are prepared to face their problems with courage. At the same time, they are not presented as infallible heroes but also have their human weaknesses. Idemudia, for example, is tempted to propose sex to Queen even though he realizes that this might adversely affect the ongoing struggle between Queen, the contractor and Idemudia's own labour union.

Yambo Ouologuem presents the working people as an amorphous mass belonging to a single social class in society. Of course he is correct to show vividly how this class was oppressed by the feudal lords of Nankem in alliance with Arab and European slave traders who came under the umbrella of a so-called civilizing mission, but he gives us the impression that the working people are lacking in any spirit of rebellion to that oppression. They refuse even to attempt to cut the parasitic sucker binding them to the local and foreign exploiters. And thus in *Le Devoir de Violence* there appears the *eternal* omnipotence of African lords and foreign colonizers.

In Festus Iyayi's novel a balanced picture is given, both of the working people and of the exploiters. Neither social class is infallible. They both show a degree of human failing and human strength, although it is abundantly clear that Iyayi is on the side of the working people. As a radical writer he is not complacent towards the plight of those who have only their labour to sell. But he does not legitimize Idemudia's attempt at beating his wife; neither does he approve of the (understandable) 'sexual methods' of Adisa, who searches for money to pay off Idemudia's hospital bill.

Certainly the creative role of labour is emphasized in Iyayi's work. Working people are essentially responsible for humanizing the natural surroundings of mankind:

> Not far off were the houses which sweat and labour had already erected. Life there was ablaze where labour had left its positive mark, the labour of hundreds of thousands of workers, working in the intense sunlight or in the biting cold or in the blinding rain, piling the blocks higher and higher and wiping the salt and the sweat from their eyes and their foreheads with the backs of their hands and all underpaid, treated no better than slaves.[14]

Unlike Ouologuem, the working people in *Violence* are not presented as an amorphous and faceless thing lacking its own goals. Instead, they are seen as indispensable agents of human progress. Iyayi emphatically rejects the presentation of a situation in which '. . . slave traders took all the credit for the achievements of the slaves'.[15] Here again is the difference between Iyayi and Ouologuem. The latter apparently gives all the social credit to slave traders and bourgeois colonizers; while Iyayi rehabilitates the image of working people as the primary historical force, and one to be politically reckoned with in society. Iyayi's radical views on working people recall Brecht's 'Questions From a Worker Who Reads':

> Who built Thebes of the seven gates?
> The history books give the names of kings.
> Did the kings haul up the lumps of rock?
> And Babylon, many times demolished
> Who raised it up so many times? In what houses
> Of gold-glittering Lima did the builders live?
> Where, the evening that the Wall of China was finished
> Did the masons go? Great Rome
> Is full of triumphal arches. Who erected them? Over whom
> Did the Caesars triumph? Had Byzantium, much praised in song,
> Only palaces for its inhabitants? Even fabled Atlantis
> The night the Ocean engulfed it
> The drowning still bawled for their slaves.
>
> The young Alexander conquered India.
> Was he alone?

Caesar beat the Gauls.
Did he not have even a cook with him?
Phillip of Spain wept when his armada
Went down. Was he the only one to weep?
Frederick the Second won the Seven Years' War. Who
Else won it?

Every page a victory.
Who cooked the feast for the victors?
Every ten years a great man.
Who paid the bill?

So many reports.
So many questions.[16]

Violence is accordingly viewed differently by the two novelists. In *Le Devoir de Violence* it is regarded as an abstract, a-historical and philosophical phenomenon. In this universe there cannot be *class* violence. This might have been the outlook of a colonial Catholic bishop. In this novel, in fact, the dominant views of members of the exploiting classes are given aesthetic preference.

In a colonial and neo-colonial situation one cannot but give empirical credence to a Fanonist view of violence. This school of thought regards violence as inextricably bound to counter-violence. But in *Bound to Violence* it is a force used only by exploiters against the exploited. In this bourgeois presentation of violence, working people did not come up even with a spontaneous response.

A deeper look at the philosophical position of Festus Iyayi on violence reveals the following points: Violence is a historical phenomenon. It has a class basis. Surplus value is forcibly extracted and expropriated from the working people by the owners of the means of production. Consequently, Idemudia feels that violence

> . . . consisted not of physical brutal assault but a slow and gradual debasement of himself, his pride as a man.[17]

Despite the constant presence of class violence pitted against the working people, the latter are portrayed as determined to overcome it within historical limits. At work, in hospitals and at home, the working people face violence of one form or another with courage and resistance.

In both *Le Devoir de Violence* and *Violence*, history and religion are dialectically interwoven. But once more, the views of the two writers on this issue are diametrically opposed. Saif and the colonial Catholic bishop could be regarded as Yambo Ouologuem's mouthpieces as regards history and religion. The history of mankind, according to them, is shaped and determined by an extra-terrestrial being. Man wanders aimlessly in the earthly desert[18] and is innately full of faults; and these faults cannot be rectified because man is permanently sick and degenerate. Thus it is not possible to resolve the problem of human misery. One has to submit without question, for redemption can only come after death. Religion teaches that Salvation is not possible in any human society and that the history of humanity is finite, whereas God's (or Allah's) kingdom is a-historical and eternal. Therefore, while on earth, man should undergo preparation for eventual acceptance in God's kingdom.

Thus man is always condemned to recommence from the beginning, and any struggle by the working people to free itself from the pedagogy of the oppressor is futile.[19] As everything is predestined by God, exploitation is natural. Therefore, one has the impression that the working people are powerless human beings who should not put into question the status quo. It may be tempting from all this to adduce that Yambo Ouologuem is on the side of the exploiting ruling classes, local and foreign, because, as Trotsky said:

> All the social illusions which mankind has raved about in religion, poetry, morals or philosophy served only the purpose of deceiving and blinding the oppressed.[20]

On the other hand, history and religion are considered by Festus Iyayi as the entire handiwork of man. His philosophical emphasis is on human labour. Man became what we know of him today as a result of labour. This is all the more reason why working people must be given their rightful place in human history. Iyayi's presentation of the truck-pushers is a good illustration of his materialist conception of history. According to him, these two truck-pushers did not think of the church. Their truck was their church and their labour was their God.[21] Unlike Yambo Ouologuem, the author of *Violence* does not give credence to any metaphysical school of thought which posits that the destiny of man is in the hands of an extra-terrestrial being. He asserts, for example, that the two children of a beggar, stretching out their hands at the doorstep of a church, '. . . were the children of the world, not created by God'.[22]

Thus we may conclude that *Le Devoir de Violence* is uneven. The feudal class and the foreign colonizers are given too much prominence. The working people only come in as a negligible and almost superfluous element in the novel. This is a serious and unacceptable amputation of historical reality. In *Le Devoir de Violence*, mankind must always submit itself to the exclusive destiny proposed by God; but we assert that art should be able to portray the potential of man to struggle against all obstacles.

Festus Iyayi's concept of art tallies with that of Fanon.[23] In his novel, he sees the working people as people always in the process of asserting their existence through struggle. They face the future with determination. At the same time, a balanced view is given of the members of the neo-colonial comprador class. They are also portrayed as human beings, but as human beings debasing themselves and others in their efforts to appropriate the surplus-value created by the working people. On the whole, Iyayi's concept of art is progressive and Fanonist because he recognizes that

> This art needs a new self-consciousness. It is above all incompatible with mysticism, whether it be frank or whether it masquerades as romanticism, because . . . collective man must become the sole master,

and . . . the limits of his power are determined by his knowledge of natural forces and by his capacity to use them.[24]

Notes

1   Festus Iyayi, *Violence*, Longman, Drumbeat, London, 1979. Yambo Ouologuem, *Le Devoir de Violence*, Seuil, Paris, 1968. I refer to this French edition. The English translation is published by Heinemann, London, 1971, under the title *Bound to Violence*.

2   Frantz Fanon, *The Wretched of the Earth*, Penguin, London, 1967. I am using the French edition, *Les Damnés de la Terre*, Maspero, Paris, 1973.

3   *Ibid*, p. 32.

4   *Ibid*, pp. 104–5.

5   *Ibid*, p. 163.

6   *Ibid*, p. 45.

7   Jack Woddis, *New Theories of Revolution*, International Publishers, New York, 1972.

8   Fanon, op. cit., p. 228.

9   See Ouologuem, p. 80

10   See Iyayi, pp. 27, 258.

11   Fanon predicted the historical inability of the African bourgeoisie to industrialize given its dependence on the foreign bourgeoisie, its role as commercial intermediary and its wasteful spending. Some radical African writers like Ousmane, Beti, Armah, Ngugi and Iyayi confirm Fanon's prediction.

12   Ouologuem, pp. 12–6.

13   *Ibid*, p. 94.

14   Iyayi, pp. 255–6.

15   *Ibid*.

16   Bertolt Brecht, *Poems 1913–1956*, Methuen, New York, Toronto, London, Sydney, 1976, p. 252.

17   Iyayi, p. 251.

18   Ouologuem, p. 200–3.

19   *Ibid*, p. 199.

20   Leon Trotsky, *Literature and Revolution*, Monthly Review Press, New York, 1974, p. 88.

21   Iyayi, p. 229.

22   *Ibid*, p. 228.

23   See especially Fanon, *op. cit.*, pp. 166–9.

24   Trotsky, *op. cit.*, p. 15.

CHAPTER SEVEN

THE SECOND HOMECOMING:
MULTIPLE NGUGIS IN PETALS OF BLOOD

Peter Nazareth

> What a homecoming! A second homecoming to an argument about
> droughts, Munira was thinking, and no questions about the drama
> they left behind.[1]

Petals of Blood is Ngugi wa Thiongo's fourth novel, the first since he gave
up being a student and returned to work in Kenya. *The River Between* and
Weep Not Child were written while he was a student at Makerere, *A Grain
of Wheat* while he was a postgraduate student at Leeds. *Petals of Blood* was
written over a five-year period, beginning while he was teaching at Northwestern University, Evanston, U.S.A. in 1970, continuing in Limuru,
Kenya, and finishing at Yalta as a guest of the Soviet Writers' Union.

'What caused things to happen?' asks Munira.[2] The novel asks this
question in the context of the dispossessed and oppressed in Kenya who
fought for independence and have lost everything. This is the same question
asked by *A Grain of Wheat*, and the quest is similiar in the two: Wanja says,
'What I mean is that perhaps we all carry maimed souls and we are all
looking for a cure.'[3] But *A Grain of Wheat*, having exposed the dynamics of
colonialism and the movement to decolonize, ends on the eve of independence. *Petals of Blood* takes up the story a decade later, when issues and
enemies are very murky. No more martyrs like Mugo or guerilla leaders like
Kihika serve as models, explain what is happening or show what must be
done.

As the situation and problems are more complex, so, too, is the question
of the right medium for the message, the right form for the exploration. Can
the author still use a specific action leading to specific conclusions as a
framework for his story?

The novel begins as a 'Whodunit', a detective mystery, the kind that
Hilary Ng'weno writes well.[4] Four people are arrested in rapid succession
in the New Town of Ilmorog: Munira, a headmaster and fundamentalist
Christian; Abdulla, a former Mau Mau, a former shopkeeper, now a seller
of oranges and sheepskins on the street; Wanja, a prostitute and madam
of a brothel; and Karega, a former seller of oranges and sheepskins, former
teacher and now trade-unionist. What for? Three pages later, we read the
headlines in the paper, the *Daily Mouthpiece*: 'MZIGO, CHUI, KIMERIA
MURDERED'. The paper says that the three were lured into a house in
Ilmorog where they were burned to death, continuing:

The three will be an irreplaceable loss to Ilmorog. They built Ilmorog from a tiny nineteenth-century village reminiscent of the days of Krapf and Rebman into a modern industrial town that even generations born after Gagarin and Armstrong will be proud to visit ... etc ... etc ... Kimeria and Chui were prominent and founding fathers of KCO ... etc ... etc ... (p. 5)

Who would kill such prominent and respectable people and why? A police inspector comes from the city to solve the mystery. His view of life is simple:

The officer had come from Nairobi to take charge of the investigation. He had served in various capacities under various heads from the colonial times to the present. Crime for him was a kind of jigsaw puzzle, ... and he believed that if you looked hard enough you could see this law operating in even the smallest gestures. He was interested in people; in their behaviour; in their words, gestures, fantasies, gait: but only as part of this jigsaw puzzle. He had read a lot and was interested in the various professions – law, politics, medicine, teaching – but only as part of his consuming interest. He was looking for that one image which contained the clue, the law of a particular crime. From there he could work out the exact circumstances, to the minutest details, and he hardly ever failed. (p. 43)

But the story is much more complex than the simple officer realizes because of political and historical continuums, unravelled by the novel, as follows:

1 Kenya had recently been under colonial rule. People had fought for independence, to get back the land, particularly as part of the Mau Mau movement.
2 The new élite, in alliance with external capitalists, consisted in the main of people who had stayed aloof from the independence struggle, or had even opposed it. In a few cases, those who had appeared to be nationalists turned out to actually be betrayers.
3 Those who had fought for independence and had lost limbs and loved ones now discovered that the fruits of independence were not theirs.
4 The ordinary people, particularly the peasants, were ignored by 'progress'.
5 When 'progress' finally came to the little village, 'outsiders' came in to dispossess the peasants of the little they had.
6 All the people carried what Ngugi calls 'secret lives', the title of his volume of short stories.[5] They have secret connections with one another, through time, and with the land.

As the elements are slowly pieced together, the characters discover their connections with one another and with history. All of the arrested four were linked with one another and with the three dead, and all meet again in the village of Ilmorog. Ilmorog, then, plays an important role in the story, and at an advanced stage in the unravelling, Wanja's grandmother, like a griot, narrates the story of the village.[6] Ngugi is very much a 'village writer'. In his first major work, the play *The Black Hermit*, the pressures are on Kiarii (Remi in the published version) to return to the village after his university education and be their leader, while he has chosen, in an ironic reversal, to be a hermit in the city.[7] Ngugi's characters always have roots in the village.[8] In *Petals of Blood*, as in his other work, people come from outside to the village, people travel from the village to various parts of Kenya but come back, and the news comes in. Ngugi deals with the whole of Kenya, and indeed the whole of the world, by focusing on a grain, a petal, a small village. The village is the hinterland, not only physically but also psychically. The four main characters had come to the village from outside, all carrying secret burdens, all searching for psychic reconnections.

The problem in Ilmorog is drought. The drought is physical, but it is also psychic and metaphorical. The people are waiting for rain because there is spiritual drought in Kenya. Every physical problem in Ngugi must have a moral and spiritual basis because, as many critics have noted, Ngugi is the most Christian writer Africa has produced.[9]

Wanting to find out why things are going wrong, Karega, once a trade unionist and a teacher, educates himself by reading books. He comes out with a solution to the problem of drought. He proposes that the whole village go to the city in a delegation to see their elected Member of Parliament to tell him about their plight. They are led by Abdulla's donkey, thus echoing Christ's entry into Jerusalem. Their journey becomes one into brotherhood, strengthening their bonds with one another, but it is also a movement into what is wrong in Kenya. They meet with hypocritical Christianity, scorn by the obscene new élite, anger by the city people, and irritation by their representatives. Their only beacon of hope turns out to be a sympathetic, idealistic (though compromised) lawyer who fights for justice within the system. As for their M.P., 'Ndieri wa Riera was the envy of most of his parliamentary peers. His area was so remote from the city that he was hardly ever troubled by endless complaints from his constituents.'[10] He has become a director and shareholder in various foreign businesses. To keep the goodies, he is involved in setting up a secret society to exacerbate tribal suspicions at the level of the ordinary people, for which Munira was tricked into taking an oath. The M.P. did not even know that there was a drought back home. He begins talking to the people like the priest that they met earlier, in clichés. When they realize that all they are getting is words, they wake up and stone him. Humiliated, he is convinced that an enemy is responsible. His mind settles on the humane lawyer. Later, the lawyer is murdered. So much for working within the system, Karega concludes.

The people of Ilmorog are arrested for assaulting their M.P. A photo gets into the paper of Abdulla's donkey, and this saves the mission:

> Donations poured in from every quarter. Within three hours of the newspaper's story, the lawyer's place was flooded with donations of food and soon the donkeycart was filled to the top. One company offered to provide free transport for the group, their donkey and cart,

and for the gifts. Rev. Jerrod called on an alliance of churches to send a team to the area to see how Ilmorog fitted into the government long-term rural development schemes: to see if plans could be speeded up so that in future Ilmorog and similar areas could be self-sufficient to meet threatening droughts. (p. 185)

With such publicity, development comes to Ilmorog: and instead of saving the people, it utterly destroys them. It is development for the benefit of outsiders, of which the most extreme example is a German concern which exports 'black ivory', young African girls sent abroad for prostitution. The Transafrican highway passes through Ilmorog, to suck up all the communities of Africa, veins in a new body of exploitation, pumping the life-blood of each village somewhere else. The plane surveying for the highway crash-lands, killing Abdulla's donkey. When aid comes in, the people are advised to register their land and take mortgages for development: the banks move in when they default to possess the land and displace the people. This is neocolonialism, control by finance capital because of rules which are not made, understood, or controlled by the people: bourgeois democracy for colonials.

The three prominent dead men held out as models of New Kenyans, we discover, were all betrayers and exploiters. Kimeria had seduced Wanja while she was a schoolgirl, impregnated her, and then cast her aside, only to use her again; he had also betrayed Karega's brother, Abdulla's companion, to the police, to have him hanged as a Mau Mau. Chui, who had once led a strike at school against European domination, had become even more white than the people he had replaced, becoming principal of the school at which first he, then Munira and later Karega had been dismissed for leading strikes. Mzigo, the Education officer, had acquired the building belonging to Abdulla and Wanja, getting the rights to the beer they made with the secret passed on by her grandmother to manufacture it in Theng'eta Brewery, a local name given to a company owned by a foreign organization. All three murdered men were metaphorically murdered men, local agents of outside exploiters.

Having shown us the connection between things, Ngugi also wants to show us *through ideas* what must be done. He says authorially in Chapter Four, Part One,

Our present day historians, following on similar theories yarned out by defenders of imperialism, insist we only arrived here yesterday. Where went all the Kenyan people who used to trade with China, India, Arabia long long before Vasco da Gama came to the scene and on the strength of gunpowder ushered in an era of blood and terror and instability – an era that climaxed in the reign of imperialism over Kenya? But even then these adventures of Portuguese mercantilism were forced to build Fort Jesus, showing that Kenyan people had always been ready to resist foreign control and exploitation. The story of this heroic resistance, who will sing it? Their struggles to defend their land, their wealth, their lives: who'll tell of it? What of their earlier achievements in production that had annually attracted visitors from ancient China and India? (p. 67)

Like Ayi Kwei Armah in *Two Thousand Seasons*, Ngugi is attempting to tell the whole story of a whole people, in living time, to restore their knowledge of themselves to themselves so that they can end exploitation.[11] For colonizers steal not only labour and resources, they also steal history. If a people believe they had no history before the coming of the colonizers, they can be exploited more easily.

However, colonialism/neocolonialism is not only out there: it has also penetrated the core, splitting the psyche. 'No', says Wanja, the author commenting that she said this 'as if she was continuing a dialogue with one of her many selves.'[12] The fragmented selves are not only in the tale but also in the teller. This is best exemplified by another well-known East African writer, a former colleague of Ngugi's, Taban lo Liyong, who has six different personalities, the key question being whether there is any central organizing principle, whether the petals have any core.[13] The chief problem with *Petals of Blood* is that in attempting to pull everything together that has been lost, to bring it into alignment with reality, to change reality, Ngugi has not realized that there are three authors in the novel who coexist uneasily in one work instead of coming out at different times in different works, like Taban lo Liyong.

First, there is the old Ngugi, the village Ngugi, the one who believes that people can change things by changing not only the outer world but also their inner selves, the Ngugi who rejects hypocritical Christianity in pursuit of a deeper Christianity, who takes the message of the Bible, particularly the old Testament, seriously, who believes that if you only trumpet the truth the walls of Jericho will collapse, whose major characters are burdened by guilt and a sense of betrayal because they have the potential for social good and messianic example. As Govind Narain Sharma, talking of Ngugi's Christian vision, says of *A Grain of Wheat*, 'the central message of the novel is profoundly Christian – the duty of each man and each society to work out its own salvation, the only way to the attainment of this salvation being through suffering and sacrifice.'[14]

The second Ngugi is a secular one of radical political ideas, black power, pan-African, Fanonist and socialist, who was born at Leeds University, ideas articulated in his book of essays, *Homecoming*.[15] (This Ngugi may have two faces: sometimes ideas of black power do not sit well with those of socialism, the former finding accommodation with black bourgeois businessmen, the latter damning them as agents of external exploiters.) These are world-wide ideas, and Ngugi brings them into *Petals of Blood* mainly through Karega, usually effectively. But sometimes Ngugi seems to get impatient and puts words into Karega's thoughts. For example, Karega thinks bitterly,

> This was the society they were building: this was the society they had been building since Independence, a society in which a black few, allied to other interests from Europe, would continue the colonial game of robbing others of their sweat, denying them the right to full flowers in air and sunlight. (p. 294)

These words could have come directly from *Homecoming*, only saved by the reference to 'full flowers', which connects with the title of the novel. But things get worse. Karega seems to be going slowly crazy with all his reading, repeating the names of various black and third world leaders:

> Children, he calls out: see this new African without chains on his legs, without chains on his mind, without chains in his soul, a proud warrior-producer in three continents. And they see him over and over in new guises: Koitalel, Waiyaki, Nat Turner, Cinque, Kimathi, Cabral, Nkrumah, Nasser, Mondhlane, Mathenge – radiating the same message, the same possibilities, the same cry and hope of a million Africans . . . (pp. 236–237)

No distinction is made in this litany of time, ideology, place, success, power in relation to a state, and race. What links all the names is that with the exception of Nasser, they are 'racially' African, though some were not even born in Africa. But Nasser is an Arab, belonging to the race that, historically, conquered and exploited the Africans, as shown in Armah's *Two Thousand Seasons*. No doubt Ngugi is catholic: he wants to get away from racial identity to commitment. Thus Ole Masai, whose father was Indian and mother Masai, chooses to be African. Thus the frequent references to the assassination of Pio Gama Pinto, who was a Goan but who chose to throw in his lot with Africans as a socialists.[16] But this is never explained to the children or the readers. Leaders like Nasser need a complex evaluation. Some intellectuals argue that in the name of socialism, such leaders pursued petty-bourgeois interests, thus not breaking free from neocolonialism.[17] Ngugi constantly gives us lists in the words or thoughts of Karega without qualification. The assumption is that the readers will immediately make the right connections as in a religious recital of the names of saints to the converted. The first Ngugi sneaks up and allies himself with the second.

Ngugi even pushes his ideas into the minds of 'non-intellectual' characters. For example, when Abdulla decides near the end to take violent action, his thoughts are described as follows:

> He was now yapping at the call of the Master. No. He was not a dog. He was Mobutu being embraced by Nixon, and looking so happy on his mission of seeking aid, while Nixon made faces at American businessmen and paratroopers to hurry up and clear oil and gold and copper and uranium from Zaire. He was Amin being received by the Queen after overthrowing Obote. (p. 315)

Given the characterization of Abdulla, it is hard to believe that he could have had such thoughts and images in his mind. Things get so out of hand that Ngugi seems to lose patience with the speechifying of Karega. Near the end of the novel, when Wanja tells Karega how she has been exploited, he gets so caught up in making a long, broad anti-imperialist speech that he misses his chance to make love to her, an opportunity offered to Adbulla moments later, who succeeds in impregnating her, one of her deepest desires.

This introduces the third Ngugi, one struggling to be born but being resisted by the first two. This is a 'Latin American' Ngugi, a writer of 'marvellous reality', a cynical, citified Ngugi who sees things going wrong in spite of the fact that writers, intellectuals and other seers keep showing what is going wrong and why, who sees people saying the right but doing the wrong things. We first meet this Ngugi in his story, 'A Mercedes Funeral'.[18] He emerges clearly in the most brilliantly written portion of *Petals of Blood*, Part Two, 'Toward Bethlehem'. When the people of Ilmorog have arrived in the city and are seeking help for the sick, they get only Christian clichés from a black priest and must move on. Munira walks up to a house and looks through a window, where he sees 'several ladies in long dresses holding glasses, talking in high animated voices.' A group then starts singing Gikuyu songs, followed by songs in Swahili and English. 'It was a truly culturally integrated party', the author says sarcastically. Then follows greater farce:

> The door was opened from the inside and Munira stood floodlit, face to face with a red-lipsticked lady with a huge Afro-wig and bracelets and bangles all over her neck and hands. He had no time to see the rest. For the lady, at first flabbergasted by the apparition, now found her voice and screamed, a loud blood-curdling scream, before she fainted on the floor. For a second he was chilled to the ground. He heard the scuffling of feet and the sound of broken glass. Chui and his friends were coming to the lady's rescue, some voice told him, and he might be manhandled before he could explain. Courage completely deserted him. He would not, he dared not wait for the consequences. He slipped into the shadows and ran as fast as he could make his legs carry him. He jumped over the outer hedge; Munira could never tell how or where he got the strength. He joined the others and urged them to move, to hurry on down the road. Behind them, they heard a gunshot in the sky and all knew without being told that Munira was involved in yet another disaster. (p. 151)

When the new black élite decoratively embraces its 'native culture', it is suddenly confronted by a representative of that culture: and it is as alienated as any colonizer. An irony within the irony is not only that the people were seeking help but that their representative in the doorway, Munira, was also an educated man, a teacher. Wheels within wheels of cynicism, which turn again when the people are arrested, freed and their mission turned from ignominious failure to fantastic success because of a photo in the papers of their donkey, the same donkey they had wanted to kill because of the drought, and finally destroyed by that very success. But this cynical Ngugi does not fit comfortably into the framework of the first, believing Ngugi or the second, radical Ngugi. The second Ngugi, being the toughest, curbs the third, getting involved and telling us what must be done to end this mess. For the committed writer cannot leave things in the air without suggesting solutions. Only once, as we have seen, does the third Ngugi sneakily defeat the second.

It is not easy for a Third World novelist to deal with the apparently confusing realities of his people in the wake of colonialism and the rise of neocolonialism. Static cynicism, such as we find in the 'African' novels of V.S. Naipaul, is an easy way out because it keeps the chaos of reality at a manageable distance from the storyteller.[19] The committed Third World novelist must deal with everything: history, politics, economics, sociology, psychology, and religion to restore a stolen people to themselves. For example, as part of the movement to self-discovery, the impersonal author tells us in loving detail how Wanja's grandmother prepared beer in the traditional way, forgotten by the younger generation:

> The old woman now set to work. She mixed the crunched millet seedlings with the fried maize flour and put the mixture in a clay pot, slowly adding water and stirring. She covered its mouth with the mouth of yet another pot through which she had bored a hole. A bamboo pipe was fixed into the hole and its other end put in a sealed jar over which she placed a small basin of cold water. Then she sealed every possible opening with cowdung and when she had finished she stood back to survey her work of art and science. Karega exclaimed: 'But this is chemistry. A distillation process.' She now placed the pot near the fireplace. (p. 206)

Such detailed, yet spare, writing captures the spirituality of life in the village. It shows the advance in Ngugi's political thinking and writing technique since his first two novels, which Murray Carlin said in early reviews tended to be misty, too dream-like.[20] As Eustace Palmer says, 'The extensive use of the oral tradition in this novel reinforces one's sense of a society that used to be cohesive and dignified.'[21]

Unfortunately, advances in some directions do not block regression on others. Ngugi reveals not only Christian humility in his novel but also Christian arrogance. Why was it necessary to put in absolutely everything, as though nobody reading his novel would have read anything else containing the truth, not even his *Homecoming*? How do we explain the long speeches and introspections of Karega, where, in contrast to the description of beer-making, the author offers us slogans and clichés, to which we are expected to have a stock response, as though we have not seen these words abused and discredited in 'revolution' after 'revolution'? In trouble as to how to end the novel, for much of third world literature must end with an artistic trick since the problem is unresolved in real life,[22] Ngugi has recourse to more clichés in the mind of Karega: 'Imperialism: capitalism: landlords: earthworms. A system that bred hordes of round-bellied jiggers and bedbugs with parasitism and cannibalism as the highest goal in society . . .'[23] Kole Omotoso of Nigeria is able to parody this kind of speech in *The Combat* and show its utter hollowness. Chuku says of his brother/enemy as preparations for battle hot up, 'Moreover Ojo Dada is the agent of colonialists, imperialists, and neo-colonialists. Through him some outside monster is going to take over the running of our lives here. I must prevent this. This is my duty and I am ready to sacrifice my life for it . . .'[24]

Omotoso has said that he writes short novels because he is aware that the writer today has to compete with other forms of the media. Ngugi writes as though there is no other media to compete with.[25] Thus the long speeches, which connect the first two Ngugis. As a good Christian, Ngugi is more concerned with the internal than the external, paradoxical as this may be for a political writer. Searching their hearts or taking down the barriers to their past, the characters in *Petals of Blood* make long speeches to one another, as though holding dialogues with their other selves. Much of the time, they do not have dialogues with one another. Ngugi prefers not to tell us what happens while it is happening: he would rather have the characters move from one introspection to another. This is a convention we can accept until the author is careless. Too often, his characters seem to remember everything said by other characters. On page 172, Karega recites a verse of twenty-six lines from Shakespeare as part of a speech made by Chui years ago. As a matter of technique, when someone tells a story within a story, he must not remember *everything* said by the person in direct speech, only what was of *particular* importance to his memory or psyche; the rest should be in reported speech.[26]

The backward and forward movement through time is not from one fixed point to another: it is spiral, taking us ever backward and ever forward. The rapid thriller opening, which could have been written by Omotoso, is stylistically misleading, and Ngugi has frequently to step in and tell us that he is taking us back through time. For example, Chapter Two of the first section begins, 'But all that was twelve years after Godfrey Munira, a thin dustcloud trailing behind him, first rode a metal horse through Ilmorog.'[27] Sometimes, the authorial movement through time is done through clichéd writing. For example:

> She started again in an introspective tone, which was *very captivating*. (p. 36, italics added)
>   The effect of their *extraordinary confession* on the present was *great*. (p. 210, italics added)

As Ngugi at his best is not a writer of clichés, his use of them here shows a failure of organic technique, an arbitrariness in the movement through time. By the end, we have forgotten the Inspector's desire to find out who committed the crime, which was what began the novel. Nor do we care who committed the crime. No doubt, it is Ngugi's intention to show us that the reality is complex, but unlike Taban lo Liyong, he is not writing metafiction. Plotting *is* important in Ngugi because there is a twist near the end as to who the murderer really is: and we still do not care that the smug inspector does not realize he is wrong.

Still, Ngugi pulls everything together with his title, taken from a poem by Derek Walcott. It refers literally to a flower whose petals look like blood because a worm has eaten it from the inside, preventing its full flowering. It also suggests the connection between the petals: the various characters are linked together at the core. What flowers today in Kenya? As a teacher, Karega sees the problem as, 'How could he enlarge their consciousness so that they would see themselves, Ilmorog and Kenya as part of a larger whole, a larger territory containing the history of the African people and their struggles?'[28] He says to Wanja, 'To understand the present, you must understand the past. To know where you are, you must know where you came from, don't you think?'[29] Munira writes, 'I had to take a drastic step that would restore me to my usurped history, my usurped inheritance, that would reconnect me with my history.'[30] This Ngugi himself has succeeded in doing. I can think of no other African novel that has explained in such detail, from a village perspective, just what neocolonialism is, how the people lose out while their cities get modernized and their political system gets democratic in the American manner, the loss being material and spiritual: not just explained but presented before the eyes and touching the emotions. But had Ngugi had more confidence in his readers, had he realized the direction his story was taking, had he recognized his many selves, he would have found the perfect form for his novel. Revolutionary content demands revolutionary form, one interacting with the other to change the consciousness. This form might have seemed cynical, it might have seemed exaggerated as in Ngugi's 'A Mercedes Funeral' or Gabriel Garcia Marquez's *One Hundred Years of Solitude*. Would such a Ngugi be anti-revolutionary? Or would he be *more* revolutionary because he would be more realistic instead of being a revolutionary romantic? Albert Memmi says of Fanon that in trying to show the failure and betrayal of the third world bourgeoisie, we cannot tell whether he was 'announcing, *forecasting* their failure or whether he was hoping it would happen'.[31] Memmi continues, 'like the revolutionary romantics, Fanon has a lyrical way of sliding over realities: because they want certain things, they end up believing that these things must inevitably happen or have already happened'.

The novelist must trust his tale and his reader. He need not hammer home his message, as when he gives characters names like 'Cambridge Fraudsham', 'Chui' ('leopard') and 'Sir Swallow Bloodall'.[32] During the Hundred Flowers Movement in China, Liu Pin-yin published a novella, *The Inside News of the Newspaper*, in which a radical woman reporter, sent to explore unrest in the mines, complains that the constant enforced meetings of the workers to discuss problems from an ideological perspective do not show confidence in the masses: on the contrary, she says, they show a lack of faith in the ability of the masses to think.[33] But the preacher, like the ideologue, does not trust the congregation: he must give long sermons about the true way. Ngugi, in his acknowledgements, thanks 'Many others/One in the struggle/With our people/For total liberation/Knowing that/However long and arduous the struggle/Victory is certain.' True, the international Christian leader wants to inspire so that his people overcome, but the form of inspiration also determines the content. Ngugi must wrestle with his other selves to find the right forms. As a good Christian, he should know that not all who cry, 'Lord! Lord!' shall be saved.

Notes

1 Ngugi wa Thiong'o, *Petals of Blood*, London, Heinemann, 1977, p. 108. All page references are from this edition.

2 *Ibid.*, p. 109. This essay incorporates a short review published in *Black Books Bulletin*, ed. Haki R. Madhubuti, Institute of Positive Education, Chicago, Vol. 6, No. 1, Spring, 1978, pp. 52–5.

3 *Petals of Blood*, p. 73. See my essay, 'Is *A Grain of Wheat* a Socialist Novel', in my*

book, *Literature and Society in Modern Africa*, Nairobi/Kampala/Dar es Salaam, East African Literature Bureau, 1972 (also published as *An African View of Literature*, Evanston, Northwestern University Press, 1974), pp. 128–54.

4   Hilary Ng'weno, *The Men From Pretoria*, Nairobi, Longman Crime Series, 1975. See the chapter on this novel in my book, *The Footnote Man*, Arusha, Eastern Africa Publications Co. Ltd., 1980.

5   Ngugi wa Thiong'o, *Secret Lives*, London, Heinemann, 1975.

6   *Petals of Blood*, pp. 205–14.

7   Ngugi wa Thiong'o, *The Black Hermit*, London, Heinemann, 1968. The play was first produced for Uganda's Independence Celebrations, 1962. The theme of the return to the village had appeared earlier, in Ngugi's first one-act play, in 1961 (published in *This Time Tomorrow*, Nairobi/Kampala/Dar es Salaam, EALB., 1971), Northcote Hall's entry in the Interhall English Competition. Unfortunately, earlier in the program, my one act play was produced for Mitchell Hall and the following exchange takes place when Karanja returns to the university as a graduate student to see Kaggwa, still struggling for his degree:

> Karanja: 'The Yellow Maize-Patch'. What's this?
> Kaggwa: Oh, you know, 'All the world's a stage.' I'm writing a play for the Interhall drama competition
> Karanja: Oh yes, of course. And you're churning out the usual play about the African village, and the chief being ill; about his son dramatically returning home from civilization in time to save his people, and all the rest of it . . .
> Kaggwa: Well, yes. You know that these plays with a traditional air always go over well – although the audience usually laughs at the wrong moments.
> 'O brave new world,
> That has such people in't!'
> I wouldn't want to disappoint them. So I take a theme from a play by Ibsen or some other dramatist and Africanize it.
> Karanja: Don't forget to throw in the usual set, with bamboos, and to dress your actors in barkcloth. That usually impresses the adjudicators.

(Peter Nazareth, 'Brave New Cosmos', in *Origin East Africa*, ed. David Cook, London, Heinemann, 1965, pp. 174–5. Ngugi never liked this play of mine.

8   Kofi Awoonor explains this in Ngugi as a sacred attachment to the Earth Goddess. (Kofi Awoonor, *The Breast of the Earth*, Garden City, New York, Anchor Press/Doubleday, 1975, pp. 282–3.)

9   For example, see Adrian Roscoe, *Uhuru's Fire (African Literature East to South)*, London/New York/Melbourne, Cambridge University Press, 1977, p. 188. Also see Narain Sharma, 'Ngugi's Christian Vision: Theme and Pattern in *A Grain of Wheat*', in *African Literature Today*, No. 10, ed. Eldred Durosimi Jones, London/New York, Heinemann/Africana Publishing Co., 1979, pp. 167–76. As Sharma notes, Ngugi's denial of his Christianity rings hollow. Like Peter, he protests too much.

10   *Petals of Blood*, p. 175.

11   Ayi Kwei Armah, *Two Thousand Seasons*, Nairobi, East African Publishing House, 1973.

12   *Petals of Blood*, p. 65.

13   See my 'Bibliyongraphy, or Six Tabans in Search of an Author', *English Studies in Africa*, ed. B.D. Cheadle, Johannesburg, Witwatersrand University Press, Vol. 21, No. 1, March, 1978, pp. 33–49.

14   Govind Narain Sharma, *op. cit.*, p. 169.

15   See the forward by Ime Ikeddeh to *Homecoming* by Ngugi wa Thiong'o, London/Ibadan/Nairobi, Heinemann, 1972.
Arnold Kettle, a well known Marxist literary critic, then at Leeds University, read the first draft of *A Grain of Wheat*, which was more explicitly socialist in ideas

than the final version. He expressed some uneasiness about the novel to me, saying that Ngugi's real talent was as a writer of fables.

16 *Petals of Blood*, pp. 78, 85, 179, 186, and 340.

17 For example, see Anouar Abdel-Malek, *EGYPT: Military Society*, subtitled, 'The Army Regime, The Left, and Social Change Under Nasser', trans. Charles Lam Masrkmann, New York, Vintage Books, 1968.

18 *Secret Lives*, pp. 113–7.
See my chapter on Gabriel García Márquez, 'The Marvellous Latin American Reality of Gabriel García Márquez', in my book, *The Third World Writer (His Social Responsibility)*, Nairobi, Kenya Literature Bureau, 1978, pp. 98–114. Also see the Afterword, pp. 164–71.

19 V. S. Naipaul, *In a Free State*, London, André Deutsch, 1971.
V. S. Naipaul, *A Bend in the River*, London, André Deutsch, 1979.
See my chapter on Naipaul, 'The Mimic Men as a Study of Corruption', in *Literature and Society in Modern Africa*, pp. 76–93, and also my chapter on the first two 'African' novels of Paul Theroux, 'Jungle Lover', in *The Third World Writer (His Social Responsibility)*, pp. 115–23.

20 See Murray Carlin's two Reviews in *Transition*, ed. Rajat Neogy, Kampala, No. 18, 1965, pp. 53–4, and No. 19, 1965, pp. 52–3.

21 Eustace Palmer, 'Ngugi's *Petals of Blood*', in *African Literature Today*, No. 10, p. 165.

22 See the end of my second novel, *The General is Up*, Arusha, Eastern Africa Publications Co. Ltd., 1980.

23 *Petals of Blood*, p. 344.

24 Kole Omotoso, *The Combat*, London, Heinemann, 1972, p. 58.

25 See my chapter on Omotoso, 'The Tortoise is an Animal but He is Also a Wise Creature', in *The Third World Writer (His Social Responsibility)*, pp. 71–86.

26 Ngugi might argue that he is writing for the masses, for whom there is no other media: he is not writing for the outside, educated reader. But, as he well knows, the moment he writes in English, he *is* writing for the outside, educated reader as well, even if he is bringing oral forms into his work such as repetition. This was one of the reasons why Ngugi turned to writing a play in Gikuyu, producing it for the masses and with mass-participation. On the other hand, Ngugi's intellectual characters want to overcome their alienation from the masses, to return to them and show the world-wide connections in their exploitation, so Ngugi cannot abandon the educated elite and say that he writes only for the masses.

27 This is what I attempted to do in my first novel, *In a Brown Mantle*, Nairobi/Kampala/Dar es Salaam, East African Literature Bureau, 1972, on the advice of Tova Raz.

28 *Petals of Blood*, p. 344.

29 *Ibid.*, p. 109.

30 *Ibid.*, pp. 127–28.

31 *Ibid.*, p. 227.

32 Albert Memmi, *Dominated Man*, Boston, Beacon Press, 1968, p. 88.

33 On the other hand, such names work perfectly in the modern animal fable, *The Amazing Saga of Field Marshall Abdulla Salim Fisi (or How the Hyena Got His!)* by Alumidi Osinya, Nairobi, Joe Publications & Transafrica Distributors, 1977. The names are consistent with the form.

34 I worked as part of a team translating the literature of the Hundred Flowers Movement of China, 1956/58, under the editorship of Hauling Nieh. Two volumes, *Literature of the Hundred Flowers*, ed. Hauling Nieh, New York, Columbia University Press, 1981. 'The Inside News of the Newspaper' by Liu Pin-yin is included.

CHAPTER EIGHT

PETALS OF BLOOD AS A MIRROR OF THE AFRICAN REVOLUTION

Grant Kamenju

> So this was the real gain. The only real gain. This was the thing for which poor men had fought and shouted. This was what it had come to: not that the whole thing might be overturned and ended, but that a few black men might be pushed closer to their masters, to eat some of the fat into their bellies too. That had been the entire end of it all.
>
> Ayi Kwei Armah, *The Beautiful Ones Are not Yet Born*

Lenin singled out as one of the characteristic features of the epoch we are living in the struggle for national liberation of the oppressed nations against the imperialism of the oppressor nations. In this struggle for national liberation led by the bourgeoisie of the oppressed nations, it was obligatory, Lenin insisted, for all progressive forces to support the national bourgeoisie of the oppressed nations in so far as its struggle was aimed against national oppression by the oppressor imperialist nations.

Lenin warned, however, that precisely because the struggle for national liberation was led by the national bourgeoisie, the 'independent' states that would emerge and that would typify the present historical stage would be states which while 'officially being politically independent' would, nevertheless, 'in fact remain enmeshed in the net of financial and diplomatic dependence' on imperialism.

Lenin further warned that by virtue of the class character of the national bourgeoisie of the oppressed nations, a situation would be brought about whereby 'a certain *rapprochement*' would be arrived at so that even 'where the bourgeoisie of the oppressed countries does support the national movement, it at the same time works hand in glove with the imperialist bourgeoisie, that is, joins forces with it against all revolutionary movements and revolutionary classes.'

Consequently, Lenin observed with profound prophetic insight that in the so-called 'independent' countries while 'the bourgeoisie of the oppressed nations *merely talks* about national revolt, in actual practice it enters into reactionary agreements with the bourgeoisie of the oppressing nations behind the backs of *and against* its own people'.

Ngugi's novel is a demonstration of the truth and validity of Lenin's penetrating analysis as applied to the post-independence state, not only in Kenya but in Africa as a whole.

Nevertheless, Ngugi is deeply conscious that imperialist finance capital is the real enemy in Africa today. As one of the characters in the novel reflects, it is because of imperialist finance capital that 'a man who has never set foot on this land can sit in a New York or London office and determine what I shall eat, read, think and do, only because he sits on a heap of billions taken from the world's poor . . .'

However, in *Petals of Blood* Ngugi is essentially preoccupied with unmasking the pornographic and obscene role of the comprador class spawned and groomed by imperialism in Africa so as to play the part of intermediary, pimping for imperialist finance capital.

At one point in the novel the obscene and obnoxious role of the national bourgeoisie as the pimps of imperialism is evoked through the hallucinatory and bitter imagination of the ex-guerilla fighter, Abdulla, while the following images whirl through his mind:

> No. He was a dog panting, wet nose, and saliva flowing from a tongue thrust out. He was now yapping at the call of the master. No. He was not a dog. He was Mobutu being embraced by Nixon, and looking so happy on his mission of seeking aid, while Nixon made faces at American businessmen and paratroopers to hurry up and clear oil and gold and copper and uranium from Zaire.
>
> He was Amin being received by the Queen after overthrowing Obote. No, he was his own donkey hee-hoo-hee-hooing and dutifully carrying any quantity of load for the master.

The novel, however, does not focus only on the puppetry of the military, political and economic elements of the national bourgeoisie. It also deals with the more subtle comprador section of the national bourgeoisie, which is constituted by the products of cultural imperialism, and, especially, those of the university and intellectual élite.

APOLOGIES FOR IMPERIALISM

The novel pinpoints the buffoonery, inanity, obscurantism and apologia for imperialism which characterize the scholarship of African professors and so-called educators trained in imperialist universities and other institutions of 'higher learning'. Hence, when the young teacher Karega tries to further advance his education he is confronted with incoherence, incomprehension and futility as he tries one area of learning after another:

> He tried political science. But here he plunged into an even greater maze. Here professors delighted in balancing weighty rounded phrases on a thin decaying line of thought, or else dwelt on statistics and mathematics of power equation. They talked about politics of poverty versus inequality of politics; traditional modernisation versus modernising tradition, or else merely gave a catalogue of how local government and central bureaucracies worked, or what this or that politician said versus what another one said. And to support all of this, they quoted from several books and articles all carefully footnoted. Karega

looked in vain for anything about colonialism and imperialism: occasionally there were abstract phrases about inequality of opportunities or the ethnic balancing act of modern governments.

Imaginative Literature was not much different: the authors described the conditions correctly: they seemed able to reflect accurately the contemporary situation of fear, oppression and deprivation: but thereafter they led him down the paths of pessimism, obscurity and mysticism: was there no way out except cynicism? Were people but helpless victims?

It is the lawyer in the novel who, in narrating his experiences as a university student in America, illuminates for Karega what lies behind this academic zombieism and intellectual flunkeyism of the national bourgeoisie:

When I saw in the cities of America white people begging . . . I saw white women selling their bodies for a few dollars. In America vice is a selling commodity. I worked alongside white and black workers in a Detroit factory. We worked overtime to make a meagre living. I saw a lot of unemployment in Chicago and other cities. I was confused. So I said: let me return to my home, now that the black man has come to power. And suddenly as in a flash of lightning I saw that we were serving the same monster-god as they were in America . . . I saw the same signs, the same symptoms and even the sickness . . . and I was so frightened . . . I cried to myself: how many Kimathis must die, how many motherless children must weep, how long shall our people continue to sweat so that a few, a given few, might keep a thousand dollars in the bank of the monster-god that for four hundred years had ravished a continent? And now I saw in the clear light of day the role that the Fraudshams of the colonial world played to create all of us black zombies dancing pornography in Blue Hills while our people are dying of hunger, while our people cannot afford decent shelter and decent schools for their children. And we are happy, we are happy that we are called stable and civilized and intelligent . . .

You had asked me for books written by Black Professors. I wanted you to judge for yourself. Educators, men of letters, intellectuals: these are only voices – not neutral disembodied voices – but belonging to bodies of persons, of groups, of interests. You, who will seek the truth about words emitted by a voice, look first for the body behind the voice. The voice merely rationalizes the needs, whims, caprices, of its owner, the master. Better therefore to know the master in whose service the intellect is and you'll be able to properly evaluate the import and imagery of his utterances. You serve the people who struggle; or you serve those who rob the people. In a situation of the robber and the robbed, in a situation in which the old man of the sea is sitting on Sinbad, there can be no neutral history and politics. If you would learn look about you: choose your side.

What the lawyer has discovered as a result of his experiences in America, the heartland of imperialism, is that education under imperialism is, as FRELIMO has succinctly put it, 'just another institution for forming slaves.'

INCONSISTENT

Despite his critical stance towards imperialist education, however, the lawyer is, ultimately, unable to adopt a consistently anti-capitalist, or thoroughgoing anti-imperialist line on account of his class allegiance as a petty bourgeois intellectual who, subsequently, opts out of the struggle. Indeed he turns out to be the embodiment and the very epitome of the petty bourgeois so vividly depicted by Marx:

> The petty bourgeois is necessarily from his position a socialist on one side and an economist on the other; that is to say, he is dazed by the magnificence of the big bourgeoisie and has sympathy for the sufferings of the people. He is at once both bourgeois and man of the people. Deep down, in his heart he flatters himself that he is impartial and has found the right equilibrium, which claims to be something different from mediocrity . . . A petty bourgeois of this type glorifies *contradiction* because contradiction is the basis of his existence. He is himself nothing but social contradiction in action.

It is to Lenin that we must turn to be able, from a proletarian viewpoint, to situate imperialist education within the class context of the system. In his book, *Materialism And Empirico-Criticism*, Lenin categorically unmasks and gets to the class roots and origin of bourgeois scholarship whether white or black:

> Not a single one of these *bourgeois* professors, who are capable of making very valuable contributions in the special fields of chemistry, history or physics *can be trusted one iota* when it comes to philosophy. Why? For the same reason that *not a single* professor of political economy, who may be capable of very valuable contributions in the field of factual and specialized investigations, can be trusted *one iota* when it comes to the general theory of political economy. For in modern society the latter is as much *a partisan* science as is *epistemology*. Taken as a whole, the professors of economics are nothing but learned salesmen of the capitalist class, while the professors of philosophy are learned salesmen of the theologians.

Petals of Blood as well as being primarily concerned to expose vividly, powerfully and memorably the client nature of the post-colonial state in Africa, is also concerned to depict the proletarianization of the African peasantry and the rest of the working masses of the continent. The setting of the novel not only in the country village of Ilmorog but also in the suburbs of Nairobi and on the edge of the Trans-Africa Highway delineates the theme of proletarianization which is part of the leitmotif of the novel.

The Trans-Africa Highway linking Nairobi and Ilmorog to the many cities of our continent is described as 'one of the most famous highways in all the African lands, past and present.'

Yet, as Lenin teaches, under imperialism, the infrastructure of roads, railways and other means of communication must be seen for what they really are: as means of gaining deeper and closer access to the natural as well as human resources of the colonial world for the purpose of the more intensified exploitation of the resources and the peoples of these countries.

Discussing the role of the infrastructure of railways in the imperialist-dominated world, Lenin wrote as follows:

> The building of railways seems to be a simple, natural, democratic, cultural and civilizing enterprise: that is what it is in the opinion of bourgeois professors, who are paid to depict capitalist slavery in bright colours, and in the opinion of petty-bourgeois philistines. But as a matter of fact the capitalist threads, which in thousands of different intercrossings bind these enterprises with private property in means of production in general, have converted this railway construction into an instrument for oppressing a *thousand million* people (in the colonies and semi-colonies), that is, more than half the population of the globe inhabiting the dependent countries, as well as the wage-slaves of capital in civilized countries.

As Lenin wrote of the railways so also for the roads. As the inhabitants of Ilmorog watch the traffic which rolls down the new Trans-Africa Highway, it is the tankers and the heavy trucks of the multi-national monopolies that thunder past bearing such names as LONRHO, SHELL, ESSO, TOTAL, AGIP . . .

DISPOSSESSION

The penetration of imperialist capital, however, takes place in compradorial alliance with the national bourgeoisie who became the new capitalist owners, not only of the town of Ilmorog but also of the former peasant lands in the neighbourhood, in the wake of the dispossession of the peasant and working masses:

> Indeed, changes did come to Ilmorog, changes that drove the old away and ushered a new era into our lives. And nobody could tell, really tell, how it had happened, except that it had happened. Within a year or so of the New Ilmorog shopping centre being completed, wheatfields and ranches had sprung up all around the plains: the herdsmen had died or had been driven further afield into the drier parts, but a few had become workers on the wheatfields and ranches on the earth upon which they once roamed freely. The new owners, master-servants of bank power, money and cunning, came over at week-ends and drove in Landrovers or Range Rovers, depending on the current car fashion, around the farms whose running they had otherwise entrusted to paid managers. The peasants of Ilmorog had also changed. Some had somehow survived the onslaught. They could employ one or two hands on their small farms. Most of the others had

joined the army of workers who had added to the growing population of the New Ilmorog. But which New Ilmorog?

There were several Ilmorogs. One was the residential area of the farm managers, country council officials, public service officers, the managers of Barclays, Standard and African Economic Banks, and other servants of state and money power. This was called Cape Town. The other – called New Jerusalem – was a shanty town of migrant and floating workers, the unemployed, the prostitutes and small traders in tin and scrap metal.

But Ngugi does not make the mistake of that self-appointed nineteenth century sage, Proudhon, who was so deservedly castigated by Marx because he could 'see in poverty nothing but poverty.'

Ngugi, like Marx, can see the revolutionary side of poverty in that poverty engenders resistance, revolt and insurgency as well as the search for a way out of exploitation and misery.

The novel affirms that, indeed, the true lesson of history is that:

The so-called victims, the downtrodden, the masses, had always struggled with spears and arrows, with their hands and songs of courage and hope to end their exploitation: that they would continue struggling until a human kingdom came: a world in which goodness and beauty and strength and courage would be seen not in how cunning one can be, not in how much power to oppress one possessed, but only in one's contribution in creating a humane world in which the inherited inventive genius of man in culture and science from all ages and climes would be not the monopoly of a few, but for the use of all, so that flowers in all their different colours would ripen and bear fruits and seeds. And the seeds would be put into the ground and they would once again sprout and flower in rain and sunshine.

Consequently, the way out of the imperialist impasse is spelt out in very clear and unequivocal terms at the end of the novel; it is the alliance of the workers and peasants under proletarian leadership:

The system and its gods and its angels had to be fought consciously, consistently and resolutely by all the working people! From Koitalel through Kangethe to Kimathi it had been the peasants, aided by the workers, small traders and small landowners, who had mapped out the path. Tomorrow it would be the workers and the peasants leading the struggle and seizing power to overturn the system and all its prying bloodthirsty gods and gnomic angels, bringing to an end the reign of the few over the many and the era of drinking blood and feasting on human flesh.

By way of conclusion it should be pointed out, however, that lest the national bourgeoisie of other African states, smugly and self-righteously, be pointing an accusing finger at their Kenyan counterparts, it would be as well for them to be reminded of the famous and wise words of the ancient philosopher when he said: 'It is of you also that the story is told!'

CHAPTER NINE

CLASS, RACE, AND AUTHORSHIP IN ANGOLA

Russell G. Hamilton

In early 1979, at a meeting of the Angolan Writers Union, a poet exhorted his fellow members to 'lower their sights'. What he meant was that Angolan writers, most of whom had their origins in the urban middle classes, should strive to communicate with the people. Although most Angolan intellectuals have supported their new nation's cultural revolution, based as it is on Marxist concepts, several writers in attendance at the meeting rejected what they saw as a prescriptive lowering of literary standards. Upwards of 85 per cent of the people are illiterate, of course; yet, there is a sizable potential readership among a new generation of students and literate workers in the cities.

The discussion that followed the poet's exhortation reflects concerns that hark back to the last decades of the nineteenth century when, in Angola, a basically Portuguese-language literature produced by Africans and *mestiços* (mixed race) began to emerge. Several European and American scholars have written precisely on the subject of the emergence of an African and *mestiço* bourgeoisie during that important period in class and race relations in the Portuguese colonies. Thus, drawing principally on the writing of such scholars as C. R. Boxer, James Duffy, John Marcum, and Gerald J. Bender, we can gain some insights into that which contributed to the interrelationship between race, class, and cultural expression in colonial Angola and in the now independent People's Republic of Angola.[1]

Selective assimilation, whereby a relatively few Africans were allowed to attain a measure of legal, social, and economic status under the colonial system, became official under Salazar's New State and was only discontinued when the guerrilla war exploded in 1961. According to this practice, which had its origins in the nineteenth century, the adult African who had learned to speak Portuguese, was gainfully employed, and had given up pagan practices and embraced the Christian faith theoretically enjoyed the same rights and privileges of any Portuguese citizen. By as late as 1960, however, less than one per cent of Angola's African population had been assimilated. Nevertheless, the 30,000 or so *assimilados*, out of a total African population of approximately 4,000,000, constituted the basis of an indigenous petty bourgeoisie, principally in the city of Luanda.

Beginning as early as the 1870's, but reaching a high point in the 1910's, Angola's as yet unofficial *assimilados* began to organize themselves around a liberal reformism strongly influenced by the Portuguese republican constitution of 1911. *Assimilado* and *mestiço* organizations, like the *Liga Africana* (African League) espoused reformist social causes; and although generally pledging loyalty to Portugal, by the early twentieth century their agitations, often expressed in an emerging African-owned press, approached a kind of proto-nationalism.

In the late nineteenth century Joaquim Dias Cordeiro da Matta (1857–1894) emerged as perhaps Angola's first significant *assimilado* intellectual. A teacher, historian, ethnographer, and journalist, as well as a poet and unpublished novelist, Matta epitomized the African intellectual who, in those early years of the colony, stood at the vanguard of a tiny, ascending bourgeois élite. Intellectual *assimilados* like Matta also stood ambivalently between the values of their newly acquired status and the African culture to which they also pledged allegiance. Thus, Matta compiled a collection of proverbs in his native Kimbundu language (1891), a Kimbundu grammar (1892), and a Kimbundu-Portuguese dictionary (1893). He reputedly wrote a novel about Nzinga Mbandi (1582–1663 – also spelled Jinga and Ginga), the queen who united several nations against Portuguese rule. The novel, which unfortunately has been lost to us, bears the intriguing title of *A Verdadeira História da Rainha Jinga* (The True Story of Queen Jinga); that it is the 'true' story suggests that, as an expression of his Angolanness, Matta wanted to revindicate the heroic African ruler. On the other hand, Matta's collection of poetry *Delirios* (Delirium – 1887) contains lyric verse in Portuguese fashioned in a style virtually indistinguishable from that of European poets of the period. Even when Matta turned to Africa for his subject, he made poetic statements essentially consistent with a European bourgeois world view. In 'Negra' (Black Woman) the persona exclaims 'Black! Black! as the wing/of the blackest, darkest raven/but in your clear eyes/you possess the purest and most limpid of gazes.'[2]

Heli Chatelain (1859–1908), a Swiss missionary who lived many years in Angola, served as a mentor to Matta. Himself the author of *Kimbundu Grammar* (1888–1889) and *Folktales of Angola* (1894), published respectively in Switzerland and the United States, Chatelain exhorted Matta and other Angolan intellectuals to found an autochthonous African literature. Matta responded within the limitations imposed on him by his developing class view in conflict with his sense of Africanness. But when he used, in poems like 'Negra', the inverted images of whiteness that characterized much of the conventional poetic symbiology he revealed to what extent he was bound to western attitudes on race.

James Duffy wrote that the officialization of cultural assimilation was an 'answer to Africanism and the ultimate hope for European colonialism.'[3] He also wrote that 'the history of the interior in both territories (Angola and Mozambique) is as much the assimilation of the Portuguese by the African as it is the reverse' (p. 161). Both observations speak to the problem of *assimilado* writers in their efforts to express African cultural values in the Portuguese language while maintaining their civilized status predicated on republican liberalism.

Portugal's short-lived republic had important repercussions in Luanda among *assimilados* and *mestiços* who often used their relatively privileged status to issue often dangerous reformist statements in African-owned newspapers. José de Norton de Matos (1867–1953), the Portuguese High Commissioner of Angola from 1921 to 1923, although lauded for his enlightened attitude toward the African masses, 'distrusted the educated Angolan African and, in order to safeguard his economic programme, he thoroughly crushed the *assimilado* associations, newspapers and unions and deported many leading Angolan figures.'[4]

Antonio de Assis Júnior (1878–1960), a co-founder of the *Linga Africana* and a journalist, lawyer, and novelist, was one of the *assimilados* who suffered deportation at the hands of Norton de Matos. Like Cordeiro da Matta before him, Assis Júnior compiled a Kimbundu-Portuguese dictionary (1941), and also like his predecessor he sought to elevate the African language by demonstrating its equivalencies with Portuguese. Unlike Matta, however, Assis Júnior, the writer, brought African culture into line with western values on a more integrated or acculturated basis. Assis Júnior is, in effect, one of the first chroniclers of Kimbundu-Portuguese acculturation although he himself, in the preface to his dictionary, inveighs against the creole speech that threatened the purity of both languages. In spite of his purist position, Assis Júnior, in his novel *O Segredo da Morta* (The Dead Woman's Secret – 1934), subtitled *Romance de Costumes Angolenses* (Romance of Angolan Customs), depicts the creolized life style that prevailed in the interior of the district (today, province) of Luanda. This novel illustrates Duffy's contention that in the interior assimilation was a two-way process. Because Assis Júnior, by virtue of his *assimilado* status, stood ambivalently between 'we' (the civilized) and 'they' (the uncivilized and uncultured natives), his acceptance of the law of cultural equivalencies was invariably a defense of a creole alternative.

The few *assimilado* authors who produced literary works between the late nineteenth century and the 1930's were essentially writing for a European audience in the colonies and Portugal. But Assis Júnior, while demonstrating to his readership that he could write in the style of Victor Hugo and Anatole France (two authors he confessed to admire), he was also attempting to dignify an African way of life based on reciprocal patterns of cultural assimilation.

The period between 1934 (taking the year of the publication of Assis Júnior's novel as a convenient demarcation) and the late 1940's witnessed a marked decrease in Africanist activities on the part of *assimilados* and *mestiços*. This decrease in activity does not mean that *assimilados* as a class completely lost their organizational base; after all, under the Portuguese New State, assimilation had become official policy. On the other hand, the state discouraged and sometimes suppressed expressions of Africanness, Angolanness, and race consciousness.

Meanwhile, in the 1930's a colonial literature, mainly exotic ethnographic novels (heirs to the travel narratives of the nineteenth century) emerged as perhaps a sign of the crystallization of Portugal's presence in Africa. The demographic changes caused by the influx of Portuguese settlers in the years immediately following World War II brought about definitive societal changes, especially in Angola's urban areas. Luanda, the capital, rapidly went from being little more than a sleepy tropical town, dominated culturally by creolized African ways, to a bustling metropolis divided into a European central city and surrounding African shanty neighborhoods (*musseques*). *Assimilados* and *mestiços* competed, generally unsuccessfully, for lower level bureaucratic positions and even service jobs, like taxi driver and hotel maid, with Portuguese settlers. Members of the indigenous bourgeoisie and the working poor found themselves on a downward trajectory of social and economic mobility. Changing neighborhood patterns forced many Africans to move from the lower city to the surrounding hills that form a semi-circle around Luanda.

During this period of change the *assimilados* in particular, but also to an extent the *mestiços*, became even more aquiescent as a political and social force. They were too busy trying to retain some semblance of their past economic status and middle class respectability to raise their voices in protest against the system that had failed them. But the worsening conditions for the indigenous middle class and working poor, along with the political and social changes of global magnitude that occurred between the world wars (the defeat of fascism, the rise of democratic and socialist states in Europe, and the emergence of national liberation movements in the newly dubbed Third World) also created new levels of consciousness among African intellectuals. In the 1940's a new breed of educated African began to organize around nationalist issues.

These intellectuals, many of whom were educated in Portugal, had a broader world view than their *assimilado* forebears. Many educated Africans, themselves from traditional *assimilado* families, rejected assimilation as a degrading sham. After all, once assimilated, the African was supposedly a Portuguese citizen with all the rights and privileges of his European counterpart. Instead, the colonial system relegated the African to the second class status of an *assimilado*. Thus, the new educated Africans saw themselves as Angolans in a way that presaged the soon to come nationalist surge.

In truth, *assimilados* were less than second class citizens; Angolan-born Portuguese, often described as 'second-class whites', as opposed to the metropolitan-born 'first-class whites', fit more properly in that category. With regard to Angola's white population, among the common criminals that Portugal deported to the penal colony there were many political dissenters, namely anti-Salazarists and communists. Some of these dissidents and their Angolan-born descendants envisioned a semi-autonomous colony or even an independent, European-governed state. Still others, seeing themselves as more African than European, closed ranks with intellectuals from the black and *mestiço* communities.

In far-off Lisbon, African university students organized, in 1946, the *Casa dos Estudantes do Império* (The Students from the Empire House). The Salazar government first gave its blessings and support to the *Casa*; but relations between the authorities and the students became strained as the latter became increasingly more militant. Several of the leaders of the liberation movements in their respective homelands received much of their political education while members of the *Casa*. From Angola, Agostinho Neto and Mário de Andrade, from Cape Verde and Guinea-Bissau, Amilcar Cabral, from Mozambique, Marcelino dos Santos, and from São Tomé e Príncipe, Alda Espirito Santo and Manuela Margarido met at the *Casa* to discuss politics and literature. The African students and their Portuguese cohorts used literature as an accessible and emotive outlet for their social, cultural, and political awareness. They published *Mensagem* (Message), a

139

literary journal, and they compiled anthologies of Angolan, Mozambiquean, and Saõ-Tomense poetry, as well as some twenty five small volumes of poetry by individual authors. Their militancy and literature of revindication and protest led the students down a collision course with the Portuguese authorities; finally, in 1964, the secret police (PIDE) closed the *Casa* and confiscated newsletters, magazines, and the literary works.

As important as Lisbon was as a setting for a coalition of anti-colonialist Angolans and Portuguese progressives, Luanda was the cradle of Angolan nationalism. According to John Marcum, writing with respect to the European, *mestiço*, and African communities of Luanda, 'all three groups contributed to the development of Angolan nationalism in general, but more particularly to the Luanda-Mbundu (Kimbundu) strain.'[5] Marcum characterizes a small active group of European anti-Salazarists as being of Marxist persuasion and as having organized and proselitized in Luanda during the 1940s and 1950s: 'they promoted the development of both white and non-white class and political consciousness.' (p. 18).

Although Norton de Matos had suppressed *assimilado* and *mestiço* organizations, and the Salazar regime kept those that remained under tight control, some of the conservative associations that continued to function harbored a nucleus of politicized, educated Africans and *mestiços* and a number of dissident Portuguese. One such association was the *Liga Nacional Africana* (National African League, a successor to the *Liga Africana* cofounded by Assis Junior) which, in the words of Marcum, pitted 'an older generation of culturally assimilated Africans, who accepted working in strictly legal collaboration with the colonial administration, against a younger generation of challengers who argued for more radical methods and advocated extension of *Liga* membership and its cultural, social, and political activities to the uneducated masses of Africans' (p. 23).

Another organization that survived persecution was the *Associação Regional dos Naturais de Angola* (Association of Angola's Native Sons), commonly known as *Anangola* (which is a corruption of the Kimbundu phrase for Angola's sons). *Anangola* housed a cultural section whose membership consisted primarily of young intellectuals of a militant bent. Several of these young men were also members of a small group of literary-minded students from Luanda's Salvador Correia High School. Calling themselves *Os Novos Intelectuais de Angola* (Angola's New Intellectuals) they launched two projects under the sponsorship of *Anangola's* cultural section: a literary campaign aimed at Luanda's *musseque*-dwellers and a literary magazine. The literary campaign did not materialize because of government opposition; the colonial authorities rightly suspected that these intellectuals were also looking to raise social and political consciousness among the poor. On the other hand, the authorities must have reasoned that because poems and short stories could only be read by the literate few, the magazine was relatively harmless. Thus, in 1951 the first issue of the magazine appeared under the same title, *Mensagem*, as its counterpart in Lisbon. This first issue did little more than announce a literary contest, the winners of which would be published in the next issue of *Mensagem*. But the combined second, third and fourth issues, published in 1952, would be the last. Apparently the authorities found some of the prize-winning literary entries too objectionable to be read even by those who were already convinced.

In 1957 another, more broadly based magazine, *Cultura (II)*, took over where *Mensagem* left off as an outlet for the literary production of committed Angolan writers and continued publication until 1961, despite occasional brushes with the official censor. In spite of the setbacks and difficulties, the *Novos Intelectuais* had definitively launched an autochthonous literary movement. And it was a movement composed of black, white, and *mestiço* writers, all with a more or less common objective.

With respect to the multi-racial aspect of Angola's literary and intellectual movement, not long after independence, in 1975, a group of specialists on Angolophone and Francophone African literature were surprised to learn that one of that new nations's most lauded writers was of European descent. Jose Luandino Vieira (born José Vieira Mateus da Graça in Portugal, and taken at the age of three, to Angola) had actively participated in the *Novos Intelectuais* movement. He, like a number of other Europeans, had thrown his allegiance to the *Movimento Popular de Libertação de Angola* (Popular Movement of Angola Liberation – MPLA), founded in Luanda, in 1956, by African and *mestiço* intellectuals with ethnic ties to the Kimbundu group.[6] Vieira, along with other notable Angolan writers from the three racial communities, paid for his nationalist activities with a long-term confinement in Tarrafal prison on the Cape Verde island of Santiago.

The surprise evinced by some outsiders upon learning that several of Angola's principal writers are of European descent reveals an ignorance of the historical realities of class and race under Portuguese colonial rule in Africa. Some Portuguese themselves attribute Angola's multi-racialism to the Portuguese supposed color-blindness. This multi-racialism is more likely the result of social, cultural, and demographic contingencies than it is the proof of Portuguese racial tolerance. Lisbon's long economic neglect of its African colonies allowed for spotty, but significant, cultural, biological, and linguistic creolization in the territories. This creolization, coupled with a history of political dissidence among segments of the socially and economically heterogenous European population contributed significantly to the multi-racialism of the intellectual group in Angola.

Intellectuals and writers from the three communities rallied around issues that affected the masses of uneducated Africans. If these intellectuals and writers were not all well versed in the writings of Marx, Engels, and Lenin, they at least had enough knowledge to analyze Angola's modern history on the basis of class struggle. Among Angolan committed intellectuals notions of class generally prevailed over race, although racism was a social reality with which the *Novos Intelectuais* necessarily had to contend. Thus, in the initial stages of the 1950s literary movement young poets exhorted Angolans to discover an African Angola.[7] In some cases this early poetry was a revindicatory evocation of an Africa symbolized in the images of ancestralism and maternal fecundity. In this vein Viriato da Cruz (1928–1974), a *mestiço*, credited with being the driving force behind *Mensagem*, wrote 'Mamã Negra' (Black Mamma), a poem that contains many of the conventional images of African ancestralism and telluric mysticism and the avowals of a universal black unity.

The *mestiço* and the educated African often evoked their African identity with the contriteness of the culturally alienated. Elsewhere I wrote that 'the fact that cultural revindication, with racial overtones, attended the first moments of Angola's (and to a somewhat lesser extent Mozambique's) cultural-literary thrust, the multi-racial composition (black, white, and *mestiço*) of the movement, and the socialist orientation of many of the writers, served to undercut the ideology of racial exclusiveness.'[8]

Starting with those first moments of the literary-cultural movement, we can divide Angolan pre-independence writing into three stages occurring between 1950 and 1975: Cultural revindication (with racial overtones); social protest; and combativeness. Obviously, it is more a question of what prevailed as a direction in a given period than that one form of literary discourse disappeared completely, giving way, at any time, to another. Therefore, cultural revindication continued even after Angolan writers rallied around themes of social protest and combativeness. Conversely, protest and combativeness are inherent in some of the early hortatory poems of cultural and geographical revindication. Although it is true that class consciousness worked against an emphasis on racial exclusivity, those members of a relatively privileged group within the colonial system had to fashion the symbols of their own identity as Angolans and their identification with the dispossessed masses of Africans.

Virtually every writer of the *Novos Intelectuais* generation has at least one poem lamenting the plight of the contract workers, those African victims of Portuguese forced labor practices. This concern with the rural masses and the equally exploited urban poor explains, in part, the choice of *Mensagem* as the title of the literary magazine. The *Novos Intelectuais'* planned literary program was one attempt to create a readership among those for whom they, ideally, intended their message. In practice, however, these writers were writing for each other, although they hoped to raise awareness among uncommitted members of the indigenous petty bourgeoisie and to reach sympathetic readers beyond the borders of Angola.

Although protest undercut some of the sentimentalism of revindication, committed writers needed to express an emotional unity with their geographical and cultural space. For a majority of these urban-based intellectuals, the most immediate and palpable space was the city of Luanda. The evocation of a creole-Kimbundu Luanda not only eased the dilemma of alienation, it also served as a cultural equalizer that cut across race and class lines.

The aforementioned 'Mamã Negra' of Viriato da Cruz may be a milestone in the history of Angolan poetry; it is, however, 'Namoro' (Courtship), another of his very few published poems, that has survived as something of a classic. True to its title, 'Namoro' is a poem about love. More important, however, is the setting against which the courtship takes place as well as the social and cultural backgrounds of the suitor and the object of his affection. The poem evokes the landmarks, neighborhoods, and lifestyles of creole Luanda where members of the three racial communities converged in real or imagined harmony. Indeed, some of the best Angolan poems and stories revolve nostalgically around Luanda topophilia.

In the 1950s and 1960s Luanda topophilia, creole customs, and a creolized language accompanied and lent emotional-ideological substance to the literature of protest and combativeness. When armed conflict exploded in 1961 a stiffening of censorship, police repression, and the imprisonment of militant writers cast a pall on the literary scene in Angola. For some the 1960s have come to be known as the decade of silence, which does not mean, however, that writers ceased to write altogether, but rather that some went underground or wrote, as it were, for the desk drawer. Others published their works in exile, and still others wrote clandestinely in prison. In Angola literary production was mainly in the hands of moderate and liberal Europeans, some of whom sympathized with the nationalist cause. Through their good offices some vestiges of the 1950's movement were subsumed under a more diversified literary activity.

The war of national liberation relegated race and class to an even lesser level of importance than existed in the revindicatory and protest stages of Angolan literature. Clandestine works extolling the armed struggle and a national unity that transcended race, class, ethnicity, and regionalism directed the aim of those writers who set their sights on a heightened sense of anti-colonialism and, increasingly, anti-imperialism. The phase in which the nationalist case crystallized allowed for an equalizing process in the ranks of the revolutionary cadres. During this period militant writers increased their efforts to get the attention of the outside world. In 1961, during the time when the final preparations for the beginning of the armed struggle were being made, the aforementioned José Luandino Vieira finished his novel *A Vida Verdadeira de Domingos Xavier*, translated into English as *The Real Life of Domingos Xavier* (1978). This story about a young African tractor driver who becomes involved in the liberation cause and who dies a martyr rather than reveal the identity of a white collaborator was only published in the original after the 1974 coup that toppled the Portuguese dictatorship. Meanwhile, the story became known abroad through Sarah Maldoror's 1972 film *Sambizanga*, which is based on a manuscript of the book spirited out of Luanda to Paris.

This story about multi-racial unity and heroism and unity in the cause of Angolan nationalism had its impact on small audiences of progressives in Europe and the Americas. But the work that had the greatest impact on contemporary Angolan literature was Luandino's *Luuanda* (an archaic spelling of Luanda – 1964), a collection of three long short stories or, better, tales (*estórias*) told from the perspective and in the creolized language of an urban *griot*. While Luandino was beginning his term as a political prisoner, his book of tales was being acclaimed as a literary masterpiece in Portugal where the Portuguese Writers Association awarded it first prize for fiction. As a result of this decision, the Portuguese authorities disbanded the Association. That *Luuanda* received its award as a Portuguese-language work is somewhat paradoxical in view of the fact that the author had attempted to produce a text in a creolized Portuguese designed to simulate the creolized Kimbundu of Luanda (this being a subject to which I shall return shortly). As a text that unabashedly represents popular speech (the *griot* speaks entire lines in creolized Kimbundu, but the author supplies no translations) without over-stylizations and depicts popular lore without resorting to exoticisms, *Luuanda* bridges the gap between the various stages of Angolan literature produced in colonial times as well as the post-independence period.

The coup in Portugal, the civil war that followed in Angola, and the final victory of the MPLA channeled post-independence literary activity along the lines of a new patriotism. Writers, many of whom returned triumphantly to Angola from exile, prison, and the guerilla war were the heroes of the cultural revolution. Their works, which had been suppressed or poorly distributed under colonial rule, appeared in print for the first time in new editions of thousands of copies. The writer-hero, epitomized by Agostinho Neto (1922–1979), Angola's premier poet and the new nation's first president, stood in the vanguard of the cultural revolution. When the MPLA pledged to lead the country to a form of socialism, under the banner of Marxism and Leninism, writers and other 'agents of culture' immediately began to define their roles as revolutionary intellectuals. This defining of roles was metaphorically the resetting of literary sights. As patriotism and political resolve ran high, in those months immediately preceding and following independence, some writers talked about the necessity of committing class suicide and supporting the emergence of a proletarian literature. And indeed, two months before independence one of Luanda's two newspapers, the now defunct *Diário de Luanda* (Luanda Daily), initiated a literary page called 'Resistência' (Resistance) as an outlet for poems, stories, and essays by revolutionary intellectuals whose only limitations, according to an editorial note, were the limited space (due to a paper shortage) and a humanizing scientific perspective that postulates man's inhumanity toward man. More to the point of a supposed proletarian literature, in April of 1976 the editors of 'Resistência' introduced a section called 'Participação – Cultura é Convívio' (Participation – Culture is Conviviality). Conviviality refers precisely to the participation of all in the production of cultural expression. This open invitation resulted in the publication of a spate of largely inept poems condemning colonialism and imperialism or celebrating independence and the new political order. Most of the contributors to 'Participação' were young students with literary aspirations (to be a writer carried great prestige in the young People's Republic of Angola), but not a few were indeed workers. The experiment in 'conviviality', although short lived, helped to keep literature in the forefront of the cultural revolution; it did little, however, to resolve the debate over what literature should be in independent Angola.

President Neto had set the tone for the pre-eminence of literature when he presided over the founding of the Angolan Writers Union, on December 10, 1975, just one month after independence day. The new Writers Union immediately became the principal forum for the discussion of the writer's and literature's role in the nation-building process. It was Agostinho Neto who set the scene for the discussion when, in his capacity as President of the Union's General Assembly, he delivered three major speeches on culture in general and literature in particular. Writers tended to hang on Neto's every word, as if waiting for directives as to how to define their roles in the emerging society. Agostinho Neto declared, in his second speech before the Union, that 'in independent Angola, headed toward a superior form of social organization, namely, Socialism, literature necessarily has to reflect this new situation.'[9] Not surprisingly, some took the President's words to mean a prescriptive policy toward literature. Some writers even talked about *pro-*

letkult and socialist realism; but Neto, aware of these murmurings, came back in another speech before the Writers Union with the declaration that 'cultural chauvinism is as detrimental as was the concept of *Proletkult* which emerged right after the Revolution of October and which Lenin condemned so vigorously' and 'the concept of socialist realism also proved to be detrimental (in the Soviet Union)' (p. 25).

Agostinho Neto did call for a literature for and of the people; and writers puzzled over what this meant in theory and practice. Without the shackles of a proscriptive policy, and despite some inevitable self-censorship, the writers of Angola began to seek the directions of a literature that would match, in form and content, the symbols and substance of their emerging society. Besides the problem of having little time to devote to their craft (most writers had skills that were in urgent demand in a nation of limited resources), these intellectuals found themselves at an impasse as they sought to define their roles and reset their sights.

Costa Andrade, the poet who exhorted his comrades to lower their sights, also declared, in an interview, that

> literary production now seems to me to be, and it has been so for quite a while now, a reflection (transitory, I hope) of a historical period that has already come to an end; and there is no concern about dealing with it in the future. Obviously, I am not referring to the question of language, which, in the case of a few has resulted in serious attempts and in a search for new propositions. But in general I do not believe that we are at this time producing a literature of national reconstruction. Those who have had something to say are saying what they could not say openly before.[10]

Andrade's assessment of the state of Angolan literature some four years after independence is essentially correct, but the parenthetical exception he makes for the role of language perhaps does not do justice to the latter's importance in the process of defining roles. Language had long been an important measure of the writer's role as a purveyor of Angola's social and cultural reality. Since the time of the first *assimilado* intellectuals, and certainly since the beginning of the 1950s literary movement, the question of language has posed something of a dilemma for the Angolan writer. In Lisbon, in 1959, Agostinho Neto delivered an address in which he lamented the absence of traditional poetry in indigenous languages in an anthology of Angolan poetry. He also called for the revindication of those African cultural values that the colonizer had denied, and he declared that Angolan poets should restore African oral traditions and incorporate them into their Portuguese-language writing.

During the colonial period committed Angolan writers could justify their use of the language of the colonizer as a weapon against the oppressor. In spite of this justification, the idea of using a 'borrowed' language tormented many educated Africans, even though in many cases Portuguese was their first (and only) language. Even for those educated Africans who did have knowledge of an African language, like Kimbundu (which was one of the first of Angola's indigenous languages to acquire a written form), there were problems involved in its use in literature. Not the least of these problems was the limited number of readers for a poem in Kimbundu; and since the days of Cordeiro da Matta, Angolan writers have wanted to communicate with the broadest audience possible. The most convenient compromise, for those who knew the language of their parents or grandparents, as well as for those who had an imperfect knowledge of that language, was to do what Agostinho Neto had called for in his speech. Thus, for many writers of the *Novos Intelectuais* movement, one means of revindicating African cultural values was to incorporate indigenous words and phrases, mainly Kimbundu, into their Portuguese-language writing. This compromise was not without its pitfalls, one being that it unintentionally resembled the style of the exotic ethnographic narratives produced by colonial writers. The problem was less pronounced in the case of the revindicatory, re-Africanizing verse produced by the *Novos Intelectuais*. African place names and words referring to local flora, fauna, musical instruments and the like lent a convincing air of authenticity to incantatory and hortatory poems. In the case of prose, however, it was often the mechanical juxtaposition of a narrative voice in standard Portuguese and un-westernized, or semi-westernized, Africans engaged in dialogues in a sub-standard form of Portuguese punctuated with native words.

Notwithstanding the writer's desire to make the African the subject of his story, the educated author ran the risk of fostering patronizing dichotomies based on class and the signs and symbols that identified one's social and cultural status. The Kimbundu-flavored Portuguese of the Luanda *musseque*-dweller carried the stigma of sub-standard. During the colonial period it was the language of the uncultured and socially uncouth; and the negative characterization of this speech as *pretoquês* (blackieguese) remained as an unspoken, but socially and psychologically potent, legacy of colonialism in post-independence Angola.

Early writers like Assis Júnior worked on the premise of the law of equivalencies between Portuguese and the African language. Some writers of prose narrative from the 1950s on wanted to revindicate both the African language and an Angolan brand of Portuguese. Thus, instead of *pretoquês*, it was *Luandense*, the Creolized speech of the *musseques* that, ideally, would eventually form the phonological, lexical, and syntactical base of an Angolanized Portuguese that would cut across race and class lines. It is to this end that Luandino and other writers of Angolan prose have sought to elevate Luanda's Kimbunduized Portuguese to the level of literature. And Luandino has simultaneously sought to codify creolized Kimbundu as a language of Angolan literature. In *Luuanda*, as well as in subsequent collections of tales, Luandino uses words and entire phrases in Kimbundu, but supplies no translations in footnotes or glossaries.[11] One of Luandino's apparent purposes was to mock those Portuguese writers who customarily interpolate untranslated English, German, French, or Latin phrases into their texts. When Luandino used an untranslated Kimbundu epigram at the beginning of *Luuanda* he seemed to be suggesting that Kimbundu was one of Angola's classical languages used to enhance a text written in the vernacular. The mocking of Portuguese writers was in a way a guerrilla tactic in the war against colonial deculturation; at the same time, Luandino, by means of cultural and linguistic integration and hybridization was seeking to transcend class and race, not only of the characters in his tales but also of the *griot*-narrator and the implied author.

José Luandino Vieira opened the way for the development of Angolan narrative discourse; his works have influenced virtually all contemporary Angolan writers. One such writer is Agostinho Mendes de Carvalho whose background and whose approach to the question of language make him quite distinct from Luandino. Carvalho is an African (not just somatically, but in the cultural, social, and psychological sense that the word *africano* denotes in Angola) who was born in the village of Calomboloca in the heart of Kimbundu country. He began his career as a writer late, when he was well over forty and, like Luandino, interned in Tarrafal concentration camp. Luandino and other writers also confined to Tarrafal helped and encouraged Carvalho in his first literary efforts. Uanhenga Xitu is the name under which Carvalho has published his two collections of stories and his two novels; and the author himself has explained that that is his name, not a pseudonym. Agostinho Mendes de Carvalho is the name of the public figure – member of the party's central committee, the former governor of the province of Luanda and also the former Minister of Health of the People's Republic of Angola. Uanhenga Xitu is the writer, the African, the cultural nationalist who cultivates his spoken and written Kimbundu with the care of a language purist.

Whereas the adopted name of Luandino is a hybridization – i.e. the Kimbundu root, meaning customs house, and the Portuguese suffix, -ino, referring to inhabitant – the binomial division Carvalho/Xitu signifies the social, cultural, philosophical, and linguistic dualities that characterize the latter's works. Luandino has attempted to elevate and dignify Luandense speech; Xitu's works flaunt Kimbundu and display the African's 'poorly spoken' Portuguese with a mixture of apology and group defiance. Xitu translates, defines, and documents the Kimbundu phrases that appear in his books in sometimes lengthy footnotes and glossaries; he wants his non-Kimbundu-speaking readers to understand every nuance of the African terms he uses. On the other hand, his narration and dialogues are an in-group code fashioned in the 'black' Portuguese of the rural interior, the suburban townships, and the urban working class neighborhoods of Luanda. Uanhenga Xitu and José Luandino Vieira, each in his separate way, converge on the level of the formulation of an innovative, authentically Angolan discourse.

Two other writers of narrative prose who have succeeded in putting forth new propositions on the level of language (remembering Costa Andrade's parenthetical observation) are Pepetela (the literary pseudonym and the nickname of Artur Pestana)[12] and Manuel Rui. Pepetela is a playwright and fiction writer whose most recent work, *Mayombe*, caused a sensation in Angola when it was published in 1979. The novel, written during the last years of the colonial period, is set in the equatorial jungle of Mayombe located in the tiny Angolan enclave of Cabinda. At the beginning of the war of liberation, the MPLA launched an important offensive against the Portuguese army in that oil-rich region of the then colony. Obviously, Pepetela, who was himself a commandant of the guerrilla forces (first in

Cabinda and later on the eastern front), had little possibility of seeing his novel published before Angolan independence, at least not in Portugal or the colonies. Paradoxically, after independence many doubted that the new nation was ready for such a provocative work, one which examines the larger ideological issues and questions the motivations of individual combatants among the guerrillas, while confronting the underlying problems of regionalism, tribalism, class conflict, the place of the *mestiço* in the nationalist cause, and other concerns that writers had hitherto glossed over when dealing with the war of liberation. What made the novel even more potentially controversial were the more or less explicit love scenes between the guerrilla leader and the fiancée of one of his younger comrades. Not only did the party and the government allow the novel to be published, the official sector conferred a literary prize on it. Angola was indeed ready for a raising of the sights that meant that literary expression could be more contemplative. In short, the discourse of *Mayombe* represents a codification (albeit a sometimes rhetorically turgid one) of the emotional-ideological component inherent in the final phases of Angolan nationalism.

Mayombe's appearance in late 1979 was like a pause that allowed revolutionary intellectuals and a rapidly growing and sophisticated readership among young Angolans to take measure of the recent past. And Manuel Rui, the second significant writer and one of a very few to actually write a work since independence, authored *Quem Me Dera Ser Onda* (Oh, To Be An Ocean Wave! – 1982), a novella that equals or perhaps surpasses *Mayombe* in controversy. The story, which revolves around a pig that a Luanda family is fattening for the kill on the veranda of their seventh-floor apartment, codifies the language generated by the rapid social and cultural transitions that came with independence. If *Mayombe* contemplates the recent past, *Quem Me Dera Ser Onda* lays bare, in almost satirical fashion, the social dynamics of the present.

The writers who grew to maturity before independence will more than likely continue to dominate Angola's literary scene for another ten to twenty five years. And the level of their aim will determine, in large measure, the sights that will be set by new writers who are already beginning to emerge from those social groups that were held in check by the social and cultural realities of colonialism. How these new groups of writers reset Angola's cultural sights will have everything to do with the issues of race, class, authorship, and, we might add, readership in that African nation.

Notes

1   See C. R. Boxer, *Race Relations in the Portuguese Colonial Empire: 1415–1825*; James Duffy, *Portugal in Africa*; John Marcum, *The Angolan Revolution*, vol. 1: *The Anatomy of an Explosion (1950–1962)*; and Gerald J. Bender, *Angola under the Portuguese: The Myth and the Reality*. Also see Douglas A. Wheeler and René Pélissier, *Angola*.

2   'Negra! negra! como a asa/do corvo mais negro e escuro/mas, tendo nos claros olhos,/o olhar mais límpido e puro!' In Manuel Ferreira, ed., *No Reino de Caliban*, vol. II, Seara Nova, Lisbon, 1976, p. 34.

3   James Duffy, *Portugal in Africa*, Penguin Books, Baltimore, 1962, p. 160.

4   Douglas Wheeler, in Douglas Wheeler and René Pélissier, *Angola*, Praeger Publishers, New York, 1971, p. 115.

5 John Marcum, *The Angolan Revolution*, vol. 1: *The Anatomy of an Explosion (1950–1962)*, M.I.T. Press, Cambridge, 1969, p. 16.

6 The Angolan Communist Party was founded in 1955, and its leaders, in John Marcum's words, 'reportedly joined in the creation of a nationalist front party, the Partido da Luta dos Africanos de Angola (PLUA)' p. 28. This party became, in effect, the MPLA.

7 *Vamos descobrir Angola!* (Let's discover Angola!) is the slogan associated with the *Novos Intelectuais*.

8 'Literary Criticism and African Writing in Portuguese: State of the Art', to be published in *Ideologies & Literature*, no. 16, 1983.

9 Agostinho Neto, *On Literature and National Culture, Lavra & Oficina* Luanda no. 20, 1979, p. 11.

10 'Inquérito aos Autores: Responde Costa Andrade', *Lavra & Oficina*, no. 8, Luanda, May 1979, p. 4.

11 Luandino's Portuguese publisher, Edições 70, convinced him to include a glossary of Kimbundu terms in the 8th edition of *Luuanda*.

12 Artur Pestana was born to Portuguese parents in southern Angola, in Umbundu territory. His nickname, Pepetela, is the Umbundu word for long eyelash, this also being a translation of the Portuguese word *pestana*.

CHAPTER TEN

THE MOBILIZATION OF WORDS:
POETRY AND RESISTANCE IN MOZAMBIQUE
Chris Searle

Oh . . . Oh, I heard the orders,
I heard the orders of the Portuguese.

Oh . . . Oh, I heard the orders,
I heard the orders of the Portuguese.
The Portuguese say, 'Men! Pay your pound!'

The Portuguese say, 'Men! Pay your pound!'
But it's marvelous, father–
Where shall I find the pound.

But it's marvelous, father–
Where shall I find the pound?

Oh . . . Oh, I heard the orders,
I heard the orders of the Portuguese.[1]

Words of resistance always broke the oppression of Mozambique's four centuries of Portuguese colonial rule. From chants which accompanied dances, like the one above, to the 'poem of combat' written by FRELIMO (Mozambique Liberation Front) soldiers and militants during the years of the armed struggle, poetry was a weapon, its words like bullets.

But the majority of these words were never written. They were part of an oral resistance – by necessity, as Portuguese colonialism only ever managed to bring literacy in Portuguese to a mere 10 per cent of the population. However, there were poets among that small, literate minority, who, like Joseé Craveirinha and Noémia de Sousa, used their poetry to anatomize and condemn colonialism in Mozambique. With their eloquence and passion they gave the oral tradition of resistance a written form in the coloniser's own language, a form which was continued and sharpened by the FRELIMO poets. Craveirinha, for example, wrote poems of huge indignation which empathized totally with the urban and rural oppressed, so much so that he was eventually jailed and tortured for words like these:

MAMANO

The voice of mufana
flooded the city with his accusing sobs
the small ghost

crossed over the night cottened with mist
and a downtrodden spirit
all his fate thrown out so desperately
in a cry full of his life:
Mamano . . . Mamano . . .

City,
What about the black boy of the streets
lost in the white and evil darkness
(white and evil, a thousand times evil)
the steam whistling through the siren in a frenzy of parting
and the holds filled with the dark, living ores?

What about the black boy, almost naked
barefoot and solitary
in that fatal night of deportation
in which the black anguish crossed the quays
covered the city with its voice
and no one heard it deflowering the silence
of the great houses of armoured cement;

City
What about the black boy, almost naked
small ghost, crying in his tongue
Mamano . . . Mamano . . .
in that fatal night that deported
fifty-three women
to the plantations of Sao Tomé?[2]

(mufana = little boy; mamano = Mummy!)

In 1962, after the foundation of FRELIMO, a national language had to be adopted that was capable of linguistically uniting all the people of Mozambique from the River Rovuma in the extreme north to the River Maputo in the extreme south, from the Indian Ocean to Zambia and Zimbabwe – an expanse of territory artificially carved out by the colonizer with no adherence to the languages and cultures of the people. A new nation had to be forged from a colony where the people spoke scores of different African dialects, where the spoken language of the north was incomprehensible to the population of the south, where the people of Tete province spoke a different tongue to the people of Sofala and Inhambane in the east.

In the event, the Portuguese language, the language of the colonizer, was adopted by FRELIMO as the language to be used by the new nation, and as the armed struggle developed and liberated areas of the country were beginning to be politically and economically organized, the need for basic literacy became crucial. Sergio Vieira tells us, in his 'Four Parts of a Poem of Education left Incomplete', of the exhilaration of learning the first words:

They were children
under the bullets

151

```
        teaching adults
            you were thirteen years
                and your eyes were opened
        with signs that you made on the floor
                and the eyes
                    meeting around your finger
        starved
            of the power which was found in them.
        and there was a huge cry
            of happiness
                marimbas and guitars
                    in the first letter
                        which was written.
        and like a machamba
            the seed was hidden,
        until that day, swaying in the wind
        there was a ripe cob of maize.
            we were like that
        at night, in the bases
            deciphering letters
        in the shadows of mango trees
            spelling out words
            under the cry of the bombs
            scribbling sentences
        with hands pained by the hoe
        paragraphs were blooming
            and we were all children
            learning from adults of fifteen years ...³
```

(machamba = field or agricultural plot; marimba = musical instrument)

From this language learned in the liberated areas – simple, concrete and applicable to the day-to-day struggle of guerrillas and peasants – there developed a new form of writing with a new intention. This was to raise the consciousness of the fighting cadres, to mobilize their determination and inspire them to future victories. Poetry, with its heightened, evocative language, its internal rhythms and visionary images, became another of FRELIMO's messengers:

```
    And later I will forge simple words
    which even the children can understand
    words which will enter every house
    like the wind
    and fall like red hot embers
    on our people's souls.⁴
```

Such poetry became the 'poetry of combat'. It was a particular genre – the poetry of guerrillas, another part of their weaponry. But it also brought a realization that language and its artifacts were common human property, they belonged to all, a part of the democratic apparatus of any thinking and practising person. When FRELIMO published their *Poems of Combat* in 1971, they prefaced the pamphlet with these words:

Thanks to the revolution in Mozambique, poetry, as with the other arts, has stopped being the privilege of an élite, of a class. The colonialists and capitalists taught us that in order to be a poet it was necessary to go to school for many years, to go to the university and be what they call an 'intellectual'. The man of the people, the peasant, the worker – so the capitalists and colonialists say – isn't capable of understanding poetry, much less express himself in a poetic form. Their contempt for the people leads them to say that the people are all coarse and devoid of sensitivity.

The colonialists and capitalists say this, but they know they are lying. They know that in every civilization, throught all epochs, the most beautiful works of art were made by the people or are the expression of the thoughts and feelings of the people. But this attitude which they have can be explained in relation to the society in which they live. In colonialist and capitalist societies there is a small group – the oppressors and exploiters – that are the owners of everything, the land, the houses, factories, banks, people's labour and even the police and the army. And not content with this, they also look for all the ways to make culture their own private property, searching for ways to exclude the people.

One of the revolution's great merits is precisely that of allowing the people to produce and set free their creative energy, which was suffocated for such a long time. And when it is freed, how this energy explodes – and we see then how the people produce marvellous things in all fields, in politics, art, technology and science.

This poetry collection we publish here is one of the first fruits of our revolution. They are all poems by FRELIMO militants, all of whom are directly involved in the armed struggle for national liberation. For this is the essential characteristic of today's Mozambican poetry: there is an absolute identification of the poet's sensitivity with revolutionary practice. This poetry doesn't speak of myths, of abstract things, but speaks of our life of struggle, of our hopes and certainties, our determination, our love for our comrades, of nature and for our country. And when the poet writes 'Forward comrades!' he goes forward himself. He is pleased to have a gun and grasps it truly, as truly as his hands are calloused from using the hoe and his feet are exhausted from long marches.

And because of this our poetry is also a slogan. Like a slogan it is born out of necessity, out of reality. While in colonialism and capitalism, culture and poetry were amusements for the idle hours of the rich, our poetry of today is a necessity, a song which goes out of our heart to raise our spirit, guide our will, reinforce our determination and broaden our perspective.

This anthology is like an exchange of experiences between our poets. It is also an encouragement for more of our comrades to write so that in the bases, in the schools, in the villages, new poems are written and recited, thus developing our cultural richness.[5]

Some of this poetry was translated and used in the English language journal *Mozambique Revolution* to explain and express the politics and ideology behind FRELIMO's liberation war. The reasons for the struggle were set down pictorially and simply, like the waves lapping on the long Mozambican coastline:

POEM BY THE SEA

It is not the sea
    casually lapping
    at the white sand

nor
    the moon shining smugly
    on the silver fronds of the palm trees.

The essential
    is the new consciousness;
    knowledge
    made the instrument of those who do not know.
    Ignorance, superstition, backwardness
    crumbling like sand-castles
    in the wind of science and materialism.

What matters
    is the union of the intellect
    with the hand
    in the collective and liberating act of working the land,
    so that for all will grow
    the undulating green of the maize field.

What matters
    is the mind and the acts and the feeling of each individual
    merging in the community
    like drops of water one by one
    creating an immense ocean that fills the world.

Near the sea
    a new poem
    for new men.[6]

The intensity of the language, belied by the uncomplicated use of words, fitted the dream of independence and freedom. Poems like the one above formed the new year messages of FRELIMO that were published in *Mozambique Revolution*. The dream becomes real as it finds its expression in real words.

How can we tell you the size
of our dream?

For centuries we waited
for a Messiah to come and free us . . .

Until we understood.

Today
our Revolution
is a great flower
to which each day
new petals are added.

The petals are the land
reconquered,
the people freed,
the fields cultivated,
schools and hospitals.

Our dream has the size
of freedom.[7]

The concrete language moved towards an integration of man – the guerrilla
– and nature, the fierce ally and camouflage which protects and sustains
him:

THE GUERRILLA

There he comes, armed and fierce,
There comes the man who brings freedom;
Ragged and dirty, but with an iron heart,
The guerrilla smiles and sings.

He has no house, little food and few clothes,
He lives through suffering.
Torrential rains beat against him
The bitter cold bites harshly.

Still he smiles and sings.
'I bring peace and freedom,
with this weapon in my hand
I'll drive out Salazar and his troops.'

It is a beautiful quiet morning.
The guerrilla awakes,
He has no water,
The dew is his water.

The birds, astonished, ask:
'Why do you suffer so, friend?'
The guerrilla smiles and sings:
'I bring Freedom for all.'[8]

Many of these 'poems of combat' were anonymous, as if they expressed the collective aspirations of the people themselves fighting for their freedom. There were poems that were clearly battle songs, written to uphold and advance morale and the combative spirit – particularly after the murder of FRELIMO president Eduardo Mondlane in February 1969.

GUERRILLA's SONG

We were born in the blood of those who died,
because the blood
    is earth where freedom grows.
Our muscles
    are cotton uniforms
    tied up with hatred.
Our step
    is synchronized in the factories
    where the machines torture us.
It was in the depths of the mines
    where the gasping air escaped
    and our eyes opened.
Us, sons of Mozambique
    for the country which carried us in its womb,
Us, the armed branch of the People,
    for the hatred which the companies taught us,
Us, the cry of the women's vengeance,
    for the widowhood made by forced work.
Us, and our will to learn from the children,
    by the hunger piled upon them, working on the cotton
We swear
    that the struggle continues
    necessary and imperative
    like the heat which the sun brings
    to the dawn.
By February's blood,
    we swear that our bazookas,
    will drink more steel,
By February's explosion,
    we swear that our mines
    will devour more bodies,
By February's wound
    we swear that our machine guns
    will open glades of hope,
By February's corpse,
By February's treason,
By the hatred that was added in February,
We cry out our will
    to free our country.[9]

Other poems drew lessons from the experiences of the liberated areas and were versified moral tales – such as 'We look for our strength in the people', which ends with:

> It's not enough for our cause
> to be pure and just.
> Purity and justice
>   need
>   to exist inside us.[10]

FRELIMO leaders who were also accomplished poets, like Marcelino dos Santos, Sergio Vieira, Amando Guebuza and Jorge Rebelo, used poetry as a new way of pamphleteering. Poetical words and images were mobilized for the Revolution. Their use for individual exploration was suspended and the imagination gave way to total reality. Poetry was to find a higher priority – the struggle for national liberation. With strong central images which were associated with growth, fertility and continuous energy – the sea, trees, flower, corn, the earth – a new vision of hope and fulfillment was starkly and simply delineated. This genre reached its highest expression in poems like Vieira's 'Poem left unfinished' and dos Santos' 'To point a moral to a comrade' and 'We must plant'.

> We must plant
> mother
> we must plant
>
> we must plant
> among the stars
> and on the seas
>
> on your bare feet
> and by the roadsides
>
> in forbidden hopes
> and on our open palms
>
> in the present darkness
> and in the future to be formed
>
> everywhere
> everywhere
>
> we must plant
>
> the reason
> for bodies destroyed
> and the earth bloodied
> for the cry of anguish
> and arms raised as one
>
> everywhere
> everywhere
> everywhere, mother
>
> everywhere

> we must plant
> the certainty
> of tomorrow's good
> in the endearment of your heart
>
> where every child's eyes
> renew their hope
>
> Yes mother
> we must plant
> we must plant
>
> along the road to freedom
> the new tree
> of National independence.[11]

Nature was the guerrilla's battlefield. It fed him and protected him. It was not his natural enemy. The sense of comradeship and oneness with the natural world, an ally which offers itself as a friend and benefactor – the great resource for the future – was a common idea in the FRELIMO poems. In the sequence 'I, the people', a series of twenty-seven poems published in the first year of independence by FRELIMO and written by a poet who called himself 'Mutimati: an individual voice which embodies the collective voice', this theme finds its most eloquent expression:

I, THE PEOPLE

I, the people
Know the strength of the earth which bursts like a bomb
    of grain.
I make this strength a faithful friend.

The wind blows with strength
The water runs with strength
The fire burns with strength.

In my growing arms I'll spread out cloths of sail
To seize the wind and take its strength into production.
My hands will grow until they make a circle of oars
To seize the strength of water and put it into production.
My growing lungs will blow the forge of my heart
To seize the strength of fire in production.

I, the people
I'm going to learn to fight at Nature's side
I'm going to be comrade-in-arms to the four elements.

The colonial tactic is to abandon the People in Nature
Making the People Nature's enemy.

I, the Mozambican people,
I'm going to know all my great strengths.[12]

Since independence in June 1975, the people chant different words as they set about building socialism in Mozambique. The peasants of the district of Salamanga now chant the words of affirmation to accompany their dancing:

> We had our land. The colonialists robbed it.
> We had our youth. The colonialists robbed it.
>
> We had our animals. The colonialists robbed them.
> But colonialism is dead!

When FRELIMO became the government of the new People's Republic of Mozambique, they immediately mapped out the lines of a *cultural* struggle that was necessary to forge out of the alienated and culturally oppressed Mozambican a new, dynamic personality. This was an extension of the personality of the guerrilla and revolutionary organizer of the liberated areas. Graça Machel, the Minister of Education and Culture, declared in 1977:

> In the liberated areas the new culture that developed consisted of a collective and common way of production, a common behaviour, a common form of expression, a common way of defining priority needs, material goods, wages: in short, a common way of facing the world.
>
> The Mozambican personality is the product of resistance that our People always showed to occupation, exploitation and oppression. Such resistance is fundamentally cultural. At any given moment it takes a political, economic and armed form, so as later to be transformed into People's revolutionary war.
>
> Through this transformation, the Mozambican personality assumes new values, the values of the worker and peasant class. Because this is so, it equally assumes the internationalist dimensions of the struggle. The launching of the armed struggle is then a cultural act. When FRELIMO took up arms it simultaneously hit out against the interest of colonialism, against its values. That is, it hit out against colonialist culture.
>
> With the definition of our culture in terms of revolution or of the revolution in cultural terms – it is also clear that foreign values in our country are all those cultural values of the ruling classes of colonialism, capitalism and imperialism. Such theories as Negritude and African authenticity are nothing more than the theories of the ruling classes of neo-colonialism, hence of imperialism. Mozambican anti-imperialist and anti-neo-colonialist culture affirms itself with a violent rupture with these racist, bourgeois and therefore reactionary theories. They are theories aimed only at diverting the working masses from the true objectives of the struggle.[13]

Simultaneously, a 'cultural offensive' was launched in all branches of the arts – dance, painting, the plastic arts, music and poetry. These cultural forms were to be mobilized throughout the country, to extend, deepen and carry the Revolution to the people. The arts were to be infused with the ideology of the worker/peasant class, taking inspiration from internationalism and the conscious struggle to emerge from a colonial past of mimicry and cultural domination. The poet Rui Nogar, who had been imprisoned during the last years of colonialism, drafted the declaration of intent for the new Mozambican poetry:

> History has offered to Mozambican poets a distinguished opportunity of serving the people who have emerged victorious from a struggle against Portuguese colonialism, and who now find themselves striving in a relentless struggle for the building of a nation in which scientific socialism triumphs in all sections of human activity.
>
> So we can conclude that *poetry*, in this phase of our revolution, must be used as one more weapon together with all those that are mobilized on the front of the cultural battle . . . it has the advantage of at any time or any place being read or recited, taking on a mobilizing role of great importance.
>
> Our poets must be concerned in educating themselves aesthetically. This is so as not to make verses which are only transcriptions of our party's slogans. There are means which already exist for this. We should say that our poets must strive to reach an artistic form suitable for revolutionary content which they want to transmit poetically.

With this commitment of poetry to explicitly serve the Revolution – although this time not as a substitute for slogans – the 'cultural offensive' also declared its aim to encourage more and more people to write and read poetry. This would result from the formation of local and workplace writing groups in a countrywide network:

> We must create groups of militant poets in which experiences can be exchanged – between themselves and the working masses, and a strategy of collective work must be organized, seeking to take poetry to the factories, communal villages, collective farms, schools, offices, houses of culture and other sectors of social production. And this task will be made easier if the content of their own poems takes the form of the material and spiritual needs of the working class.[14]

So poetry inhabits almost every aspect of the Mozambican Revolution. Open the papers and journals and there will be poems to bolster production, poems of solidarity with the people's struggles in Namibia and South Africa. Other poems will be recited at political meetings and rallies. Poems will try to explain new socialist ideas to the people. On a 'people's newsboard' outside a government office in Maputo in December 1978, I read this 'poetic' attempt to illustrate the ideas of 'socialist emulation', which at that time were being introduced by FRELIMO to improve the national level of production particularly with the cashew harvests:

> If you put two seeds into the ground,
> I'll put in three – to see if you'll put four,

So that I'll put five afterwards
in this challenge of Emulation.

When there are children who have no bread
It's not enough for us to belch with over-eating
And say, 'This country's rich!' –
What we need is to increase Production.

And we mustn't lose even a grain of corn,
Nor waste a drop of water.
And just because we live in the city –
It's not enough just to work,
We need to increase austerity.

Workers, peasants – our strength's vanguard!
It we're going to level this mountain
If we're going to pull down the rock
or re-direct the course of rivers –

Let's raise our tools
for the Revolution,
make new fields and factories –
and shout out loud,
FORWARD EMULATION!

In schools, poetry flows through the classroom notice boards, school meetings, Portuguese lessons and sessions of political education. A student might
write a poem to express to her colleagues the joy and satisfaction she felt
while working with the peasants in a communal village during her school
holidays:

NAJACA

It was on that spot of earth
where I reaped such rich experiences,
experiences which can serve
for a future with more meaning.
Yes, Najaca –
With your bush
so beautiful, so green –
you have in you
a welcoming communal village.
You awoke in me
things that were sleeping.
In you I made firm steps,
and each step which I made
was an advance,
was a lesson which I learned.[15]

Another student may, during a school meeting, use poetry to remind his
colleagues of their disciplinary responsibilities inside and outside the school:

Student!
Side by side
with the worker and the peasant
the student works
destroying the separatist obstacles
which divide them.

Student!
You are a child of the People
You came from the People,
and it is to them
you must transmit your knowledge –
to your *own* people.

Student!
You are present
in the reconstruction of your country,
present in the People's mobilization
present in the struggle
against nakedness and hunger!

Student!
Forget the corruption,
join yourself to the Revolution!
Take the weapon of combat
against all injustices![16]

Or a group of students may combine to write a collective poem – in this case on the anniversary of the massacre of Soweto – to declare their love and solidarity for their South African brothers and sisters:

Soweto
 Your streets are great rivers of blood
 Pregnant with corpses!

Soweto
 The cries of children
 Calling to the Power of the People
 That neither the hostile faces of the guards
 Or the guns managed to smother –
 This great desire
 This flame of freedom!

The united hands
Of this great People
Firmly clenched
Shall lay in ruins the foundations of Apartheid!

It is more than saluting
the voice of reason

It is more than seeing
the reason of the struggle

It is more than being certain
of the awaited victory

We are with you – only one People
Of the one Africa
Who arise from the long night
To destroy the chains of oppression –
We are with you![17]

Thus poetry itself becomes a part of Mozambique's revolutionary rhythm and process. It becomes genuinely popular and non-élitist, with a clear and unequivocable *function* to carry and affirm the ideas and practice of the revolution. Thus poetry also becomes an organ of democracy, available for the people's use at any time, integrated in the participatory nature of socialist government.

To meet and to participate
Are our duties and our rights –
Like the fisherman goes to the sea,
And wells are opened in arid lands.

If I put up my hand and say 'yes',
but make no comment on the words which you suggest –
I will be depriving myself of myself.
and defrauding the cause of millions.

We need to coldly analyze each detail
To be able, at last, to take the right decision.
And if this isn't true for everybody here,
We may have persons together – but a People, never![18]

This function of poetry is one of affirmation, often a celebration, of the Revolution. This means that often its previous *critical* function during the colonial time remains suspended. The passionate and incisive voices of the latter colonial period – those of, for example, Craveirinha and Noémia de Sousa – which railed against cruelty and alienation with such huge imaginative and critical power, have been temporarily under-exposed – although Craveirinha still writes in Maputo and the National Institute of Books and Records has plans to produce a new volume of his poetry. There is a continuing tendency to place a great importance, even in this post-revolutionary period, on the 'poems of combat', and recently two volumes of poems written during the armed struggle were published. Such poems may continue to fortify the combative spirit for the continuation of the class struggle and the building of socialism, but they could also have the tendency to make the poetic development among the young writer-militants static and nostalgic for the 'heroic' past rather than inspire the critical and divergent qualities needed to solve the massive material problems facing the Mozambican people now.

For poetry is the language of wit and insight as well as inspiration and vision, and these former qualities must eventually fuse with the others to form the emphasis of a developing poetic offensive in Mozambique that will

163

help to lay the foundation of an imaginative and resourceful application of socialist ideas:

> ... words like grenades
> leaving the shrapnel of ideas in our bodies
> bursting walls of ignorance
> and patient
>   and strong
>   and constant
>   they explained
> and in the words we discovered the truth![19]

Notes

1 Quoted in *Livro de Leitura*, 8th Year, Maputo National Institute of Books and Records, (1977).

2 From Chris Searle (ed.), *Sunflower of Hope: poetry from the Mozambican revolution*, London, Alison and Busby, 1982.

3 *Ibid.*

4 From Margaret Dickinson (ed.), *When Bullets Begin to Flower*, Nairobi, East Africa Publishing House, 1972.

5 From the Preface to *FRELIMO, Poesia de Combate*, 2nd edition, Maputo, Instituto Naçional dos Libros e dos Discos, 1979.

6 From *Mozambican Revolution*, a journal in English published by FRELIMO during the armed struggle.

7 *Ibid.*

8 *Ibid.*

9 Sergio Vieira, poet, from *Sunflower of Hope*, op. cit.

10 Jorge Rebelo, poet, from 'We look for our Strength in the People', from *Sunflower of Hope*, op. cit.

11 From *When Bullets Begin to Flower*, op. cit.

12 From *Sunflower of Hope*, op. cit.

13 Quoted in Chris Searle, *Beyond the skin: how Mozambique is defeating racism*, London, Liberation Books, 1979.

14 From the Mozambican daily newspaper, *Noticias*, May 3, 1977.

15 Poem by school student Sarita Andade, quoted in Chris Searle, *We're Building the New School* London, Zed Books 1981.

16 Poem by school student José Maria Pereira, quoted in *We're Building the New School*, op cit.

17 Quoted in *Beyond the skin*, op cit.

18 Translated from Orlando Mendes, *País Emerso*, FRELIMO, Maputo, 1975.

19 Sergio Vieira, poet, from *Sunflower of Hope*, op. cit.

CHAPTER ELEVEN

SURVIVE THE PEACE:
CYPRIAN EKWENSI AS A POLITICAL NOVELIST
Peter Nazareth

The man most responsible for the growth and development of modern African literature has been the most damned and vilified of all African writers. Phrases like 'hired to debase literature', 'models his work on fourth-rate Western writing,' 'appreciated only by those who have not been exposed to better writing' and other insults have been heaped on the work of Cyprian Ekwensi like bombs dropped from a plane, without regard for what is destroyed. Very few critics have stopped to analyze Ekwensi's work. For such critics, the literary history of Africa is modeled on F. R. Leavis' 'Great Tradition'. Ekwensi's role was to play John the Baptist to Achebe's Jesus and then to disappear from the scene.

Ekwensi is still around. Reading from his fiction, he holds his audience spellbound, until he chooses to release it, while other certified African writers bore their audience to tears. Could this be a careless, fourth-rate writer? Or is there something wrong with the perceptions and values of the critics? Why does Ekwensi continue to be one of the most popular writers in Africa if he is no good?

Now comes a chance to analyze Ekwensi's work afresh: the publication of his first novel in a decade, *Survive the Peace*.[1] The setting of the novel is the end of the Nigerian civil war and its aftermath. The protagonist is James Odugo, a senior news reporter on the Biafran side. The opening lines take us straight into the situation:

> Laughter in the midst of tragedy can never really be funny. Yet they had been bandying jokes that afternoon, soon after the air raid on the Biafran town.
>
> James Odugo, Senior Reporter *News* had been there in the newsroom with his colleagues, tense as a bow-string, frightened with that hollow fear of ever-impending sudden death in war-time. One of the boys at the typewriter – he could not remember which – had made a prediction.
>
> 'When this war will end; it will be like the abomination of desolation which was spoken of by Daniel the Prophet, standing in the Holy Places, he that heareth let him understand . . .' (p. 3)

This is taut, careful writing. We can see and hear it. Ekwensi grows out of an oral tradition. He was told stories and folktales by his parents, Igbos who lived in Northern Nigeria but who wanted their son to know their traditions. Later, he worked in radio: an extension of the oral tradition into modern times. In sound, before an audience, one must make one's point quickly or one will lose the audience. As Ekwensi told me some years ago, when he was a member of the International Writing Program, he believes that the novel should entertain.

The beginning of *Survive the Peace* contains what is to come: the civil war, the end of the war, the religious values by which the end and indeed the whole war will be judged, the problem of survival, and the contrast between appearance – the formal presentation of the news – and reality. James Odugo forms a good link between these various elements. He is a reporter and wants to witness everything. When he realizes that the war is coming to an end, that Biafra has been defeated, he feels, '*Lost the war*. But why stand here, like one mesmerized? Why not run? No, I'm a newsman. I must witness it all.' Like other Ekwensi protagonists, then, James Odugo is a witness to society, social forces and social disintegration. But unlike Ekwensi's most famous protagonist, Jagua Nana, Odugo is almost dwarfed by events: they are too large for him to be able to shape, manipulate or fully resist.

What is Odugo a witness to?

THE ABOMINATION OF DESOLATION

The epigram to the first section of the novel is from Aristotle: 'We make war that we may live in peace.' This is not a statement of what we find in this section or the novel as a whole. It is an expression of hope. The whole novel is concerned with the question of survival; surviving the war and surviving the peace that is to follow. Can one escape the war because it has stopped?

On the contrary: the underlying structure of the novel is a nightmare, a descent into hell. This happens gradually. First we see scenes of the damned from real life while Odugo and his lover, Vic Ezenta, are running away:

> In the half-darkness they saw streams of silent people fleeing, mainly on foot, with headloads. Men, women, children, sliding past like so many black ghosts. Odugo discovered that the other girls in the car had escaped, leaving him alone with Vic. (p. 16)

Later, when they are at the village of Obodonta,

> It was as if this was all happening in another world. Refugees were marching three deep, thousands and thousands of them. Men with beds on their heads to which cotton mattresses had been bound, women with two children on their backs, weary faces, anguished eyes, haunted eyes, dragging feet, they plodded or trotted or galloped in one final effort to keep life burning. The ordeal was killing even to see. (p. 23)

Then we see the full abomination, the horror of modern war:

> The words coincided with multiple booming explosions, followed by

the cacophony of strafing, and the belching of smoke from oil-storage tanks. Odugo felt, rather than saw, wings – huge, shadowy wings – glide overhead in one smooth and frightening sweep, and felt the acrid jet of hot wind in his throat and nostrils. The earth trembled and opened up beneath him. The staccato sound of strafing ricocheted against everything standing. The vultures collided in mid-air and came tumbling down, and cattle, a politician, a trader, a student . . . he could be Ibo, or Hausa, or Yoruba, or Efik or Rivers . . . no one can tell now. Now he is just a bony skeleton. He will not fight again, he will not be insulted, he has returned to his Maker, he will not conspire with anyone to overthrow any government. Mark you we shall all . . . all of us one day be like him. *Definite*! (p. 74)

For Captain, the nightmare represented by this skull is a lesson on the levelling process of a war from which nothing is gained. He says,

While you remained here, Benne, wiggling your bottom at loafers and deserters, crawling into bed with strangers . . . do you think I do not know you? But, it will all be a waste of time – and this is why I called all of you together. It will all be a waste of our time and blood if after this there is no peace . . . if we do not get the government we desire . . . a government to give us good food at a cheap price, clean water, comfortable houses, paying jobs, education for our children who survive, medical attention, everything that means that Africa is independent, that we understand why people go to war. Above everything else – peace. Peace to trade and train our children, peace just to sit and do nothing. (p. 74)

His three children had died of kwashiorkor during the war and he blames Benne for carelessness. Saying he has to begin all over again, he begins to beat her up with the teeth of the skull.

Captain is to serve as a constant reminder of the indiscriminately destructive lessons of the war, with the skull as his companion. He becomes a religious savior of souls.

RELIGION

The novel has a religious subtext. It is full of ironic religious reversals. In the Bible, Samson is the strong man who brought the Temple down. In *Survive the Peace*, Samson is the helpless leader of a platoon, fighting against hopeless odds after the war has ended without knowing the end has come. His prayer just before the final action becomes an eloquent plea against all war:

Bless my dear father and mother at Obodonta. *Chineke*, if this should be the way it must end, I will come to you swiftly and painlessly and in peace. I do not blame you for bringing war to our land. As long as men live and lust for power, so long must there be wars. And we the soldiers are the currency for war. But, Lord, let me pray to you that those who survive will learn from our sufferings. It is only we mortals who fight wars and die hoping to make life better for those we leave behind. If their lives are no better than ours, then we have sacrificed ours in vain. *Chineke*, bless all my brothers wherever they may be – in Germany, Nigeria, Britain, the United States. I shall never see those lands. But they also sometimes fight wars . . . Bless my fighting companions. (p. 48)

As we shall see later, it is no accident that all of Samson's brothers are in various parts of the Western world. The sacred python that Samson prevents one of his men from killing becomes the only witness to their death. The sacred becomes sinister while death is dictated by the machine:

Samson and his men choked under the suffocation of hot lead and suddenly one of them threw away his empty gun and yelled and everyone of them knew it was time to do the same, but the machines were typing out their names with bullets of death that seared into their stomachs and shattered their hip bones and back bones and head bones. Then every living thing became quiet in the Umunevo River basin except for the Umunevo python that coiled round a thick tree whose roots dipped into the river. There the python remained silent, licking his lips with a forked tongue and listening to the thunderstorm without rain. (p. 49)

Things have fallen apart. Echoes of Achebe in *Survive the Peace* are no accident but references to social contexts. Ekwensi is more subtle than he is usually credited with being. There are few explicit references to foreign involvement in the Nigerian Civil War, but this involvement is implied, as in the last prayer of Samson, going back to the very beginning of European technological imperialism. Thus in the passage describing the death of Samson and his men, death 'types out' the names of those who are to die while Samson's brothers are all in the white man's world. Perhaps this war was doomed to happen from the time the white man set foot in Nigeria . . . We stumble upon Okonkwo in *Survive the Peace*. It is the name of a very political priest, who attacks foreign involvement at the burial service for Samson, referring not only to the Nigerian war but also to Vietnam. Odugo thinks this sermon is more political than religious. When Odugo returns home, his father greets him with his given name: Okonkwo. Thus the priest is really Odugo's alter-ego, that side of himself that he is not aware of and has not embraced. Odugo's moral consciousness is inadequate.

ODUGO'S MORAL CONSCIOUSNESS

Odugo is our witness to what is happening during the war and after. The size of the horrors he sees may blind us to the fact that he must also be looked at carefully. He is a reporter, but he disclaims responsibility over the war. He is merely a passive observer, he says, an innocent man caught up in a war declared by others. As a journalist, he merely serves his master. His relationships with women are also casual. This is partly so because of the war – he needs the comfort of a woman to survive – but there is the suggestion that he is generally too casual with women. He impregnates Gladys, has an affair with Vic, and has sex with Benne, although she is the wife of his host's nephew. Yet when he meets up with his wife after the war and finds she is pregnant with another man's child, he is angered, his manhood is wounded.

Odugo keeps insisting that he is not responsible for the war, like everyone else; but he must share the blame, something he refuses to see. He has avoided all moral responsibility. He was willing to issue lies in the news while he knew the reality was quite different. Throughout the novel, there is the juxtaposition of slickly incorrect news reports with the reality. Would Samson have died if he had heard from his radio that the war had ended instead of news like, 'Gallant Biafran forces today flung back an attack on the Umunevo Bridge . . .'? Odugo once comes close to acknowledging his guilt. 'We know how to sell ideas, people, products,' he says, 'even governments.' Unfortunately, he draws the wrong conclusion from this discovery. 'But this time, when I sell such things, I don't pay with my blood,' he says, 'I get paid in good cash.' He has pulled back from social responsibility into selfish individualism, like his brother Patrick, who pursued his own business interests from Cotonu without any regard even for his family. We need Captain to remind us that the war has shattered souls. As Captain says, it is necessary not only to reconstruct the body but also the soul. James Odugo has actually opted for the very course of action that would lead to the same situation. Defying advice to be cautious, he decides to drive back to Pa Ukoha to get back his documents because he wants to claim back his land. His reason? It is not sacred or sentimental: he wants his share of 'the national cake'. The novelist says, 'If he sold some plots of land and had cash, it would do a lot towards the recovery of the whole family. Many landowners were selling and land speculation was rife throughout the war area.' On his way to the documents, Odugo is waylaid and killed by some young men with guns that had probably been thrown away by the Biafran soldiers.

However, Odugo has made one important moral decision. This is after Gladys catches up with him and tells him she is pregnant with his child. She asks whether she should keep it or remove it. Odugo thinks that if this had happened before the war, it would have been scandalous. But now he asks Gladys whether she can carry it through. She begins saying, 'If you wish – ' but he interrupts, 'I wish!' He thinks,

> No nation can survive on deaths. It is the new generation that must make for continuity. Let the baby come. This is the time most of our women are running away from us because they believe we will not survive. Now Gladys is coming forward to me, with a child in her arms. Bless her! (p. 111)

The child is born after his death, to carry on his life. The child is a girl. She is given the name, Nkikura, which means, 'That which lies ahead is greater.'

THE WOMEN

Ekwensi's great strength is his ability to create a whole range of characters from ordinary life, including women. In *Survive the Peace*, there are four important women characters, all connected with the protagonists: Vic Ezenta, Gladys Nwibe, Benne and Juliette. Each is or has been Odugo's lover. Vic is his lover until he goes to search for his wife and family. While staying with Pa Ukoha, Vic begins to have an affair with Flight-Captain Abdul Gana. She quietly leaves with him for the city. Odugo thinks bitterly:

> Now the truth was coming out. If you are a defeated man, without a job, without power, how do you retain the loyalty of your women? Men with jobs and power will take them from you. It is only natural. Vic has told you that she wants the good things of life, and fast. At least it is clear she cannot find what she needs in Obodonta. And she is not your wife. (p. 79).

Benne too wants the good things of life. She is married to Captain, away at war, but keeps on having affairs. She even seduces Odugo, while Vic is around. Gladys Nwibe, who was mentioned earlier in the novel and who resembles Vic in Odugo's mind, turns up later. Although she had slept with him only once, she is pregnant. She finds him just before he tracks down his wife, Juliette – who is pregnant with another man's child.

All the major women characters in the novel seem to be promiscuous, 'bad women' and no doubt they will give some critics the opportunity to grumble again about the breasts you constantly find in Ekwensi's writing. Although Ekwensi seems to go along with popular values and sometimes makes moral comments growing out of the popular value-system, he often presents a face of his characters that surprises us. He makes us suddenly sympathize with characters we would have condemned in real life, particularly if we belonged to the society he is writing about and for. In the case of all four women, there comes a time when we are made to sympathize with each because we suddenly see things from their perspective instead of Odugo's or that of the society. For instance, Vic leaves Odugo, and he thinks it is because she wants the fine things she cannot get from a powerless, defeated man. Yet he forgets that he has been searching for his wife so there can be no room in his life for Vic. They were brought together by a common need during the war. They helped each other survive. Now they must part. Odugo is selfishly trying to have things both ways. Furthermore, he is rather casual about the fact that he has been having intercourse with Benne although he is staying in the house of her husband's uncle.

Benne is condemned by almost everybody, including her husband's relatives, for being promiscuous; and she is very sexy. Yet, she says, her husband was just as promiscuous, but nobody condemned him. She goes with the soldier-conquerers. The novelist says, 'Her need for the warmth of male company was insatiable. The sight of any kind of military uniform got her on heat like a bitch in a rut.' This looks like the author's judgement of Benne, but in fact it is the impersonal author's comment, a reflection of the society's condemnation. Actually, Benne uses her sexual charms to get things from the soldiers which she shares with the family: 'the family shared the loot and Benne acquired a special importance for her efforts and this importance made it difficult for anyone, having tasted of her loot, to reprimand her.' When her husband comes back, he beats her up with the skull for being unfaithful and leaves her. When Odugo is also going to leave, she tearfully presents a case for herself: 'Go! – and leave me alone! It is my luck! I give myself to you men and you always throw me away when you have satisfied yourselves.' She goes on to say, 'Captain left me here, no money, no food, no plan. I will go and look for my own survival. I don't want anyone to control me.'

When Odugo meets Juliette, he is shocked to find her pregnant. He accuses her, conveniently forgetting that he has impregnated Gladys. Juliette counter-accuses, 'Have you been a Saint?' He replies, 'Did I say I was? But while I may marry three or four wives, you cannot have more than one husband at a time!' This is an inadequate defense, and it is hypocritical. The hypocrisy does not come from Odugo alone: it comes from the society, which is patriarchal. Ekwensi is questioning the popular morality, and blaming it. There follows a heated exchange, which gives Odugo a shock:

> 'God above! This war has really done something! Do you know that what you are saying is an abomination in Iboland! You will take Ifoma and your unborn child to the new man –?'
> 'Which new man?'
> 'The father of your child.'
> 'I do not wish to be under any new man, can't you understand?'
> 'Under –?'
> 'Not under, not by the side, not *controlled* by any man. I want to be my own boss, and see what God has in store for me.' (p. 141)

All our sympathy is now for Juliette. Odugo has made a male-chauvinist assumption: that she will go to another man. Here is one change the war has brought about: the emancipation of women. Juliette is going to be independent, like Benne, having been so during the war and survived.

SURVIVAL

Survival is the obsession of all the characters in the novel. There are many survivors at the end of the war. But a high price has been paid. Sometimes the wife was on the side of Biafra and the husband on the side of Nigeria. Families have been split.

Odugo tries to gather his family together. When he finds his wife, however, he discovers she has been impregnated by another man. He himself has impregnated another woman. He realizes that there is no going back. The war has scattered families, a phrase that is a refrain in the novel; in fact, 'Scattered Families' was the draft title of the novel. When Odugo meets his wife, although he feels the bonds of traditional marriage cannot be dismissed lightly, he thinks, 'This woman was not his wife, but a strange product of the war.'

Ironically, survival becomes more difficult after the war. This is because, as the novel indicates, the war did not just start and then just end. The war was the consequence of events and decisions that went before. Thus in Part II, Chapter 7, we are taken into Odugo's past. He was in love with a girl, Jokeh, but her family did not want her to marry him. They snatched her away and sent her to the United Kingdom 'for further studies' because they wanted 'to improve her eligibility for a judiciary class of husband.' This is an example of what has been called 'class-formation' in Africa. It is one of the many causes of the war: too many people seeking their own material interests, not enough seeking the interest of the nation as a whole. Ekwensi is not a political ideologue, yet we see that there is a political sub-structure in the novel. It becomes difficult to survive the peace because in a sense, the war has not ended: many people go back to the old business of trying to pursue their own material interests, like vultures.

What, then, is survival? While the people are thinking of material survival, that of the body, Captain stands as a reminder that a more serious survival is necessary: that of the soul. This is the soul of the individual, but as part of the larger community. Everywhere, people seem to be forgetting too soon. 'We do not love ourselves,' says Stephen Odugo. 'We have faced every kind of suffering. Today, we have forgotten.' We are given example after example of new business ventures, exploitation of Nigerians by Nigerians, like before.

The phrase 'One Nigeria!' is used cynically by most of the characters in the novel, but Ekwensi is not a cynic. There are some remarkable examples of a return to normality at the end of the war. For example:

> Many more cars in the Obodonta bush remained concealed and immobilized to avoid commandeering by the military. These were the cars which later invaded Enugu city to surprise the relief and rehabilitation organizations which had broadcast a call for the return to work and had thought that all the cars in Iboland had been destroyed. (p. 88)

It is praiseworthy that people like Odugo are readily accepted by friends on the other side. He is even given back pay, money to start him off in life again.

But the problem of survival cannot be so easy, the novel says. The deepest criticism of the war comes from a traditional perspective.

TRADITIONAL VALUES

Some traditions have survived the war, though shakily. When Odugo enters the house of Pa Ukoha, they decide to split the kola nut in the traditional way, but they cannot decide who should do it: the older one or the younger. Finally, they compromise: the elder delegates the younger to split it. There has been a terrible spiritual loss. The novelist says,

> Odugo could not help thinking: the old men who gave us life, they lived by faith. They did not go to college but they had faith. *We went to college and lost our faith.* He thought of Pa Ukoha in Obodonta and of Pa Ezenta in Ifitenu. These men belonged to a generation that was dying away, and with them went traditions. If there was one good thing to be learnt from them, it was their power of survival which depended on the undying faith that sustained them. (p. 113)

For the older people, moral values are solid. Thus the chief lesson of the causes and consequences of the war is presented in the words of Pa Ukoha, talking to Odugo after the death of his son Samson:

> Our people do not speak with one voice,' Ukoha lamented. 'What we need is one voice, less greed ... everyone wants to be rich, but that is not possible. God did not intend it like that'.
>
> Odugo said, 'But the whole world is like that!'
>
> 'Like what?'
>
> 'Everyone wanting to get rich.'
>
> 'Yes, but it is worse in our people. No patience, at all! We poor men, we do not ask for much,' said Pa Ukoha. 'No matter who is ruling us today, we ask for good water to drink and to wash. Good roads to carry our yams and cassava. Good schools to train our children. Good maternities to care for our wives in labour. Give us a place to worship our God – no, that one, we can build for ourselves. Finally, let us have peace, no more killing.'
>
> 'And you will not envy the rich man, if you have all these?'
>
> 'What for? More money, more trouble, that's all!' And his eyes almost twinkled.
>
> Odugo smiled.
>
> Pa Ukoha said, 'Do you know ... we have lost everything by this war. Who gained, but the foreign powers? We black people faced every kind of suffering. They say that war should refine people, make them fear God. Our war has made us into *usu-agwu* – '
>
> 'What's that?'
>
> 'Don't you know *usu-agwu* in Iboland?'
>
> 'No, pa.'
>
> 'It is a kind of *usu*, a bat. Not bird, though it has wings. Not beast, though it has hairs. *Usu-agwu* grows one nose, every year. It has a small face. In five years, it has five noses.'
>
> 'Terrible!'
>
> 'Truly! When a small boy picks *usu-agwu* in the bush, he is too frightened! He cannot make out what it is. He runs home to tell his mother the terrible thing he has caught.'
>
> 'I understand,' said Odugo, 'So the war has multiplied our ugliness.' (p. 57–58)

Unfortunately, Odugo has not really understood the call of the elders of the society to turn away from material and spiritual violence.

VIOLENCE

How does the artist handle violence in an artistic form? How can he present a horrible violence from real life in an art form? How can he communicate the experience effectively without turning the reader off?

Ekwensi has used various techniques, some of which we have already seen such as the effect of nightmare and the traditional consciousness-making judgements. The most important method is to describe violence off-stage so that we see it obliquely. Buying a chicken, Odugo sees the woman staring in horror:

> At first he thought he had said something offensive. The woman stared straight ahead past him, over his shoulder, and her mouth remained open with the voice rattling within and no words coming out. (p. 5)

The other women stare the same way. Odugo turns to see 'a spectacle that put fear in him'. He sees thousands of Biafran soldiers streaming in, running away. The soldiers remove their uniforms and put on ordinary clothes:

> Before all eyes, he untied the bundle. It contained civilian clothes. In a few minutes the soldier had transformed himself into a civilian complete with crumpled cloth cap and innocent smile.
> 'If you see me for army uniform again, make you shoot me!'
> He had become his true age, about eighteen. His acquired military bravado, and his haughty bearing had been shed like a snake-skin on the grass, and there it lay in a heap on the market-square, dead and useless. (p. 10)

We experience here the feeling of cataclysmic violence, yet we do not *see* any graphic physical violence. We *feel* the violence of young, innocent boys forced to become soldiers. We *feel* the violence of the 'innocent smile' the soldier puts on like his cap: we doubt the innocence of the demilitarized soldier, and it prepares us for the killing of Odugo later by 'innocent' young people using guns cast off by such ex-soldiers. The reference to the shedding of clothes like a snake prepares us for the python that will witness the death of Samson.

Although there are many references to rape, the first rape takes place off-stage. The girl runs into the Obodonta compound with her clothes torn, in tears. At first incoherent, she finally stammers out her story. She had been bathing at the stream when she was raped by the soldiers. The other girls ran away instead of trying to save her. We are not told much, yet we feel the violence, physical as well as to the spiritual values of the community. Ada Ukoha says, 'Now who said the war has ended when such evil comes to our village? Men and woman bathe naked side by side, and no one attacks the other.'

When we finally meet a few incidents of violence on-stage, they have an impact beyond what the accumulation of graphic incidents on-stage could have had. The death of Anna in an air-raid is horrible, more so because we do not know for a while what has happened to her. We feel the tension of Vic and Odugo as they search for her in the mortuary. When they find her body, it has a deep slash in her neck, where the bomb fragment is embedded; and the body is naked. Again, we do not see much, but we feel the violence.

From his handling of violence, one can see that Ekwensi is a fine artist, a careful craftsman, conscious of the overall shape of the novel as well as the metaphorical significance of language. For example, the soldier distributing relief is called 'the relief-selling soldier' because he is selling off the relief supplies meant to be distributed free to the people.

THE PEOPLE'S NOVELIST

Ekwensi has been correctly identified as a popular novelist, but critics have tended to conclude that this somehow makes him inferior to 'serious' novelists like Achebe and Ngugi. Let us look at the virtues of being a popular novelist.

Ekwensi told me that he always had a specific audience in mind, the Nigerian audience, although he tries to make his writing clear so that others outside Nigeria can also understand it. He is aware of the increasing level of consciousness in his audience and feels he is in communion with this audience. He bears a social responsibility towards this audience. Thus he has written several children's novels. Thus, too, he worked as a broadcaster and journalist: he says that when *he* deals with the issues of the day, this has a great impact on the people. Although Ekwensi says the job of the writer is to entertain, we notice that he is not really in opposition to Achebe, who said in a frequently quoted lecture that the duty of the African writer is to teach. Ekwensi believes in teaching by entertaining. He therefore writes about recognizable people in a language that can be easily understood. His favorite authors express things simply, and he himself believes the work should be written as simply as possible. However, he believes that the work should be complex in *thought and ideas*.

While some of the moral comments in *Survive the Peace* grow out of popular morality, Ekwensi actually questions some aspects of that morality. But he does not do this through psychological introspection, through painful self-questioning by the protagonist, unlike Ngugi: he does it through the story. Talking of the writers who influenced him, he says, 'I liked adventure. I liked people doing things, fighting or digging for gold, not just beating their breasts in remorse about something they could have done but did not do.'[2] His use of simple language actually covers a complexity. His description of the nightmare as the war ends could have come out of Kafka, except the story *moves* as it would in an oral performance.

Ekwensi has read popular literature of the West and acknowledges his debt to it.[3] But a more basic debt is to the African folk-tradition. In a symposium on *The Novel and Reality in Africa and America*, he defined the function of the African novelist as follows:

> The journalists in their own way mirror the times but sometimes they do not hold the mirror very fully to the event for obvious reasons. The mirror is tilted to its side and it gives perhaps an image distorted in favour of the particular moment. Now if the writer were accepted in African society he would be rather like the bird in the folktale that always appears on the wall and pipes a particular tune. When you hear that tune you know that there is a tragedy somewhere; someone has died or something quite serious is happening. The bird disappears and within a moment you get the illumination of the bird's visit. The writer is this kind of bird. He pipes the tune which gives the warning.[4]

The tune piped by the bird may sound clear, but its meaning must be worked out by the listener. In *Survive the Peace*, the protagonist is a journalist who holds up a mirror to reality: but we make a mistake if we take his observation to be the full truth. As we have seen, as the story progresses, he is presented for criticism, and his vision and morality prove to be inadequate. When he is dying, his last word is, 'Darkness . . .' Gladys has to puzzle out its meaning, and so has the reader, just as we have to work out the significance of the last words of Kurtz in Conrad's *Heart of Darkness*. Reality is not simply understood. For Ekwensi, as for Conrad, the ultimate purpose of the novel is moral discovery: but in social terms.[5] Ekwensi says, 'We Africans are in need of knowing ourselves. We don't really know ourselves well enough, and the writer who writes with immediacy serves to bridge this gap of self-knowledge, which I think is very vital to understanding ourselves and our relationship with others.'[6] In bridging this gap of self-knowledge, the African author inevitably writes a political novel. 'And we are getting quite close to the political,' says Ekwensi, 'which we cannot divorce from present day life in Africa. At this particular moment of time we live in politics and economics.'[7]

Survive the Peace is a fine political novel, one of Ekwensi's best in a long and distinguished career working for the people of Nigeria. Why, then, has there been such an attack on his work? Perhaps it is plain malice on the part of some critics. Possibly it is an inability to see that several good African writers can exist simultaneously, all writing in different ways. Most likely, academically trained critics do not realize the nature of work to be *heard* by an audience. An audience listening to a speaker must be given a few moments to relax its concentration before the tension builds up again. In drama, this would be called comic relief. In a novel, this would be a paragraph or two where a great deal happens without the author taxing us with psychological or dramatic depth. Such paragraphs analyzed in print may appear to be careless. One such 'lapse' in *Survive the Peace* is as follows. Odugo is returning from the stream to Pa Ukoha's home when he sees a seductive woman. She accompanies him back. The novelist says,

> As they neared the Ukoha home, Odugo found that she too was walking in the same direction. After that he saw her again and again in different outfits, and suddenly he realized that she was Benne. (p. 64)

At this point, the reader finds it improbable that Odugo would not recognize Benne unless more time were spent telling us why. He also finds it improbable that Odugo would suddenly realize it is Benne when she has been living in the same compound all the time. I suspect that hostile critics have tended to select all such passages from Ekwensi's work, to dismiss them as badly written, and to say that Ekwensi therefore gets all his models from fourth-rate Western writers. After all, one does not find such 'weak' passages in Achebe. But if one looks at the oral tradition, one can understand why there are such 'lapses' in Ekwensi's work after several pages of beautifully crafted paragraphs. The weakness of Soyinka, for instance, is that in being profound, he becomes virtually imcomprehensible. Soyinka could do with a little of Ekwensi's kind of relationship with his audience.

Ekwensi told me that the critic's business is not only to interpret but also to evaluate the work, to assess and direct the attention of the author to ways of realizing his intention as well as to direct the reader to things he should be looking for. In other words, said Ekwensi, the critic should be a kind of agent between the producer and consumer of writing. I hope I have fulfilled the function of the critic and drawn attention to a fine political novel to have come out of the tragic Nigerian civil war. I hope I have also illuminated the strengths of Cyprian Ekwensi, the people's novelist, who has labored long and hard for over thirty-five years without respect from the very critics and academics who owe their livelihood to this pioneer of modern African writing.

With *Survive the Peace*, Cyprian Ekwensi confounds all those who buried him with 'the first generation of Nigerian writers.' He belongs to the present generation. He has survived.

Notes

1 Cyprian Ekwensi, *Survive the Peace*, Heinemann African Writers Series, London, 1976. Ekwensi has written an earlier novel about the war entitled *Africhaos*, which has not been published.

2 Bernth Lindfors, ed., *Dem-Say (Interviews with Eight Nigerian Writers)*, African & Afro-American Studies and Research Center, The University of Texas at Austin, Austin, Texas, 1974, p. 34.

3 *Ibid.*, p. 24, p. 34.

4 *The Novel and Reality in Africa and America*, ed. Dr. Theophilus Vincent, Department of English, the University of Lagos, Lagos, Nigeria, undated, pp. 9–10. The publication is a full transcript of a symposium held on January 26, 1973 at the University of Lagos on the occasion of the visit of John Updike as a Lincoln Lecturer.

5 See my essay on Conrad in *Literature and Society in Modern Africa*, East African Literature Bureau, Nairobi/Kampala/Dar es Salaam, 1972. (American edition: *An African View of Literature*, Northwestern University Press, Evanston, Illinois, 1974.)

6 Lindfors, *op. cit.*, p. 33.

7 *The Novel and Reality in Africa and America*, p. 9.

CHAPTER TWELVE

THE POLITICAL-ECONOMIC FACTOR IN URHOBO SONG-POETRY

Godini G. Darah

> Works of literature and art, as ideological forms, are products in the human brain of the life of a given society.
>
> Mao Tse-Dong[1]

> If one is to regard the process of poetic creation only as a combination of sounds or words, and to seek along these lines the solution of all the problems of poetry, then the only perfect formula of 'poetics' will be this: Arm yourself with a dictionary and create by means of algebraic combinations and permutations of words, all the poetic works of the world which have been created and which have not yet been created.
>
> Leon Trotsky[2]

The opening citations are intended to draw attention to the essential thesis of the Marxist theory of art and literature in general. Marxist criticism recognizes the primacy of the sociality of every artistic endeavour and insists that the evaluation of any artistic work be guided by a knowledge of the human world that conditions the production and reception of that work.

The methodological question posed by Marxism has generated lively controversy in the ranks of African literature in European languages. This controversy has crystalized into two main schools of criticism: the bourgeois formalist or art for art's sake on the one hand, and on the other, a Marxist and anti-imperialist tendency.[3] Hovering between these two positions is a radical, pan-Africanist tendency. For reasons not unconnected with the relative novelty of African oral literary scholarship, differences of approach have not assumed a confrontational form as yet. Many students of the oral literary tradition have pointed attention to the social context of the literature.[4] At any rate, the production and performance techniques of oral literature compel some sociological perspective in its criticism. But among those who recognize the significance of the social environment, the dominant effort has not strayed very much beyond the appending of ethnographic data to the literary material. More often than not the dialectical interaction between the literary product and the social world it portrays is never explored in analyses.[5] This critical practice is unable to account for important changes in themes and techniques which occur in the literary culture due to the socio-political dynamics of the producing society.

One other common shortcoming of African oral literary criticism is the indiscriminate lumping together of societies under such loose rubrics as 'non-literate', 'traditional', etc. Even when national labels such as 'the Yoruba', 'the Wolof', or 'the Hausa' are provided in the discussion of the literature, the entire population in the language areas is often presented as manifesting a monolithic and undynamic ideological outlook and artistic sensibility. The use of the omnibus labels shields from focus important socio-economic or class differences among nationalities; differences which have profound implications for the kind of literature practised by the various groups.

In the rest of the paper we shall attempt a review of Urhobo song-poetry traditions in the context of the political and socio-economic developments in the Niger Delta area of Nigeria. The period covered stretches from the establishment of colonial rule in the late nineteenth century to the present. For the Urhobo-speaking peoples, this period is certainly the most momentous in their history. Like most African peoples in the post-Berlin Conference phase of Western European imperialism, the Urhobo suffered the loss of political autonomy between 1900 and 1930. Consequently, the people became severely disabled in their struggles to lead a dignified existence.

Our source data are songs because, unlike the more stable forms such as drama and tales, songs usually provide more reliable evidence of the various ways Urhobo people have responded to the ruptures in their material and superstructural situations due to the influence of colonialism.

THE URHOBO IN DEMOGRAPHIC PERSPECTIVE

The Urhobo number about a million and live mainly in the Delta area of the Bendel State of Nigeria.[6] About a quarter of this number lives in 'diaspora' in the oil palm and forest belts of most of western and eastern Nigeria. Colonies of Urhobo emigrants live in the ghettoes of Ekotedo quarters in Ibadan, and Mushin and Ajegunle in Lagos.[7] A sizeable proportion of the Urhobo may be found in the fresh water and mangrove swamps between the Cameroon border in the east and the Lagos lagoons in the west. A vast majority of those living in 'diaspora' comprises the bulk of the virile, labouring population.[8] This demographic peculiarity and its attendant social insecurity problems provide the most enduring theme for Urhobo song-poems.

UNDERDEVELOPMENT, POVERTY, AND THE MIGRANT PHENOMENON

A condition of want or wretchedness is referred to by the Urhobo as *obevben*. In order of gravity, *obevben* is second to mortality (*ughwu*). These two plus witchcraft (*orhan*) and childlessness (*egan*) make up what we may call the four principal contradictions in the life of the Urhobo. The essence of Urhobo common prayer embodies these four items. In all occasions for prayer, supplication to the gods and ancestors always includes a request for children, material prosperity, and long life, in that order. A morphology of these issues reveals that they are all rooted in central contradictions of underdevelopment that exists in Urhoboland. The genesis of this crisis is traceable to the two cardinal factors of: (i) neglect and plunder by colonial authorities, and (ii) land hunger. A brief comment on these factors follows.

The colonial scenario

Wherever the colonial enterprise is established, it reaps bountiful harvests in profits and leaves behind abundant misery and wretchedness. The fact that colonialism develops underdevelopment is now widely accepted even by apologists of the system.[9] The backwardness of Urhoboland today is a direct consequence of its contact with capitalist Europe. Let us explain this further. Throughout the eighteenth and nineteenth centuries, European merchants operating on the Atlantic coast were prevented by Itsekiri[10] middlemen from reaching the Urhobo in the hinterland. Ironically, the Urhobo were, and are still, the main producers of palm oil and kernels on which the coastal trade was carried. Thus, although the Urhobo were linked to Europe for a long time through the oil business, the price at which the Urhobo producer sold to the European buyer was determined by the Itsekiri middlemen. Consequently, whatever prosperity mercantilist capitalism brought to this part of Nigeria during the period never really reached the Urhobo. In this sense, the Urhobo people experienced two forms of imperialism – one by Europeans and the other by the Itsekiri.

When finally the Europeans, in a more aggressive phase of their presence, broke through the Itsekiri cordon following the punitive expedition against the leading Itsekiri merchant, Nana Numa, in 1894,[11] trade and colonial administration were already in 'unholy alliance'. The consequent 'opening up' of Urhobo territory for European penetration in the late nineteenth and early twentieth centuries, rather than bringing 'prosperity', expanded the avenues for more rapacious plunder of the area. The situation was made worse by the depression in the capitalist economy of the twenties, an event which pushed the Urhobo palm produce worker farther below the poverty line.

Following a temporary decline in rubber business in south-eastern Asia during the forties, European firms dealing in the commodity encouraged West Africa to produce it. Most of Urhobo territory was found suitable for plantations. A boom in rubber trade increased the cash-earning opportunities of the peasant population. But the boom was shortlived, and by the mid-sixties the price of the commodity had plummeted to a point where it was no longer profitable to engage in production. Meanwhile, the plantations had consumed vast tracts of land needed for food production. As the shrinkage in the acreage of arable land coincided with an increase in the working population, the practice of migration (*ukale*)[12] reviewed below was the inevitable consequence.

The land question

The dispersal of the Urhobo in the areas mentioned earlier was initiated by the search for palm trees. Fishing, for which the Urhobo are also famous, gave further impetus to the migrant inclination. The economic slump that

180

accompanied the two world wars drastically reduced the earnings from palm produce work. By the middle of the forties, productive effort was diverted to the distilling of gin (*udi* in Urhobo or *ogogoro* as it is popularly known in Nigeria) made from the liquor of rafia palm (*ogoro*). Rafia palm trees abound in the southern areas of the country. It was to these areas that gin distillers moved in search of trees to exploit. This set in motion waves of migration which caused a kind of 'demographic haemorrhage' in rural Urhobo. The effect of this on the literary culture will be shown shortly.

The pervasiveness of mass poverty in the Urhobo-speaking part of Nigeria should be explained in the context of the political economy reviewed above. But as we shall see below, the people often show contradictory responses to the crises in the society. However, the most popular response is the one that explains the crises in idealist and metaphysical terms. Poverty (*obevben*), for instance, is believed to derive from two main sources: inauspicious destiny and/or sorcery (*orhan*). All cases of premature or accidental deaths are believed to be caused by malefic magic or sorcery. An *ukale* expedition that ends in failure is hardly explained in economic terms. Any such endeavour that is unsuccessful is blamed on either an inauspicious destiny, or witchcraft, or the anger of an offended ancestor.

THE CLASSICAL AND MODERN TRADITIONS OF POETRY

For the convenience of this discussion, Urhobo secular song-poetry can be divided into two traditions: the classical (*ile ahwaren*) and the modern (*ile okena*).[13] The *ile ahwaren* tradition embraces all songs performed by village- or quarter-based dance ensembles at annual or periodic dance-song festivals. Songs of this tradition were usually critical and satirical in intention. This tradition suffered a decline in the early sixties. The modern, or *ile okena* tradition is used here to refer to all types of songs owned and performed by professional or semi-professional groups. The songs are produced as commodities. Whereas the songs of the old tradition were satirical, the *ile okena* are distinguished by a strong panegyric temper. This is why most Urhobo people refer to these songs as *ile ejiri* (lit. praise songs).

THE SOCIO-ECONOMIC ORIGINS OF THE PANEGYRIC TRADITION

The decline of the *ile ahwaren* and the rise of the *ile okena* traditions are traceable to two distinct but related factors – one demographic and the other economic. As already mentioned, secular song-poetry performances in Urhobo were organized on a collective basis. In *Udje* (one of the most developed of the classical forms), for instance, every able-bodied male in every community participated. The songs were satirical, with one village or ward using its neighbour as target. Associative dance ensembles which flourished in the forties and fifties adopted the *Udje* organizational pattern, except that the recruitment of members was according to age-grade or sex profiles. Given the collectivist approach in these musical practices, the human resources outlay was to be severely reduced by the waves of migrations discussed above. In fact, the population depletion caused some kind of 'artistic drought' in most of rural Urhobo.[14]

The panegyric tradition began during the Nigerian civil war years (1967–1970). It was at this time that the Urhobo entrepreneural élite broke loose from the economic isolation mentioned in the previous section. Before the civil war Igbo traders dominated the commercial and cultural life of urban centres of Warri and Sapele to which rural Urhobo forms an immediate hinterland. The outbreak of the war changed the situation suddenly. The exodus of the Igbo to eastern Nigeria created a vacuum in the cultural and business life of the cities mentioned. The vacuum was filled by the Urhobo mainly. Warri was the focal point. Oil companies fleeing from the war zone set up operational bases there. Many Urhobo traders hitherto quarantined in depressed rural economy moved in searching new prospects. Demand for accommodation increased. Pressure on the scarce urban land intensified; so did litigations over it by competing Urhobo and Itsekiri families. Of the three ethnic groups – the Urhobo, the Itsekiri, and the Ifo – that lay claim to Warri, the Urhobo had a greater share of the boom that the war period created. The Itsekiri in particular were seriously hampered in the scramble for land when a powerful Urhobo family won in a land case against a rival Itsekiri family in the late sixties.

Most Urhobo saw the reverses suffered by the Itsekiri as well-deserved measures. The reasoning then (and even now) was that the Itsekiri had for too long enjoyed patronages vastly out of proportion to their numerical strength; first during the colonial period, and later during the Action Group-led government in the old Western Region (1952–1966). The Urhobo merchant élite, especially, saw the turn of events in the late sixties as a vindication of Urhobo manifest destiny. This feeling of triumph of a nationalistic dream certainly influenced the emergence of the panegyric tradition.

The sudden rise to affluence of many Urhobo merchants at the time was greatly facilitated by a programme of Nigerianization of certain economic activities embarked upon by the military regime in the early seventies. This opportunity as well as a thriving smuggling trade during the war, transformed small retailers to big speculators in real estate – a branch of business made the more lucrative by the increased demand for housing at the time. The achievements of the Urhobo *nouveaux riches* provided ready material for the panegyric musicians. Presently, there is a kind of competition amongst the musicians for 'big names' to proclaim in song.

MUSIC-MAKING AND PROFIT MOTIVE

The ascendancy of the Urhobo merchant class sketched above has introduced new production relations in the life of the people. Even the rural economy which was based on subsistence has now been over-run by a capitalist ethic of the profit motive. This new, commodity economy (*akpo igho* as the Urhobo call it), has profoundly affected the career of the musician (*obuole*). In the old tradition of music practised by the peasants, aesthetic gratification for both artist and audience was the prime inspiration for participation. Now an *obuole's* success and fame rest not so much on the aesthetic merit of his songs as on his material reward as well as the prestige value of the personality on whom his songs are made. Music has become a commodity, a merchandise subject to the same 'blind forces' of supply and demand operating in the business world. This situation is underlined in the following excerpt from an interview with Mr Ogute Ottan, one of the leading avant-gardists of the new tradition:

> ... It is not true that we sing in celebration of rich people only. We also praise those who have made their mark in other spheres of life ... However, most of our songs are about rich people. Afterall, we don't make music just to show that we are gifted singers; *we are concerned primarily about financial reward. What does it profit a man to be a good musician and remain a pauper?* This is why we concentrate attention on financially 'weighty' people. The public image of such persons ensures rapid sales for every record produced ...
>
> At the moment we demand a minimum of a hundred naira from whoever requests to be praise-sung. But if the applicant is well-to-do we ask for no less than six hundred naira. This is what it costs the applicant to have his name immortalized in song. When we first started we chose names of those we considered deserving of praise. Nowadays we sing in praise of a person only after he has formally applied to us.
>
> There has been remarkable improvement in my life since I became a praise-singer. The house where we are holding the interview now was built out of the proceeds from the sale of our records. Both Damijo (my assistant) and myself depend solely on music-making for a living ... (emphasis added)[15]

Ogute's remarks reveal another important aspect of the matter under review, that is, the erosion of the artist's autonomy in a capitalist society. This subordination of the artist's freedom and his products to the sway of the market is aptly described by the Mexican Marxist aesthetician, Adolfo Sanchez Vázquez:

> In capitalist society, a work of art is 'productive' when it is market-oriented, when it submits itself to the exigencies of the market, the fluctuations of supply and demand. And since there is no objective measure by which to determine the value of his particular merchandise, the artist is subject to the tastes, preferences, ideas, and aesthetic notions of those who influence the market. Inasmuch as he produces works of art destined for a market that absorbs them, the artist cannot fail to heed the exigencies of this market: they often affect the content as well as the form of a work of art, thus placing limitations on the artist, stifling his creative potential, his individuality.[16]

The rest of this essay will examine the specific ways in which the socio-economic factors identified above have affected the song-poetry culture of the Urhobo in recent times. We shall look at the composition and location of the target audience, the mode of production and strategies of propagation, and the peculiar style of a few representative texts.

THE AUDIENCE

Prior to the civil war, most Urhobo music was produced by and for the rural population. This restricted focus was consequent on the demographic peculiarity of Urhoboland. With the exception of Sapele and Warri, no settlement had more than 10,000 inhabitants as at 1963. Even in these two urban centres, the ethnic diversity was such that a clear-cut domination by a single language group was impossible. After the exodus of the Igbo group already referred to, the ethnic balance altered radically in favour of the Urhobo who came from the countryside in large numbers.

Unlike the classical tradition, the panegyric one began as an urban phenomenon. Mr Ogute Ottan, credited with popularizing the form, was living at Ibadan at the time.[17] His first songs were directed at colonies of the Urhobo in Ibadan, Lagos, and Benin City. The post-war concentration of the Urhobo in Warri shifted the bulk of the audience to Warri and its immediate environs. As the Urhobo merchants began to assume a dominant position in the business life of Warri, Sapele, and semi-urban places such as Ughelli, Ephron (Effurun), Agbarho, and Kokori, the dimensions of the target audience began to expand rapidly. Soon, the new music penetrated most of Urhoboland, thanks to the battery-operated cassette players.

Needless to say that this development opened an extended market for the foreign manufacturers as well as the local distributors of the electronic devices connected with the music. The role of the distributors is significant in another respect. Given the heavy financial outlay in the production of a new record, a musical group with a weak financial standing is perforce dependent on assistance from successful business people. The assistance varies from bringing pressure to bear on the recording firms, to actually paying the deposit amount demanded of the artists by the manufacturing companies. This relationship between the artists and their financiers partly explains the practice of making songs in praise of people of incontestable credit-worthiness.

Both the population movements and the production techniques of the music resulted in the replacement of the public arena as venue for broad-casting new songs. In the classical tradition new pieces were performed at dance-song festivals climaxing several months of intensive preparations by groups. Between two festivals, even the informal performance of new compositions was prohibited. Also, the fame or praise arising from such performances was credited first to the group and then to the individual artists in it.

Now, all that has changed. As a result of the depression in rural life and the relative maturation of a cash-oriented economy, there are hardly any festive artistic displays solely for the entertainment of the broad masses. Whereas authorship of the songs of the old tradition were usually anonymous, the panegyric song (*ule ejiri*) openly advertises the name(s) of the composer(s). This form of propriety is in consonance with the ethics of private property accumulation now in vogue. In place of communal or associative dance *ensembles* of old, we now have groups of between two and several members operating on professional basis. As some of the practitioners interviewed on the matter admitted to me, no group seriously concerned about remaining in business can afford a large group; especially because of the cost of transporting the members to and from Lagos or Ibadan where most of the recordings are done.[18]

FROM SATIRE TO EULOGY

Perhaps the most significant of the changes under review is the switch in temper from the satiric to the panegyric. The former, as we have already noted, runs like a red thread through all genres of Urhobo song-poetry before the late sixties. Among such forms in which satire was the dominant outlook were *Udje, Igoru, Ijury, Ighovhan, Adjuya,* and *Overen.* In view of the fact that the new tradition is aimed at celebrating the 'heroic achievement' of those who, rightly or wrongly, are seen as harbingers of a prosperous and modern world, it would be untactical to expose their vices and follies, even when the character celebrated is a notorious one. As the Juju/Udjabo Group of Aladja puts the matter metaphorically in one of its songs, the mortar and the pestle are never made from the same wood; that is, criticism and eulogy cannot go together.[19]

The rural/urban dichotomy already referred to also expresses itself in the area of artistic attitude. In the few villages where group performances are still held there is a growing divergence between a rural-peasant outlook on the one hand, and an urban one on the other. The village of Orhunghworun, a few kilometres from Warri, provides a good illustration of the matter. Here, there are at least three groups famous in the panegyric tradition. Some of the members in these professional groups also participate in the *Udje* satirical tradition.

The Orhunghworun scenario is interesting in another respect. In the *Udje* convention, any individual, regardless of his/her social status, is a potential victim of vicious attack. In fact, *Udje* satirical practice is conducted in form of a warfare amongst communities or wards; hence the higher the social standing of an individual the greater the chances of being attacked in song. But since the pangyric genre gained prominence several years ago, the principle of indiscriminate attack has been revised somewhat. A subtle attempt is now being made to redefine the social composition of the '*Udje* satirical net' to exclude 'successful and illustrious' citizens who are known to have achieved great heights in the business world of the cities. These individuals are, in the opinion of the practitioners, worthy sons and daughters of the village who should not be smeared with the mud of satire. For example, of the forty or so songs I recorded at the Orhunghworun *Udje* carnival in 1977, there is none in which an affluent indigene of the village is satirized.

The panegyric disposition which was hitherto alien to *Udje* has begun to infiltrate some of the latest *Udje* songs. Perhaps for the first time in the experience of Orhunghworun *Udje* practice, the 1977 carnival featured songs in which the activities of certain citizens were celebrated instead of being censored. The opening lines of one of the pieces, titled 'Orogun' makes the point more unambiguously.

> In the modern era praise songs are the vogue
> The illustrious ones in Urhobo, these we shall now praise in song
> The late Orogun was an illustrious son of Orhunghworun
> His achievements as leader of the community
> This year we shall proclaim them in song

This is not just a case of giving the dead due respect. In the typical *Udje* songs, even the dead can be 'recalled' by the satirist to account for their actions on earth. The following excerpt from another song by the same community is a case in point:

> When the dead elders of Ughere (ward) arrived in the Ancestral World
> The ancestors arraigned them before a jury
> All of them were found guilty
> And were jailed in the remote regions of the Ancestral World . . .
> Hence during ancestral feasts they are not worshipped

Despite the tendency towards a fusion of tempers which these examples point to, the tension between town and countryside remains a strong, contrasting feature in the songs of the two traditions. Let us illustrate this with three existential issues which recur in the songs. These are: (i) response to colonialism, (ii) attitude to poverty and wealth, and (iii) response to postcolonial politics.

Response to colonialism

Poets in the classical tradition always displayed an attitude of protest to the white man and his culture. Of course the protest was not uniformly outspoken in all instances. There are remarks in some songs which seem to betray a tacit admission of white superiority. Such remarks should be seen in the context of the psychology of a conquered, subject people, rather than an uncritical acceptance of a 'higher civilization'. (What with gun-boat diplomacy, sacking of resistant communities, murder of nationalists, and outright confiscation of peasant land!) In the main, however, colonialism was portrayed as cultural pestilence. The two passages below exemplify this attitude. The first indicts colonialism for 'turning the world asunder':

> The white man has ruined the world
> Every haloed custom has lost value
>
> (from 'Verbal Challenge' by the Owahwa community)

The second passage focuses on the problem of prostitution among teenage girls and situates it in the context of colonial culture:

> The white man improved the world to a point
> And left it totteringly

Left it on a shaky balance
Girls now go to school, too!
How would they ever get married?
This is the life girls have been longing for
A lantern is lit in a room
Some men are engaged, others queue for their turn!

(from 'Makpoghiehwe' by the Edjophe community)

The poets of the panegyric tradition do not make direct reference to the colonial era because of its relative remoteness in time. But the enthusiasm with which they ascribe attributes of superiority to Europeans and cultural achievements certainly points to an outlook of adulation. Two testimonies from the Ogute Ottan repertoire will illustrate this. The first is taken from a song titled 'Okumagba Layout', a chart-burster number produced a few years after the Okumagba family of Okere quarters, Warri, won the land dispute between it and an Itsekiri family. A housing estate built on the land is compared in the song to the architectural marvels in the United States of America:

You go to Okumagba layout and behold marvels!
It is laid out like European quarters
In the United States of America; what creativity!

Our second testimony is taken from a song in praise of Chief Michael Ibru, chairman of the Ibru Organization.[20] The image of Africa in the song is similar to that popularly painted by imperialist historians and anthropologists:

Even white men who civilized us
Are employed by Ibru...
Michael Ibru is Mungo Park
Who first discovered Africa
His name, who can ever forget it?

In another section of the song, Chief Ibru's mother is compared to Mary, the 'virgin' mother of Jesus. If you stretch the implication of this analogy a little further Chief Ibru becomes an Urhobo Jesus!

Attitudes to poverty and wealth

References to these twin issues abound in songs of the two traditions. But there is a remarkable difference in the reactions of the respective poets. In the classical songs, ostentatious lifestyle is unambiguously censured; so too is abject poverty. However, with regard to the latter, the comments are usually more analytical. In the panegyric songs, you are poor because you are lazy. You are poor and lazy, and therefore ugly. You are poor, lazy, ugly, and therefore foolish! But if you are well-to-do, you are an embodiment of virtue and wisdom.[21] The positive imaging of the rich class is well summed up in the popular Urhobo saying: *Igho sh'emu sua* ('with money all things are possible'). This expression has become a kind of formulaic refrain in many songs exploring the theme of material contentment. The excerpts below, taken from representative texts of the two traditions, elaborate the matter further:

The classical tradition:

>   If a poor man has wisdom
>   He commands more respect than the rich does

>>>   (from 'Verbal Challenge' by Owahwa community)

>   Consider the vanity of parents. . .
>   When parents talk of children
>   You would think they originated sex
>   The same is true of the rich
>   When the prosperous talk of money
>   You would think they were the first to labour

>>>   (from '*Tomi*' by the Ubogo community)

>   The poor man gets money no doubt
>   It is his *Erhi* (Fate) that scatters the yield
>   Whether it is here or there the money goes
>   The poor does not know

>>>   (from 'Oloya Family' by the Edjophe community)

The panegyric tradition:

>   The poor man suffers a lot
>   Like a boat at the port
>   A boat without a lock
>   Everyone paddles it at will

>>>   (from a song by Ogute Ottan)

>   With money all things are possible
>   Money carried the poor shoulder-high
>   And dumped him at the rich man's feet

>>>   (from 'Igho sh'emu sua' by the Juju/Udjabo Group)

>   The modern trend in living conditions is already clear
>   Whoever has no money will experience hardship
>   He will lose his right to talk in public
>   If God helps one to prosper
>   Then he talks confidently in a peers' gathering
>   Whenever the poor addresses a community meeting
>   His speech interests no one
>   Money is sugar in a rich man's mouth
>   Every utterance he makes appeals

Tastes pleasantly like honey
Whenever occasion for deliberation arises
He must be present before business begins
Whatever suggestion he makes is always right. . .
The poor man's jaws always cave in
Like the toothless man wearing a tie
The poor man's jaws are never friendly with a mirror

(from 'Life of the Poor' by the Adama Group)

Response to post-colonial politics

The views of the panegyric poets on the contemporary neo-colonial order
are implicit in the foregoing analysis and excerpted passages. As already
pointed out in note (19), these poets occasionally denounce immoral behaviour. But their criticisms do not seem to derive from an honest sense of
offended morality which is essential to satire. More significantly, in their
exposure of human follies, the poets often make the class of the poor their
target. Lament over a declining communal moral order is also a favoured
subject of most panegyric songs. This is very noticeable in the songs of the
Johnson Adjan, Omokomoko, and Okpah Ariboh groups. But viewed
against the background of the extravagant praises the same groups shower
on the beneficiaries of the triumphant capitalist order, these laments are
hypocritical like the cry of romantic poets over a glorious past.

In contrast, the poets of the classical tradition who are nurtured in a
pre-capitalist morality react differently to the rupture of the 'more humane
past' by the 'turbulent present'. The *Udje* song-makers, for instance,
endeavour to relate the present woes of the masses to contemporary political
and economic conditions. In the opinion of these poets, the gravest crises
afflicting the poor today are: (a) tyranny of irresponsible governments, (b)
neo-colonial urbanization, and (c) post-Udoji awards inflation.[22] The passages reviewed below show how the issues are reflected in the songs of this
tradition. The first example is from the song, 'Independence and Tax
Raids', in which the Aladja community laments the hard times experienced
by most rural people after Nigeria became independent in 1960. In place
of 'life more abundant'[23] promised by politicians, the masses had 'suffering
in abundance'. In the body of the song the trickster politician, the police
tormentor, the 'Mark Anthony' campaign experts – all are castigated and
held responsible for the woes of the times. The up-welling of the peasants'
feeling of disappointment comes to a climax in the last twenty two lines
describing the drama of constant tax raids. The section deserves quoting
in full:

Demo, Power! Zik[24] *Okokoroko* (the cock)[25]
The more you sink a calabash the more it floats
The campaign fever was everywhere
Scarcely two years later tumult of tax raids brought sleepless nights
　　to all
'The police are in town, let no one brave the streets'

189

With characteristic naughtiness, the children would taunt defaulters:
'*Kikighwo*, run fast!'
And everyone would join in a stampede
Those who ran into gullies were innumerable in Urhobo
The injured were a multitude
The fleet-footed escaped paying for a year
Oh, a debt does not grow mouldy with time
Soon angry murmurs filled the air:
'Are we to excrete in the house for fear of tax?
The so-called progress is now a curse
We tread stealthily like a fox prowling for a stray fowl
Independence has brought us misery'
While we fumed over this, orders came from Benin[26] that government
    was broke
Tax receipts for four, six years were demanded;
For the poor, life became a nightmare
Demo! *Okokoroko*! One Nigeria!

The sarcasm in the last line needs explaining. The words 'Demo' and '*Okokoroko*' were the respective slogans of the Mid-West Democratic Front (MDF), and the National Council of Nigerian Citizens (NCNC). These two and the Action Group (AG) were the dominant political parties in the then Mid-West Region. The NCNC campaign rallies were begun and concluded by a tumultuous shout of 'One Nigeria! One Destiny'. (It is an interesting coincidence that the National Party of Nigeria (NPN) which ruled the central Nigerian government from 1979 until 1983 used the same phrase as a slogan). From the mock-heroic tone of the song, there is no doubt that the masses were aware that in bourgeois politics, slogans purporting a community of class solidarity are mere pretences.

THE CRISIS OF URBANIZATION

The popular image of the city in the songs is a repulsive one. This attitude has its origin in the colonial times when the city represented all the inequities that came with foreign rule. Since independence, negligence by generations of the neo-colonial bourgeoisie has worsened the social and hygienic conditions in the urban areas. This has made them more dreadful to the average rural dweller who is used to more open, and therefore, more hygienic environments in the villages.

In most of the songs, comments are focused on Warri. This is so partly for its proximity to the area under reference, and partly because Warri graphically illustrates the main contradictions of urban life in neocolonial Nigeria. In the first of the two passages below, Warri is depicted both as a filthy place as well as a haven for those given to lewdness:

(a) Imagine a refuse dump in Warri township
    It smells offensively; that is what Ughere is like

(from 'Ughere's Wretchedness' by Orhunghworun community)

The following lines allude to class differentiation between rural dwellers and those who live in urban areas:

(b) It is commoners who perform rituals at Urhiephron festivals
The affluent ones enjoy themselves in Warri
Behold the wonders of life!

(from 'Udoji Inflation and the Gods' by the same community)

THE 'UDOJI INFLATION'

The third subject that features prominently in the songs is the inflation in the economy occasioned by the Udoji salary review exercise in 1974. Whereas most establishment economic analysts commended the government for the exercise, nowhere in the songs do we find an expression of joy by the peasants for the raise in pay. As is commonly the case in most dependent capitalist economies, the government gesture brought misery to the working class.

Orhunghworun, from which we draw our illustrative texts, is a source of cheap labour for employers in Warri. The experience of Orhunghworun people, like that of places such as Ephron, Aladja, Ovbian, Ugborikoko in the outskirts of Warri, typifies the rapid marginalization of the peasantry in Nigeria. Thus, although the rural dwellers did not share directly in the 'Udoji bonanza', they were nonetheless submerged in the inflationary floods it occasioned. Also, a few Orhunghworun people who had salaried jobs received the awards which, like the proverbial Midas gold, turned into ashes within a short time. The uncomplimentary remarks on the awards reflect the plight of the recipients. For the rest of the story, let us hear the poets themselves. (All the songs referred to were performed at the 1977 Udje festival already mentioned.)

The first example laments the decline in festive activities due to rural poverty:

Drinks are so expensive these days, festival drums are hardly audible
Three gods now share a pint of drink; how wonderful!
You have to buy drinks and then a fowl for five naira
No wonder those due for offerings are negligent!

(from 'Udoji Inflation and the Gods')

The second passage focuses on the problem of child-bearing in the era of inflation:

The Udoji inflation escalated the prices of all goods
Turned parents into obejcts of pity
Whenever one's wife is pregnant
One does not feel comfortable
Living suddenly becomes a burden
For thought of how to cater for the children
Let matters be so, let them be so
Because of the Almighty Udoji!

191

In the hundreds of panegyric songs produced in Urhoboland so far there is none in which one encounters this kind of perceptive depiction of socio-economic issues. What is at stake here is more than the simple question of 'to every poet his imagination'. As we have pointed out in the relevant sections above, the same song-maker can display a contradictory attitude to the same issue, depending on which poetic tradition he is exploring. No doubt, extra-literary factors are involved in this matter. The musicians who alternate between satire and panegyric express this contradiction more tellingly. The output of groups like Ogute, Omokomoko, Juju/Udjabo, Johnson Adjan, and Gometi/Badia/Taxe shows clearly that the composers are as gifted as their counterparts in the classical genres. The reason why the panegyric poets employ their creative and intellectual resources to extol only the prosperous minority in the society cannot be found in the realm of art alone. A fuller explanation must be sought in the context of the political-economy of contemporary Nigerian society and the social relationships it has engendered. As we have tried to show with reference to Urhoboland, this is a society of nascent capitalism, a world endowed with the power to convert 'the physician, the lawyer, the priest, the poet, the man of science, into its paid wage-labourers'.[27]

Notes

1 *Talks at the Yenan Forum on Literature and Art*, Foreign Language Press, Peking, 1965, p. 18.

2 'The Formalist School of Poetry and Marxism' in *Marxists on Literature: An Anthology*, David Craig(ed), Penguin Books, London, 1975, pp. 370–1

3 In Nigeria, for instance, the first open 'clash' between the two schools was at the 1977 'Workshop on Radical Perspectives on African Literature and Society' held at the University of Ibadan. It was organized by the 'Ibadan-Ife Group'. What looks like a prelude to that encounter began several years earlier with Omafume Onoge's 'The Crisis of Consciousness in Modern African Literature: A Survey' which appeared in the *Canadian Journal of African Studies*, Vol. VIII, No. 2, 1974. At about the same time, Chinweizu, Jemie, and Madubuike came out with their provocative 'Toward the Decolonization of African Literature' in *Okike* No. 6, and later in No. 48 of *Transition* which also carried Wole Soyinka's rejoinder titled 'Neo-Tarzanism: the Poetic of Pseudo Tradition'. Chinweizu *et al.* reacted to this with 'Soyinka's Neo-Tarzanism: A Reply' in *Okike* 14, 1978. Chinweizu and others have since published their decolonization thesis in book form as *Toward the Decolonization of African Literature I* (Fourth Dimension Publishers, Enugu, 1980).

4 The social context is emphasized in three of the essays in *The Traditional Artist in African Societies*, W. L. d'Azevedo (ed.), Indiana University Press, 1973. They are: 'The Musician in Akan Society' (J. K. Nketia), 'A Sociological View of Hausa Musical Activity' (D. W. Ames), and 'The Bala Musician' (A. P. Merriam). Chapter 4 of Ruth Finnegan's *Oral Literature in Africa* (Oxford University Press, 1970) also has useful information on this aspect.

5 One of the few examples of notable departure from this approach is Dan Ben-Amos' *Sweet Words: Storytelling in Benin*, Institute for the Study of Human Issues Inc., Philadelphia, 1975, which combines a stylistic analysis of prose narrative texts with a detailed description of the superstructural institutions in Benin society.

6 For more details on the Urhobo people, see R. E. Bradbury, *The Benin Kingdom and the Edo-Speaking Peoples of South-Western Nigeria*, International African Institute, London, 1970, pp. 127–64, and Onigu Otite (ed.), *The Urhobo People*, Heinemann Educational Books, 1982. J. W. Hubbard's *The Sobo of the Niger Delta*, Gaskiya Corporation, Zaria, 1948, and Obaro Ikime's *Niger-Delta Ravalry: Itsekiri-Urhobo*

Relations and the European Presence, Longman, 1969, also contain valuable information on the Urhobo.

7   The squalid conditions in these ghettos are a pointer to the lumpen and precarious life led by Urhobo emigrants in these cities.

8   For a continental survey of this phenomenon in Africa, see for instance, Y. M. Ivanov, *Agrarian Reforms and Hired Labour in Africa*, Progress Publishers, Moscow, 1979.

9   Among the numerous books written on this matter, the following are relevant for the area under consideration: Walter Rodney, *How Europe Underdeveloped Africa*, (Bogle-L'Ouverture and Tanzania Publishing House, 1978), R.I. Rhodes (ed.), *Imperialism and Underdevelopment: A Reader* (Monthly Review Press, 1970), Ola Oni and Bade Onimode, *Economic Development of Nigeria: The Socialist Alternative*, (Nigerian Academy of Arts, Sciences and Technology, Ibadan, 1975, esp. chs 1–3), Peter Gutkind and Peter Waterman (eds), *African Social Studies: A Radical Reader* (Heinemann Educational Books, 1977), and Gavin Williams, *State and Society in Nigeria*, (Afrografika Publishers, Idanre, 1980, esp. chs II and III).

10   The Itsekiri are the western neighbours of the Urhobo in the Niger Delta. They speak a dialect of Yoruba, although their political organization shows strong Benin influence. Being coastal people, the Itsekiri had an early and advantageous contact with Europeans. Several centuries before British colonialism was established in Nigeria in the late nineteenth and early twentieth centuries, there were Itsekiri princes and merchants fluent in Portuguese and English.

11   Chief Nana Numa was a powerful Itsekiri merchant whose activities on the Benin and Ethiope Rivers in south-western Nigeria challenged the monopoly of European firms in the second half of the nineteenth century. Although Nana was finally conquered and deported to the Gold Coast (Ghana) in 1894, his influence and that of Chief Dore (another Itsekiri merchant-politician of the period) brought the small Itsekiri nationality into international focus. This is what partly explains the powerful political leverage which the Itsekiri have had over other larger nationalities in the Delta area of Nigeria.

12   The word *ukale* or *ukane* is said to be a corruption of 'Ikale'. According to Bradbury in his work referred to in note (6), the 'word is apparently derived from Ikale, the area in the southern part of Ondo Province (State) in which a large number of Urhobo and Isoko have settled. Thus "O kp'ukane" means "he has gone to Ikale". Nowadays, the word is loosely applied to all types of migration from home for the purpose of fending for money.'

13   This is a loose grouping based on the principle of time. A more precise typology must await a full-scale study of Urhobo song-poetry genres, religious and secular.

14   More details on this may be found in my '*Igho sh'emu sua*: Note on Capitalist Ideology in Urhobo Oral Literature' in *Theory and Practice* (Journal of the Nigerian Academy of Arts, Sciences and Technology, Ibadan, No. 2, 1977), and also *Battles of Songs: A Study of Satire in the Udje Dance-Songs of the Urhobo of Nigeria*, Ph.D. thesis, University of Ibadan, Ibadan, 1982, pp. 180–95.

15   From the text of an interview with Messrs Ogute Ottan and Damijo of the 'Up Ogute and His Lucky Stars', Warri, August 8, 1976.

16   *Art and Society: Essays in Marxist Aesthetics*, transl. by Mario Riofrancos, Monthly Review Press, 1973, p. 84.

17   Although Mr Ogute has never admitted this, there are strong reasons to believe that his artistic outlook was influenced by the Yoruba *oriki* (heroic poetry) tradition. He lived in Ibadan for about twelve years, first as a petty trader, and later as a part-time musician. This point deserves stressing because, before he moved to Ibadan, Ogute was a leading poet-singer in the satirical traditions for which his community, Orhunghworun, is famous.

18   Lagos and Ibadan are 618 and 475 kilometres respectively from Warri.

19   On rare occasions some of the *ile ejiri* musicians mediate the extravagant flattery in their songs with denunciation of anti-social behaviour. But these derisive remarks do not compare in effectiveness with the 'lethal' invectives and negative portraitures that characterize the satirical songs.

20   The Ibru Organization comprises more than twenty enterprises specializing in a wide range of activities such as distribution, servicing, and manufacturing. Chief

Michael Ibru himself is rated the richest Urhobo entrepreneur and certainly among the top ten in Nigeria's millionaire circle.

21 See Marx's anatomy of 'The Power of Money' in section XLI of his *Economic and Philosophical Manuscripts* in Karl Marx and Frederick Engels, *Collected Works*, vol. 3, Progress Publishers, Moscow, 1975, pp. 322–6.

22 In 1974 the military government increased the salaries and wages of all workers in Nigeria in the hope of shoring up political support for itself. The review commission was headed by Chief Jerome Udoji. Known as 'Udoji' for short, the exercise brought so much cash into circulation that it set in motion a high rate of inflation which has been on the rise since then.

23 This was the vote-catching slogan used by political parties during the first civilian regime, 1960–1966.

24 Short for Nnamdi Azikiwe, one of the leading nationalist politicians of the time. He was founder and leader of the NCNC, the first political party to stir up Nigerians for anti-colonial struggle in the forties.

25 The cock was the symbol of the NCNC.

26 The seat of the then Mid-West Region (now Bendel State) government which in the opinion of the song-makers epitomized the iniquities of post-colonial administration in Nigeria.

27 Karl Marx and Frederick Engels, *The Manifesto of the Communist Party*, Progress Publishers, Moscow, 1977, p. 45.

CHAPTER THIRTEEN

LITERATURE AND POPULISM IN SOUTH AFRICA:

REFLECTIONS ON THE IDEOLOGY OF STAFFRIDER

Michael Vaughan

RACE AND CLASS IN SOUTH AFRICAN LITERATURE: THE DOMINANCE OF POPULIST CONCEPTS AND STRATEGIES

In this paper, I want to bring certain questions to bear on the literary role of the magazine *Staffrider*. Now, much of the debate over this role that I have read or listened to seems to have been provoked by an anxious defensiveness of behalf of the 'traditional' status of 'literature'. Thus, the polemicism which has been so prominent in the literature of *Staffrider* has been criticized, as leading to a compromise of aesthetic quality. It has been argued – largely in certain white academic circles, but not only there – that *Staffrider* literature is politically prescriptive, in such a way as to inhibit the necessary intuitive freedom and spontaneity of the writer. From my point of view, this type of debate is quite reactionary. It is based on the idea that aesthetic quality is somehow independent of social determination, and thus mystifies the processes by which aesthetic criteria are actually established.

The questions that I want to bring to bear upon the literary role, or character of the magazine *Staffrider* are not of this type. It is no accident, though, that *Staffrider* has provoked such reactions amongst 'traditional' intellectuals. *Staffrider* has made a very interesting and significant intervention into the contemporary South African literary scene. The literature published in *Staffrider* has, to a degree, both challenged and transformed the social image and meaning of literature in South Africa. It has achieved this by means of its relation to a black, township reading public. The inception of the magazine was closely associated with its recognition of and response to this reading public. The dominant, or characteristic concepts, idioms and images of the magazine are both directed towards, and about this public.

This connection between the literature of *Staffrider* and a black, township reading public – a connection which is ignored in the usual, academic debates over aesthetic quality – needs to be made more precise. It is a specific kind of reading public that *Staffrider* has addressed itself towards, and helped call into being. There are, of course, other types of reading matter available in the townships, which address themselves towards and help to constitute different reading publics (although the actual membership of these reading publics will probably involve a good deal of overlapping). The literature of *Staffrider* needs to be distinguished from journalism, on the one hand, and from the exclusively market-oriented genres of the 'popular' press, on the other. The distinction between the literature of *Staffrider* and journalism is clear, although it is less sharply defined than is the distinction between most academically recognized literature and journalism. It is the polemical populism of the magazine that dictates that this distinction is not as sharp as it might be. Thus, for example, the short story genre, as employed in *Staffrider*, allows a good deal of space to polemical documentation: documentation of the conditions of oppression of the people. The magazine also gives a significant place to the documentary genre of the interview: the interview with some known and exemplary character of the township. The place given to this genre within the magazine derives from the ideological concern to articulate the voice(s) of the people of the townships in the widest possible sense, and hence to include those voices – the voices of the oral cultures of the townships – that do not normally have access to, or are not normally recorded within the genres of written literature. The literature of *Staffrider* converges, then, with those documentary genres that might be encountered in a polemical journalism. *Staffrider* is, however, distinguished from journalism by the centrality accorded in the magazine to 'fictional' genres/genres of 'the imagination'. The genres of the short story and of poetry dominate the magazine. This means that the primary literary activity of *Staffrider* is not an activity of documentation, at any rate in the journalistic sense. It is rather an activity of the transposition of the material of documentation – of the conditions of oppression of the people of the townships – into a material of the imagination. It focuses upon the way in which *individuals* experience conditions of oppression: the way in which individuals encounter imaginatively these conditions.

At the same time, the literature of *Staffrider* can be distinguished from those market-oriented genres of the 'popular' press that deal in fantasy and 'entertainment'. These genres arise purely in order to exploit certain given market conditions. It is integral to the *modus operandi* of these genres that their reading publics should be conceived of as passive consumers of 'entertainment' . The distinction between the producers and the consumers of these 'entertainment' genres is hidden from perception, in that the conditions and imperatives of production are mystified within the genres. Despite some degree of convergence with this 'popular' literature – for example, there is a strong romantic love theme in a number of the stories in *Staffrider* – the literature of *Staffrider* is markedly different in its polemical populism. In the absence of legitimate conditions of political activity, the function of this literature overlaps with politics: it is directed not simply towards 'entertainment', but towards 'consciousness-raising'. *Staffrider* literature offers itself both as the voice of the people of the black townships, and as the polemical activation of that voice. Within such conceptions of the role and character of this literature, it is important for the writers and artists to declare themselves, to make themselves visible, to indicate exactly where they are situated within the life of the townships (that is to say, it is absolutely essential that they should not hide behind a mystique of their creativity).

Indeed, in its populist polemicism *Staffrider* literature goes so far as to challenge the distinction between the creator and the consumer that is intrinsic to the literature of the market. There is no reason in principle why any reader of *Staffrider* should not become a contributor. To contribute, it is essential only to possess a certain degree of literacy, combined with an experience of the conditions of oppression that are endemic for blacks in South Africa, and a polemical attitude towards this experience (and the genre of the interview establishes a relation between the *literate* expression of such experience, and the *oral* expression).

That *Staffrider* literature is predominantly for and of a black, township reading public, polemically organized in terms of its populist opposition to endemic conditions of racial oppression, and using literature as its polemical instrument – while at the same time being individualist and 'literary' enough to employ as its central modes of expression those genres of the imagination, poetry and the short story – is the reason why this literature has come into conflict with 'traditional' aesthetic criteria, as established within a white, liberal reading public. In recent years, the hegemony of these 'traditional' values over literature in English in South Africa has been threatened from a number of directions, and most significantly, perhaps, in relation to the development of the black, township reading public I have been discussing. The literary concerns – the thematic priorities and their attendant idioms – of this black, township reading public are, naturally, vastly different from those of the 'traditional' white, liberal reading public. *Staffrider* literature has, I think, developed largely in an 'organic' way in relation to its township public, and without paying much overt attention to the traditionally hegemonic demands of liberal aesthetic criteria. On occasion, however, this traditional hegemony over literature has provoked a polemical reaction from a *Staffrider* writer. An example is this one by Mothobi Mutloatse:

> We will have to *donder* conventional literature: old-fashioned critic and reader alike. We are going to pee, spit and shit on literary convention before we are through; we are going to kick and pull and push and drag literature into the form we prefer. We are going to experiment and probe and not give a damn what the critics have to say. Because we are in search of our true selves – undergoing self-discovery as a people.
>
> We are not going to be told how to re-live our feelings, pains and aspirations by anybody who speaks from the platform of his own rickety culture. We'll write our poems in a narrative form; we'll dramatize our poetic experiences; we'll poeticize our historical dramas. We will do all these things at the same time.[1]

Well, I have gone a long way round about to indicate the type of question I do *not* want to put to the literature of *Staffrider*. I don't want to question *Staffrider* from the standpoint of 'traditional' literary standards. This type of approach seems to me to stem largely from a reactionary desire to perpetuate the hegemony of a certain public and its aesthetics. On the other hand, this does not mean that I am entirely in accord with everything that

197

Mothobi Mutloatse says about what *Staffrider* literature stands for.

The type of question I want to raise in connection with *Staffrider* concerns the nature and significance of the *populism* of the magazine. This populism is given a rather characteristic expression in Mutloatse's polemical assertion, *vis-à-vis* his reaction to traditionalist aesthetics, that 'we are in search of our true selves – undergoing self-discovery as a people'. In the first place, the oppressed are postulated as possessing an immanent unity, the unity of being 'a poeple.' Secondly, the relation between *Staffrider* literature and this people is formulated as a relation of unity: a relation of self-expression. These populist conceptions – of the immanent unity of the oppressed as 'a people', and of the relation of a specific body of imaginative literature to this people as involving the self-expression of the people – need, I think, to be critically examined. It is possible that they actually *obscure* certain very important dimensions of social experience and social struggle.

What I have in mind is the question of the relation between race and class in South African social experience, in political and ideological forms of social struggle. The populism of *Staffrider* belongs within a whole, tremendously powerful tradition of political and ideological struggle against the South African apartheid State. At this point, I would like to quote at some length from a paper that, to my mind, puts very clearly some of the crucial issues in the relation between popular struggle and class struggle in South Africa:

> South Africa's history has been characterized by great repression and the major political and ideological *instrument* for this repression has been *racism*. Yet the major effect of this repression has been to very rapidly establish a large capitalist economy.
>
> Racism and the violences and injustices associated with it is a very stark and clear form of repression. Alongside this only about 5–10% of the population has ever had the franchise. Clearly, therefore, there is a very identifiable oppressive force and the major political task of the oppressed peoples has always been to attack that oppressive and racist regime.
>
> So what has developed in South Africa is a very powerful tradition of popular or populist politics. The role of the great political movements such as the ANC and the Congress Alliance has been to mobilize the masses against the repressive minority regime. In such a situation mass mobilization is essential so as to challenge the legitimacy of the State both internally and internationally.
>
> Where virtually all the population is voteless and oppressed by a racial minority then a great alliance of all classes is both necessary and a clear political strategy. Furthermore, building such an alliance was a great task.
>
> The ANC had to overcome racial division so as to rise above the divisive racism of the oppressors. They had to deal with opportunistic tribal leadership, to organize thousands upon thousands of people and they had to do all this in the face of harsh repression by the State. In achieving this there is little wonder that the ANC rose to be one of the great liberation movements in Africa . . .

In these circumstances the progressive trade unions became part of the popular struggle against oppression. They did not and probably could not have provided the base for working class organization. There is of course no doubt that their activities have been very, very important in creating the conditions that led to the emergence in the last ten to fifteen years of the present progressive trade unions. However, these unions are operating in a different environment.

Workers and their struggle became very much part of the wider popular struggle. An important effect of this development was that capital could hide behind the curtains of apartheid and racism. The political energies of the oppressed masses and of international critics were focused on the apartheid regime and its abhorrent racism. The government and Afrikanerdom became the focus of attack. In fact the position was such that learned liberal academics saw in capital the great hope for change despite the fact that capital and its lackeys were undoubtedly the major beneficiaries of apartheid.

Capital did its very best to keep in the political background and as a result this helped prevent the creation of capital's logical political opposite which is a working class political movement. However, of crucial significance was that capital was growing rapidly and changing its very nature into a more monopolistic, technologically advanced and concentrated form. Its links internationally were growing as was its importance for international capital.

We find, therefore, that behind the scenes of the great battle between the apartheid regime and its popular opponents that the capitalist economy has flourished and capital emerges now as a powerful and different force.[2]

A number of points, made with clarity and economy in the above quotation, provide terms of reference upon which I wish to draw for my own argument. The first point is the acknowledgement of the necessity and power of popular strategies of resistance to racial oppression in South Africa. The second point is that these popular strategies of struggle have subsumed within their more prominent and powerful categories the specific terms of class struggle (thus the 'progressive trade unions' became a subordinate element within the popular struggle, instead of concentrating their energies upon developing specifically working class forms of political organization). The third point is that capital has been the major beneficiary of the apartheid State, so that it has developed rapidly during the present century, and established itself in advanced and concentrated forms (this has the corollary that the industrial working class has grown in importance into the major actual or potential source of opposition to the forces of oppression and exploitation). A further point, which is really implicit in those already made, is that capital has been able to 'hide behind' apartheid, and that the black working class has remained very undeveloped, in terms of either political or ideological self-organization.

The argument of Joe Forster, the General Secretary of the Federation of South African Trades Union (FOSATU), has its own polemical thrust: that of the urgent necessity of a strong development of specifically working class forms of political and ideological organization. Why? The forging of a popular unity amongst the oppressed peoples is a vital strategy, and a tremendous task, in the struggle against oppression. The possibility of this unity is grounded in the generic and brutal conditions of political and material deprivation that are the consequences of racial oppression. But this does not mean that there are *no* elements of class struggle amongst the oppressed: that the oppressed majority in South Africa is undifferentiated, in terms of class. To what extent will the struggle against racial oppression involve also a struggle against capital – against the exploitation of labour? To what extent will the leading forces in the struggle against racial oppression be able or willing to resist co-option into the capitalist system? It is possible to conceive of a victory over apartheid which will lead to a 'colourless' form of capitalism in South Africa, with the great majority of the people still oppressed and exploited – although this does not mean that the transition from a racial capitalism to a 'colourless' capitalism would be easy or welcome for the present agents of capital, either. The popular liberation struggle in other African states has, more often than not, resulted in some form of co-option by, or alliance with international capital. In South Africa, the chances against this may perhaps be the greater, precisely because capitalism is so developed here, and has proletarianized vast numbers of the oppressed peoples, thus creating some of the preconditions for a powerful oppositional working class movement. The relative strength of the black working class – as a self-organized body – within the popular movement against racial oppression will surely, therefore, have a crucial role to play here.

It is in the context of this conception of the role of the black working class that I want to consider the nature and significance of the populism of *Staffrider* literature. I am taking it that the black working class is at present in a relatively weak, though developing, position within racial and class struggle in South Africa. After all, only a small percentage of even the urban industrial workforce is unionized and capable of fairly organized actions *vis-à-vis* capital. It is not surprising, therefore, that *Staffrider* literature, which is overwhelmingly popular or populist in its orientation, should pay little overt attention to the struggles of the black working class *as a class*.

Even so, for reasons already indicated, it seems important to examine the populism of *Staffrider*, in order to ascertain to what degree connections are being made between opposition to racial oppression and developing class struggle in the prevailing ideology of the magazine – or, in other words, to assess the degree of awareness of/relation to working class struggle which is articulated in *Staffrider* literature. An analysis of this kind should sharpen our sense of the sort of contribution that *Staffrider* is making to the ideology of popular struggle.

Only very recently, it seems, has a literature of the black working class (in the specific sense of a written literature) started to emerge in South Africa.[3] Black South African literature has increasingly addressed itself to 'the people'. This stance is clear in the quotation I have already cited from Mothobi Mutloatse, where *Staffrider* literature is proclaimed as the self-expression of the people, in their process of coming to full self-consciousness.

At the recently held 'Culture and Resistance' symposium at Gabarone, an exiled writer asserted that:

> The Black poet, in most cases, has accepted that he (sic) will not be recognized by the pseudo-academic or critic as a poet. He does not write from an ivory tower for an élitist minority. He regards himself as a poet of the people, from the people, and uses words understandable to all.

'The people' is not, however, an entity identical to that of 'the working class'. Depending on whether the writer is addressing 'the people' or 'the working class', he/she will be – in actuality – using different words, different arguments, different forms; will be addressing different interests. This is not to deny that the working class is also contained within the people, shares its membership with the people, and is involved through its membership in the people in the common struggle against racial oppression. It is simply to remind that while 'the people' refers to the totality of the oppressed population in its immanent unity, it also in actuality represents a developing alliance, in the common cause of racial liberation, of diverse social elements. The leading social forces in this alliance do not *necessarily* have interests absolutely identical to those of the working class membership in the alliance.

Because the racial oppression of the vast majority of the population of South Africa has given rise to very powerful populist traditions of political and ideological resistance to the apartheid State, and because racial oppression has been the essential instrument for the substantial proletarianization of the oppressed population, and for the development of capitalism, the language of class struggle has been subsumed within the language of the popular liberation struggle. The popular liberation struggle directs itself both against racial oppression and against capitalist exploitation. The strength of this connection in the struggle – as against both racial oppression and capitalist exploitation – depends in reality, however, upon the relative strength of working class organization within the popular alliance.

Reference to the language of the class struggle is easy to find in recent South African literature. Often, though, it seems to me, this type of reference occurs without any real analytical development, so that the language of class struggle alluded to fails to get a purchase in the literary context. What really provides this literature with its cogency and momentum is the far more powerful language of popular opposition to racial oppression. Some of the novels of Nadine Gordimer are examples, I think, of the language of class struggle being introduced into literature because of the populist commitment of the writer, and of class achieving a somewhat deceptive emphasis within this literature. (The novels of J. M. Coetzee are a different case. There the enslavement of the people of one race by the members of another race – which is explored in terms of a fascination with the infinite psychological permutations of the master-slave relation – becomes a total subject-matter. There are – *in the last instance* – no classes, only races.)

The relatively wide circulation of *Staffrider* – in consideration, that is, of the type of literature the magazine contains: predominantly, those genres of 'the imagination', poetry and the short story – indicates that this literature is less socially exclusive than have been earlier black imaginative genres of this type. One reason for this must be that 'Bantu Education', miserably inadequate as it is in its educational provisions, has provided access to at least some degree of literacy for a greater percentage of the youth of the townships than under the old mission school system of black education. The mission school system produced a small, well-educated élite. Widely separated from the rest of the community in terms of its educational provision, this élite developed a distinct petty bourgeois class identity. With 'Bantu Education', the basic skills of literacy – of writing and reading – have been both more widely and more shallowly disseminated. Literacy has therefore come to signify something less élitist than previously. Racial oppression also inhibits the development of a black petty bourgeoisie, and forces individuals down into the working class, who might otherwise have had access to petty bourgeois occupations. These factors have contributed to the specific character of the populism of *Staffrider*. This magazine evinces a commitment to recording a relatively wide range of township 'voices'. For example, access to publication in the magazine has not simply been decided according to traditionalist aesthetic criteria – it has not been made dependent upon the execution of exclusive literary skills and techniques, upon the exercise of literary sophistication and 'finish', and so on. Much writing has been included that a traditionalist editorial policy would have rejected – or sent back for revision – as raw and unfinished. The inclusive editorial policy of the magazine would seem to indicate that *Staffrider* is not simply being run as the organ of a black petty bourgeoisie, by means of which members of this class establish their credentials as ideological leaders of the popular struggle, in terms of their possession of a relatively exclusive political and literary culture. The emphasis of the magazine is not upon *finished* literary skills, but upon *developing* skills, employed polemically in illuminating the conditions of racial oppression and of the popular resistance to them. The implication is that any reader can become a contributor. The visual imagery of *Staffrider* – particularly in the early numbers – has, equally, emphasized the inclusively 'popular' commitment of the magazine. This imagery focused the predicaments of commuters, hostel-dwellers, squatters, workers, etc., rather than highlighting specifically petty bourgeois themes.

It would seem, then, that the emergence of *Staffrider* has been associated with a certain 'democratization' of imaginative literature, and of the image of the writer or artist. It is this downward social reference of the literature of *Staffrider* which, in conjunction with the resurgence of organized black working class activity in the last decade that has made black trade unionism – along with the subversive activities of the exiled liberation movements – the major target of state repression, seems to me to give a special point to a consideration of *Staffrider* in terms of the magazine's degree of rapprochement with proletarian, as well as broadly popular issues.

IDEOLOGY IN *STAFFRIDER*

Space does not permit a comprehensive analysis of the literature, by a great number of authors, that has been published in *Staffrider*. I shall confine myself to commenting upon a few literary images that, I think, bear a specially significant ideological charge. The first such image comes from a story 'from a novel in progress' published in the first issue:

> The boy had instantly warmed to this character of the back-streets. Liso felt instinctively that only good could come from this man. He of the checked woollen cap, the faded denim trousers, the canvas shoes which showed the toes and the shirt the original colour of which was now impossible to tell, due to long use and its state of cleanliness. He of the red, fearful, jumping eyes. The one who knew how to get onto trains without a ticket; he who could discourse for hours upon the virtues of keeping your eyes open. The one who would give you the best advice on how to avoid trouble. He introduced himself as Magawulana. Whether it was the first name or the surname you did not know, and you instinctively knew you were not supposed to ask. This one knew how to bruise the law and how to avoid its consequential retaliation. He was the maestro; Machiavelli reborn. He was truly master of any situation. You knew he would captain the ship; you knew where your place was with him. In any situation you had to take the back seat and he would drive, for, you see, difficult situations were his speciality. Only practical experience can give these qualities to any man, and experience was what Magawulana certainly had.[4]

This sketch of the protagonist Magawulana is closely related to a conception of what life in South Africa is like for the black population Magawulana is a folk hero figure, in that he concentrates in himself the basic condition of the black population as a whole – a condition of poverty and oppression – while at the same time representing, in some sense, a victory over this condition. Magawulana is a character of 'the people'. He is a very simple and basic figure, in that he is not complicated by any form of social status (he has, of course, sexual status). He is poor: that flexibility of movement that is so vital an aspect of this strategy for survival – for he is always on the move – is possible because he is absolutely unencumbered by any sort of wealth or possessions. He has no formal educational qualifications: he is not the voice of an educated minority. His 'assets' are entirely 'human'/'popular': generic attributes of 'the people', acquired or sustained through generations of experience of, and struggle against, an enduring oppression. They consist in 'experience' and an innate goodness. Magawulana's goodness is really a form of generosity, derived from his character as a man of 'the people'. He never forgets that he is a member of 'the people'. He is always ready to distribute freely those assets he has acquired through painful and dangerous experience. He is not a hoarder or accumulator, but a sharer or giver. Magawulana exemplifies, therefore, the virtues of communalism: he has a sense of solidarity with the suffering individuals whose paths he crosses, as derived from their membership in a common oppression.

Magawulana's whole wealth consists in his knowledge of how to survive. Within this strategy, it is an important victory 'to get onto trains without a ticket' or, simply, 'to avoid trouble'. The implication is that the system of oppression in South Africa is a very radical one indeed. Oppression takes the form of a constant and dangerous harassment. The system is not only out to impoverish you, to exploit you; its aim, ultimately, is to kill you. To survive, you have to break the law: it is illegal to survive. Magawulana is therefore an adept at knowing 'how to bruise the law and how to avoid its consequential retaliation'.

The image of Magawulana as an inveterate traveller – 'one who knew how to get onto trains without a ticket' – is an especially rich one, in the populist context of *Staffrider* ideology. The image of blacks as a *travelling* population within South Africa bears a complex reference to the effects of racial oppression. The black population of South Africa is conceptualized by the apartheid State as a foreign population, necessary to the interests of the State only in the form of a migrant labour force. It is on the basis of this conceptualization that blacks are denied political rights, as well as other social capacities, in South Africa. Access to the sites of labour is heavily guarded by a multitude of repressive and restrictive laws. Thus the black population's experience of *travel* is, in many ways, an immediate symptom of the power of the apartheid state, whether this travel takes the form of commutation between the ethnic township and the site of labour in the 'white' city, or between the 'homelands' and the workplace, or of 'forced removal', or of 'resettlement', or of flight from the law, or of search for work. In every case, the necessity to travel is a reflection of the alienation of the black population from political and social self-determination *within* South Africa, and of the constant interventionary power of the apartheid State. It is not surprising, therefore, that the image of blacks as *travellers* is a recurrent one in *Staffrider*. It is an important motif in the stories of Mtutuzeli Matshoba. It is present, of course, in the very title of the magazine, which refers to Magawulana's practice of getting onto trains 'without a ticket'. Indeed, a second image I want to discuss, and connect with the image of Magawulana, also concerns a 'staffrider' figure. It is developed in 'Staffrider, a poem', published also in the first issue of the magazine:

> Black boy
> no recreation centre
> no playing grounds
> no money for lunch at school
> not enough schoolbooks
> No proper education
> no money for school journeys
>
> but
> one Saturday morning
> my father gave me
> one shilling and six pennies
> he said
> my son
> go and make enough
> for a living
>
> with eleven pennies

I bought a return ticket to town
the remaining seven for provision
good enough

I was one of those
carry-boys at the municipal market
caddy at the golf course
selling oranges and peanuts
illegally on the trains

money money money
that's not enough for a boy
what about entertainment

right
I am seventeen by now
waiting on a station platform
waiting for the conductor's
whistle of command
waiting for the train
to roll on its permanent rail

now steel wheels of an electric train
start playing a tune of
percussion and trombone
from the middle of the platform
pulling myself from the crowd
waiting for the tube to the north

like a bebop dancer
I turn around twice
and I open the window
push up the frame with my elbow
grab the frame between
the window and the door
listen to the improvization
from my dirty oversize
canvas shoes
pha – – phapha – phapha –
pha – phapha – phapha –
phapha – phapha –

listen to the shouting
and whistles
from the audience in that tube
when I swing on the outer handle
and rest on the bottom stair

THAT'S THEATRE HEY

they see me once
but only once
I'm on top of the coach

lying eight inches under
the main power lines

ACROBATIC HEY

they see me once again
but only once
I'm under the coach
lying on a steel frame
next to the wheels

CIRCUS HEY

fifteen stations
stupids packed
sardines in the tube
phapha – pha –
poor black eyes on me
– phapha –
home station
– pha – phapha – phaphaphaphapha

WA SALA WENA

– phaphapha –
railway police chasing me
I jump the platform
the railway line
the fence
across the river
towards home
I'm safe

this is the Saturday programme
and till we meet again
thank you brothers and sisters,
thank you.[5]

This poem provides us with an extremely complex and sharply developed image of the 'staffrider' figure. There are evident points of similarity and difference between this image of the 'staffrider' and Magawulana. The protagonist of the poem is not quite the generic folk hero represented by Magawulana; he is, more precisely, a youth who has had some experience of 'Bantu education', but who has had to abandon his schooling because his family could no longer afford to pay his school fees, and has consequently been forced to learn to fend for himself – to learn the arts of survival. The poem has an obvious relation – of a certain kind – to the Soweto revolt of 1976. The two basic themes of the poem relate to crucial issues of the revolt: in the first place, criticism by black pupils of the educational provisions of 'Bantu Education'; secondly, a broadening of the agitational platform to include the township community as a whole. The staffrider protagonist of the poem links these two phases of the revolt biographically, as he is transformed from a pupil to a 'staffrider'.

The poem also involves an interplay between the two themes of 'money' and 'entertainment'. Money is associated with subsistence, with survival – you can't survive if you don't have access to money. Entertainment is associated with self-expression, with self-realization. There is a dialectical tension in the poem between the pressures of mere survival in conditions of racial oppression – pressures which focus upon the need for and the scarcity of money – and the necessity to develop a critical, polemical perspective on these conditions of 'mere survival'. This tension is apparent in the perception of the black commuters as both 'stupids' and 'brothers and sisters'.

The poem opens with a criticism of 'Bantu Education'. It brings into laconic focus a characteristic dichotomy in the attitude of the apartheid State towards African education. On the one hand, a generalized structure for the provision of formal education to urban Africans is established: 'Bantu Education'. On the other hand, this provision is made ineffectual, or of minimum effectuality. The protagonist of the poem is a victim of this characteristic dichotomy. This dictates the evolution of the poem: from the expression of a specific type of criticism of the apartheid State, related to its educational provision for the youthful members of the oppressed urban population, to an engagement with the broader predicament of the urban community as a whole. Aspirations associated with education are thwarted by poverty, and lead the pupil into a new direction.

The second and third stanzas of the poem read like a parody of petty bourgeois Emersonianism – of an emphasis on the capacity of the individual to determine his/her own fate, according to energy and initiative and hard work. The solemnity of

> my son
> go and make enough
> for a living

is counterpointed by the meagre precision of

> my father gave me
> one shilling and six pennies.

At any rate, the protagonist proceeds to carry out the demands of this parental exhortation – in a way that parodies them. He acquaints himself with the casual, illegal and interstitial ways of surviving that are available to the township youth. He learns about subordination and defiance, as different modes of survival. This transformation of the aspirant scholar into the resourceful township urchin alludes to a whole dimension of urban black experience. The township youth, after a brief acquaintance with formal education, is thrown onto the labour market. In circumstances of chronic unemployment/underemployment/restrictive legislation, this youth is likely to be forced into membership of an urban lumpenproletariat, existing precariously through illegal or informal employment picked up in the interstices of the apartheid State. The protagonist, sent out to 'make enough/for a living,' is forced into a battle of wits and daring with the agents of state repression simply in order to survive.

207

The sixth stanza turns on a juxtaposition between the theme of 'money' and the theme of 'entertainment'. The emphasis shifts, in other words, from the problem of survival – conveyed, with wry irony, as involving an obsession with 'money':

> money money money
> that's not enough for a boy –

to the problem of self-expression and self-realization. This shift towards the issue of self-awareness, of *consciousness*, can of course be related to the central preoccupations of the Black Consciousness movement, though Motshile Nthodi's way of conceptualizing the 'Black Consciousness' role of his protagonist is a novel one. The protagonist becomes a 'staffrider'. Becoming a staffrider is an 'organic' development of the previous struggle for survival, but Nthodi frames, or alienates this role of staffrider by treating it in terms of the theme of 'entertainment'. The protagonist was denied adequate recreational facilities as a school pupil, and now the search for entertainment re-emerges in a different, more 'popular' context, amongst the characteristic crowds of black commuters which so well represent the status of the black population as a foreign population in South Africa. The protagonist is turned, perforce, into a popular entertainer, a 'street theatre' artist. The materials of this 'art' are drawn from the endemic conditions of travel of this *migrant* population: the 'percussion and trombone' of the electric trains gives rise to the peculiar contortions of the 'bebop dancer'.

The weekly exercise of the protagonist as a staffrider is a graphic kind of theatre, which speaks eloquently of oppression. The staffrider shows how survival involves a constant and dangerous battle with the forces of repression, an exercise of courage and skill in the face of deadly risks. The affirmation of black identity, of black consciousness, involves a fight to the death with the system of the apartheid State! 'Home' is a place you arrive at only after evading a desperate pursuit. For the commuters, alienated in the routine of a ceaseless to-and-fro between township and place of work, the activities of the staffrider provide a welcome distraction, a piece of entertainment. There is a tension in the latter part of the poem – a tension related to the issue of 'raising' a fully affirmative black self-consciousness – between the perception of the mass of commuters as

> stupids packed
> sardines in the tube

and *distracted* by entertainment, and these same commuters as 'brothers and sisters', whose life is *realized* in the actions of the staffrider.

This discussion of the literary image of the 'staffrider' figure can be extended into the visual imagery of *Staffrider* magazine. There is space here only to refer to one striking series of photographs by the late Ralph Ndawo, published, once again, in the first issue of the magazine. The cover of this issue features a photographic image, in which a youth in black silhouette is shown in the process of clearing – arms stretched out to balance, legs bent for landing – a formidable, high, wire-netted barricade topped by thorn-like projections and by strands of barbed wire. Behind the barricade is a still, black mass of figures, where the individual shapes of people are blurred into one dark, continuous entity, although a strong sunlight streaming across from the right highlights the contours of some heads, shoulders and sides. The spectator of this image looks from *outside* the barricade *in* to the mass of people, the sunlight catching on the wire netting emphasizing the barrier. The front page of the issue shows only this dark mass of people behind the barricade: the back page, over which the image continues, reveals the youth jumping clear. Inside the issue, six further frames are shown, in which the youth is carefully picking his way from the 'enclosed' side of the barrier to its 'free' side, the jump representing the culminating moment of freedom.

These photographs by Ralph Ndawo clearly articulate a potent populist mode of symbolism. The material of the photographic image, like the material of the staffrider image in the poem by Nthodi, is derived from a 'popular' imagery of township life and culture. The photographs are of a crowd at an NPSL soccer match in the townships. The images, however, alienate this moment of popular entertainment by making the spectator perceive the barrier that separates the crowd from the game being played as a symbol of oppression. By a reversal of perspective in which the reader of the magazine is confronted with the predicament of a mass of spectators, rather than sharing their distraction from that predicament in the drama of the game, the context of an 'entertainment' is superimposed by a symbolism of oppression. The crowd appears as the inmates of a detention camp. The point is clear: the life of the ghetto is a life of internment: the language of naked repression of the apartheid State can be heard everywhere. The youth jumping clear is escaping to 'freedom'.

Ndawo identifies the imagery of the apartheid State in an unlikely context, and thus exposes the universality of its presence. Indeed, the origin of the formidable fences erected between the crowd and the field at football grounds in the townships must be sought in the repressive conditions of the apartheid environment, which mean that even soccer matches can turn into explosion points of mass protest and 'violence'.

The youth clearing the barrier is a visual counterpart to the verbal 'staffrider' figure discussed earlier. I want now to try and pinpoint the ideological significance of this figure who is so recurrent in the early literature of *Staffrider*. I want to do this in terms of my concern with the degree of compatibility between populist conceptualizations of racial oppression and popular struggle, and awareness of specifically working class experiences and perspectives. My reason for focusing upon the 'staffrider' figure in relation to this concern is that the image of this figure seems to me perhaps the closest that *Staffrider* literature gets, in its imaginative genres, to dealing with proletarian issues.

The 'staffrider' figure is not, however, a specifically proletarian figure. More obviously, he is a broadly 'popular' figure. He is always to be found in juxtaposition to images of the people, the masses, the suffering and oppressed multitudes, the community – rather than in juxtaposition to images of class-defined collectivities. The reason why the 'staffrider' figure has something of a 'proletarian' ambiance is that the black working class, after all, makes up such a significant component of the racially oppressed peoples. The experience of the black working class largely overlaps with the experience of the oppressed peoples. Whether working class experience is conceptualized *as* working class experience, or simply as popular experience, can, however, have important implications within political and ideological strategy. I hope that this point will be borne out in the subsequent argument.

What does the image of the 'staffrider' figure, as developed in *Staffrider* magazine, actually signify in social terms? What is the *social* relation of this figure to the popular experience of racial oppression? The 'staffrider' figure is clearly not petty bourgeois. He is not, in any immediate sense, a symbol communicating the ideological legitimacy of the idea of petty bourgeois leadership of the struggle of the oppressed masses. On the contrary, the 'staffrider' is in social terms a very humble figure. He is not so much pro-letarian as a member of the lumpenproletariat. That is to say, he is inti-mately associated with an interstitial/informal/illegal mode of existence. It is this association with the lowest of the low, with the barest conditions of survival, that enables him to become the authentic symbol of the oppressed masses of the black population. His 'folk hero' status is the corollary of his association with degradation. His poverty and illegitimacy are the condition of a personal flexibility and freedom of strategy that can be interpreted as a mode of pure opposition to 'the system'. His life, his chosen or forced stratagem of survival, is very evidently always a fight, a struggle, a hit-and-run affair with the repressive agents of the apartheid State, a constant ex-ercise of experience, vigilance, cunning and daring which can be understood as self-affirmation in the face of appalling odds. In this sense, he can be seen as an assertion of 'black consciousness' – of the qualities of the people that have enabled them to sustain a positive and integral identity despite depri-vation, denial and humiliation.

I want to argue that this conception of the 'staffrider' figure as a rebel/survivor/folk hero gives very strongly *individualistic* connotations to the conceptualization of social struggle. Before I develop this point, however, I would like to suggest some reasons why this lumpenproletarian/interstitial figure *does* have strong connections with the experience of members of the black proletariat in South Africa. Racial oppression has obviously played an integral and complex role in the process of class formation, and in the experience and perspective of individual class agents, in South Africa. Thus, repressive State legislation and action have placed exceptional difficulties in the way of black working class organization and consciousness. At the level of individual experience, the vulnerability and weakness of working class organization has the corollary of great insecurity of personal status. For very many individual members of the black working class, the threat is unlikely ever to be far away of a loss of employment, and a demotion to the vast ranks of the 'reserve army' of the unemployed, or even to those of the 'surplus population' of the unemployable. In such cases of demotion, those concerned have to adopt other ways of 'making a living' – in the words of Nthodi's poem – than that of offering their labour-power to capital for exploitation. Huge numbers of the black working class in South Africa must have gained enormous experience of the movement between 'formal' and 'informal', 'legitimate' and 'illegal', structured and interstitial modes of existence. The same persons may therefore, at different times, be 'workers' and 'staffriders'.

The ideological prominence of the 'staffrider' figure in the literature of *Staffrider* is perhaps, to some degree, a symptom of the *weakness* of working class identity and resistance in South Africa. The weakness of working class *organization* gives rise to the prominence of more informal modes of resistance, with individuals moving between and within such informal modes, on the basis of personal 'experience' and the existence of *popular* networks of communication. The 'staffrider' figure seems to address himself to this type of circumstance.

On the other hand, the 'staffrider' figure in the literature is also associated with a certain type of *individualism*. Of course, the individual figure of the 'staffrider' is connected to images of the people, the community, and so on. The 'staffrider' is a humble/popular figure, who does not rise above the level of the people, in terms of any social attributes or qualifications. This is particularly strongly stressed in the presentation of Magawulana, whose essential attribute is that of generosity. Magawulana is essentially a helper of those in need: he shares his wisdom of experience absolutely spontaneously with anyone who requires its benefits. In this way, he is an embodiment of the virtues of community, of communalism. Though connected to the people, the community, the 'staffrider' figure is, however, the figure of an individual. His help or his significance is directed, also, towards the people as specific individuals, informally encountered. The emphasis, with this figure, falls upon the informal encounters between individual members of the oppressed population. The strengths of 'the people' are seen to be transmitted and developed within this type of encounter. Individual agents, as bearers of the 'popular' virtues of courage, cunning, toughness, generosity, honesty and so on, exemplify and communicate these virtues in their informal interactions. The point is that the concept of 'the people' 'the community' is always exemplified at the level of individual agency. There is no significant concern with formal structure or organization – this 'absence' is the symptomatic counterpart of the preoccupation with individual agency in the 'imaginative' genres of *Staffrider* literature.

Ralph Ndawo's sequence of photographs juxtaposes a youth jumping clear of a formidable barrier to a mass of people penned behind that barrier. In this juxtaposition, Ndawo perceives an image of the oppression of the people, and of the necessity for a struggle of liberation from this oppression. But what is the relation between the youth and the mass? The mass is trapped in a repressive structure; the youth is engaging in an unstructured, self-reliant activity which leads to his 'liberation'. The youth seems to offer an inspiring *personal* example to the mass. The relation between the young 'staffrider' and the mass of

> stupids packed
> sardines in the tube

in Nthodi's poem, seems somewhat similar. In its concern with personal agency, and its corresponding lack of concern with questions of structure and organization, *Staffrider* literature often promotes an individualistic and voluntaristic view of liberation (an analogous point can be made about the more 'Black Consciousness' side of *Staffrider* literature – developed mostly through poetry – in its preoccupation with individual self-consciousness, and its 'liberation' through an affirmation of 'Blackness').

The highlighting of the role of individual agency in *Staffrider* literature – as embodied especially in the figure of the 'staffrider' – is, I think, much more compatible with a broad commitment to the popular struggle against racial oppression than with a developed awareness of specifically working class terms of struggle. The fondness of writers for 'staffrider'-type imagery can be seen not simply as conditioned by the general prevalence of populist ideology over ideology based in class struggle, however, but, more specifically, as derived from the social context of the production of such (written) literary genres as poetry and the short story. The themes of generalized racial oppression and of the national liberation struggle against this oppression naturally contribute a great deal to the ideology of such genres, in the *Staffrider* context – but they do not entirely controvert the effects of the social context of such literary activity, and hence of the ideology which accompanies it. When I refer to the 'social context', I mean that the relation of the writer of poetry/the short story to his/her work is very different from the relation of the worker to the product of his/her labour. Whereas the worker alienates his/her labour-power to an employer, and only by means of such a contract is brought into connection with the instruments of labour, the writer of the type of literature under discussion exercises an immediate personal control over the activity and the instruments of writing, and enjoys immediate personal possession of the product of the labour-process of writing. In this sense, the production of written literature is a characteristically 'petty bourgeois' activity, in that it bears reference to a relatively self-contained or 'autonomous' process, neither immediately in the service of nor hostile to the interests of capital. The generalized racial oppression of the apartheid State has certainly determined the consistently downward social reference of black literature in South Africa, as writers have made common cause with the mass of the people in the struggle against racial oppression, and focused upon ever more humble images of the authentic basis of such a struggle. It is nevertheless to be doubted whether the conception of the role of the Black poet propounded by an exiled writer at the recent Gabarone Symposium, already referred to, is anything more than a populist slogan:

> He regards himself as a poet of the people, from the people, and uses words understandable to all.

In what sense are the poems and stories of *Staffrider* accessible and relevant to the experience and struggles of the industrial working class of the townships, let alone to 'all' the black population? It seems to me that the 'staffrider' image so prominent – in one or other guise – in the pages of the magazine is evidence of a tendency amongst the writers to interpret the forces at work in the popular struggle against oppression in a form that is more or less analogous to their own relatively autonomous, 'petty bourgeois' mode of activity. The 'staffrider' figure can be read as a symbol or analogy of the social role of the writer or artist.

It would seem that only a conscious recognition of the part of writers of the nature and demands of *class* struggle – of the emerging strength and significance of the black industrial working class, in particular – could lead to a thorough rejection of the individualism and voluntarism so endemic to the ideology of 'imaginative' genres of literature. It is certainly true that the ideological demands of *popular* struggle have led black, township writers – *Staffrider* writers – to a partial criticism of individualism. Thus the notion of the writer as an 'aesthete', responsible primarily to the immanent criteria of the literary craft, has been given a thorough pummelling. We have seen the significant emergence of writers' groups in the townships. Here, the declared objective has been to establish a strong collective of committed writers, who collaborate with each other towards common ends, rather than simply a loose association of individual writers drawn together on the basis of their 'craft' activity. Writers in the townships have also countered the severe limitation imposed upon their interaction with the popular community by a preoccupation with publication, by involving themselves directly in political and ideological events in the townships (by poetry readings at political meetings, at funerals of individuals who have died as a result of state repression; by popular theatre, etc.). This criticism and transcendence of literary individualism has been born out of the pressures of *popular* resistance to the apartheid State.

As I have tried to demonstrate, however, by means of an analysis of the 'staffrider' theme in the literature of *Staffrider*, the populist-inspired rejection of individualism has been only a partial one. An individualistic and voluntaristic view of social struggle still seems to have a powerful fascination for writers – and this type of fascination is associated with the neglect of any significant concern with the analysis of the role of structures and organizations in the struggle. As I have argued, popular struggle is exemplified essentially in terms of *informal* interactions between individual agents. In a similar way, the forces of oppression are characterized in terms of malevolent human agency. Whereas the protagonist of popular struggle is a humble individual, within whose social anonymity lie embedded the popular qualities of wisdom, cunning, endurance and generosity, the protagonist of the apartheid State is the complete negation of these qualities, being arrogant, brutal, sadistic and cowardly – an exemplification of a *sick* humanity. Some examples of this way of representing the agents of the apartheid State can be drawn from the stories of Mtutuzeli Matshoba. A WRAB (West Rand Administration Board) official:

> At last she was sitting of the bench before one of the superintendents, a middle-aged man with a beaky nose, thin down-turned lips, a pale pinkish, leathery, veined complexion and impersonal grey eyes. He kept toying with his pen on the blotter while his underscrapper buzzed around arranging the house files and the rubber stamps on the desk so that his lordship could reach them without straining himself.[6]

Police reservists in the townships:

> A person who has spent some time in Soweto will doubtless have guessed by now that the characters I am referring to are none other than some of the so-called police reservists who roam our dirty streets at weekends, robbing every timid, unsuspecting person, while masquerading as peace officers to maintain law and order in the community. There are no greater thieves than these men of the law, men of justice, peace officers and volunteer public protectors in the whole of the slum complex because, unlike others in the same trade of living off the sweat of their victims, they steal out in the open, in front of everybody's eyes. Of course nothing can be done about it because they go out on their pillaging exploits under the banners of the law, and to rise in protest against them is analogous to defiance of the powers that be . . .
>
> They split into twos when they arrived below us. Two of them, a tall chap with a face corroded by skin-lightening cream and wearing a yellow golf cap on his shaven head, and another stubby, shabbily dressed, middle-aged man with a bald frontal lobe and a drunk face, chewing at a cooked sheep's foot that he had taken from one of the grannies, climbed the stairs on our right hand side. The younger man took the flight in fours. The other two chose to waylay their unsuspecting victims on the street corner at the base of the left hand staircase. The first wave of the people who had alighted from the train was in the middle of the bridge when the second man reached the top of the stairs.[7]

This characterization of agents of the apartheid State is a corollary of the way in which agents of popular struggle are represented. The agents of the apartheid State are, naturally, characterized in terms of their deficiency in human virtues – or, more specifically, in the virtues of the people, the community, 'the brotherhood of men'. Those blacks who are seen to occupy roles of collaboration with the apartheid State are an especially prominent target of ideological condemnation. The black police reservists in the quotation above are seen as betrayers of the people, and their alienation from the people is the basis of their human degradation. The narrator of the story in which the reservists appear is also a significant protagonist. His position is the polar opposite of that occupied by the reservists: he exemplifies at a very humble, yet ineradicable level, the virtues of human fellow-feeling, and communalist solidarity – virtues that are, in the populist perspective, the very basis of popular struggle. This narrator is, indeed, a very good example of Matshoba's distinctive contribution to the 'staffrider'-type motif in recent township literature that I have been discussing. The story opens with this self-declaration on the part of the narrator:

> By dodging, lying, resisting where it is possible, bolting when I'm already cornered, parting with invaluable money, sometimes calling my sisters into the game to get amorous with my captors, allowing

214

myself to be slapped on the mouth in front of my womenfolk and getting sworn at with my mother's private parts, that component of me
which is man has died countless times in one lifetime. Only a shell
of me remains to tell you of the other man's plight, which is in fact
my own. For what is suffered by another man in view of my eyes is
suffered also by me. The grief he knows is a grief that I know. Out
of the same bitter cup do we drink. To the same chain-gang do we
belong.[8]

Just as the themes of popular struggle are exemplified – as with the 'staffrider'-type motif – through the informal interactions of individuals, then
so the role of the apartheid State is characterized through its malevolent
human agents. There are good reasons, within a popular perspective, for
this preoccupation with agency. On the one hand, an intensive ideological
campaign against 'collaborators' is an important strategy. On the other
hand, the characterization of agents of – or collaborators with – the apartheid State in *Staffrider* literature is at a relatively humble level. The agents
of the State who appear in the literature are those who are the immediate
executors of the power of the State. They are the ones who are in immediate
contact with the inhabitants of the townships, the members of the 'popular
community'. They are the ones who bear in their own persons the authority
and power of the State, and whose personal conception of their roles may
have immediate and drastic implications for the township inhabitants with
whom they come into contact. They are the ones with whom some form of
contact is customary, frequent, inevitable and dreaded. They may be brutal, or they may be bribable. In short, at the level of popular survival and
resistance, it is a vital matter to understand these agents of the State, to
know how best to avoid their strengths and to exploit their weaknesses.

The malevolence and brutality of the apartheid State, in its effect upon
whole oppressed populations, has obvious implications for the malevolence
and brutality of its agents. The ideology of racism, for example, gives in
effect an extra-legal sanction to the exercise of power by whites over blacks,
however 'informal' the context of this power. Brutality and degradation are
endemic to such an environment.

Despite these very good reasons for a preoccupation with malevolent
human agency in the characterization of the apartheid State, from the point
of view of a recognition of class struggle and of the basic interests of the
developing black working class, there are serious limitations in a critical
strategy – a popular strategy – that fails to go beyond this type of characterization. This type of characterization of the apartheid State tends to
imply that the real nature of the State, its oppression of the vast majority
of the population, and the malevolence of its personal agents can be explained in terms of – racism. It is racism that produces the human malevolence that is so strongly castigated in contemporary black literature.

Racism is understood as an aberration of human nature. It is an aberration, or disease of humanity that has extraordinary, cancer-like malignancy, ramifying from the original diseased cells and quickly eating into
every aspect of social life. Racism, in other words, is a force that can explain

anything to do with oppression and exploitation, and leave no need for further analysis. Explanation of the apartheid State in terms of racism sees the way whites hold power over blacks in South Africa in terms of a general delinquency. The white ruling group is an embodiment of arrogance, greed, selfishness, sadism, cowardice, etc. – these vices running into and coalescing with each other as an expression of the generalized, cancerous malignancy of racism. This view is very clearly put across by Mtutuzeli Matshoba, in a powerful, populist-oriented story about the convict labour system:

> So we rambled on and on about whites. It had started when I told them what had taken me to Trannfontein.
> 'But what are they made of that they are so indifferent to, or rather delight in, the suffering of other people?' queried the one they called Temba.
> 'It's greed that makes them like that. In order to satisfy their greed they have no choice but to insulate themselves against the sufferings of those they exploit by convincing themselves that the latter are not really human beings but something less than that. They liken us to beasts that they can force to do anything they will upon us,' Thabo said.
> 'But if it had been that way, there would have been no need to keep us in subjugation with guns. We would simply serve them without argument – it being only natural to do so,' another one added.
> 'How much longer do they think they can maintain the status quo, without inconveniencing everybody with an unnecessary war?' asked another one.
> 'Who knows. I heard once that Hitler wanted to try a similar thing for a thousand years. It took twelve years, after which he learned the hard way how wrong he had been; but not without having robbed the world of thirty million lives. Perhaps that is how they blackmail the world,' came still another voice, trying to answer the puzzle.
> I saw that we would never arrive anywhere trying to pinpoint or diagnose the disease that was eating away part of our mottled human society, placed by fate in a most beautiful country to learn to appreciate it in amity, but failing to do so, to the utter dismay of the rest of humanity. 'It's just no use trying to find out these things. But at least let me give my opinion too. I think it's pride, an insane pride that makes them refuse to accept in the face of humanity that they are wrong. On the other hand it's cowardice, a fear of accepting failure and losing face. But then think of how great the man would be who would stand up and declare that they were indeed wrong'[9]

This does not mean that there are *no* elements of class analysis in Matshoba's story. The following conversation – a significant medium, in itself, in Matshoba's stories – takes place two pages after the previous quotation:

> 'Here starts the second day of slavery,' sighed Thabo as we started off to the granary.

'Every day of your life has been a day of slavery. You were born for that,' I corrected him.

'If only I had gone to school when I was young. I would not be here now; I would be in an office working with a phone and a pen,' Thabo went on.

'Ha. You'd still be serving, and you'd still not be satisfied. That would be just another form of slavery. Leashed with a tie to a desk doing the same thing half your life to make a white millionaire even richer. When a black person goes to school he does it in order to earn a certificate to serve at a better place, not for the sake of gaining knowledge to use for the betterment of his own people or to widen his scope of thinking so as to be able to analyse the world and find himself a place in it. We who serve the harder way with physical labour need not go to school for it, that is, there are no certificates sold to dig trenches and sweep streets. We're ready made as such,' I answered.

My words sparked off some interest in Jabulani, the man who had started the whip dance the previous day. 'What about doctors and lawyers? Don't they work for themselves, those people? They don't serve anybody, *mos*.'

'You're absolutely right – they don't serve anybody but themselves. The doctors rob sick people and the lawyers make money out of the distress and ignorance of people. Both have a common aim of leading jet-set lives and looking down upon other people. I don't say all are like that, but most of them are.'

'Of course you might be right, *mfo*,' agreed one of the other two men. 'You know, people don't trust the educated because they hunt with the wolves and graze with the sheep, mostly.'

The fifth man also broke his reticence. 'Ya – who can trust them when they keep only to their 'high societies' and boast to the people about the money they make? They live on whisky, champagne, women and lust; vice is the mark of many an 'educated' person. It must be disappointing for some of the old men who worked their hearts almost to a standstill to buy their children what they never had themselves, an education which they hoped their sons and daughters would use to recover what was lost by our forefathers.'

'So you agree with me that education or rather knowledge is used by blacks only to serve the whites, if not to steal from their own brothers who have not had the same opportunities to go to school for many reasons that are beyond their control,' I said, trying to drive my point home but not knowing the right way to put it. 'The betterment of mankind is a dead virtue. Educated people should be an investment in the futures of those around them, but it is they who are posing the greatest threat to the dignity of man with their class consciousness. Instead of raising the man at the bottom, they tend to keep him there for fleecing, or deliver him to white wolves for fleecing,' Jabulani concluded. We would have liked to pursue the subject further but had arrived where we were going to work.[10]

217

The group of convict workers which holds this conversation has been re-duced to a condition of transparent 'slavery' – a condition which is simply the bottom term of their whole existence as members of an oppressed population. Despite their predicament, the convicts readily become absorbed in a political discussion. The subject of their conversation is the black petty bourgeoisie or professional class, and its failure to deliver the promise of a commitment to emancipate the people from oppression. This petty bourgeoisie is seen as having revoked its obligation to devote itself to the improvement of the condition of the poor and oppressed majority of the black population – it has betrayed this obligation by preoccupying itself with consumerism, display and degenerate appetites. The class is profound-ly untrustworthy because, though it employs when the occasion suits it a language of popular rhetoric, its real impetus is acquisitive and rapacious: 'You know, people don't trust the educated because they hunt with the wolves and graze with the sheep, mostly.' The educational system itself – a condition of access to petty bourgeois status – becomes highly suspect, since it appears to exist only to fill places within the present set-up, and to foster the individualism and élitism of a select minority. The condition of the vast majority of the people will not be changed by the educational system, since education is not necessary to the labour functions that this majority per-forms: 'there are no certificates sold to dig trenches and sweep streets.'

Although social distinctions amongst the black population are empha-sised in this extract from *A Glimpse of Slavery* – and although the extract develops a radical dissatisfaction with the role of the black professional class *vis-à-vis* popular aspirations – the perspective is populist rather than class-based. The concept of 'the people' works in such a way that class analysis is prevented. 'The people' is taken as the basic, organic entity of social analy-sis. Those individuals who acquire education, and become doctors and lawyers, are seen as agents of 'the people' – agents intended to advance the general cause of 'the people', but sometimes – too often – deflected in the direction of self-advancement. This deflection is understood as deriving from a system designed for the enrichment of *whites*, and requiring the mor-al complicity – or degeneracy – of individual blacks.

There appears to be no reference in this passage – except in very broad terms – to the existence of a *structure* of economic relationships, within which the behaviour of black doctors and lawyers can be understood. This be-haviour does become readily comprehensible and without reference to any moral degeneracy, once the place assigned to these professions within the capitalist order is taken into account. These essential social services are also private enterprises. Considering this, and the time and money that are in-vested in acquiring the practising qualifications of these professions, it is clear that only exceptional individuals will withstand the pressure to use these qualifications as sources of self-enrichment. *Not* to use them in this way is to work in contradiction with the system.

Preoccupation with the personal agency of individuals, in relation to the cause of 'the people', prevents the role of the structure of economic re-lationships in South Africa – essentially, the structure of capitalism – from being identified and analyzed. It seems clear that the convict workers in the above extract from *A Glimpse of Slavery* do not really challenge this structure.

At most, their discussion can be read as an exhortation to members of the black petty bourgeoisie to remember the cause of 'the people'. It is interesting, for example, that these workers do not make the demand that would be the logical outcome of their criticism of the black petty bourgeoisie, within a class context: they do not demand *free* legal aid and *free* medical care on a generalized basis. This would have been a structural demand.

THE IDEOLOGY OF *STAFFRIDER* AND CLASS STRUGGLE

I have tried to demonstrate that the ideology of *Staffrider* literature – despite its inclusion of proletarian, or more properly, lumpenproletarian imagery – is overwhelmingly populist. The strength of populist ideology within this literature means that class analysis is very undeveloped. The black working class belongs, of course, within a larger and looser alliance of the oppressed peoples of South Africa, and in this way the experiences, struggles and aspirations of the members of this class are recognized in the literature – in their popular character. So far as the more class specific activities of the most conscious, organized and militant sectors of the black industrial working class are concerned, however, it cannot be said that *Staffrider* literature reflects any real awareness of or rapport with these activities. Commensurate with this lack of connection with organized working class struggle, there is a significant lack of commitment in *Staffrider* literature to the analysis of the role of capital in the maintenance of the apartheid State, or, in other words, to the structure of capitalist economic relationships, as articulated with racial oppression, in South Africa. *Staffrider* literature, which is committed to an ideological assault upon the racism of the apartheid State, appears unwilling or unable to take on the capitalist system.

I have identified the populist texture of the ideology of *Staffrider* literature in terms of the prominence of certain themes or motifs: the 'staffrider'-type motif, the concept of 'the people', the preoccupation with individuals, either as 'agents' of 'the people' or of the apartheid State, the fore-grounding of informal and immediate interactions, rather than the analysis of structures and organizational preconditions, the identification of the apartheid State in terms of racism rather than capitalism. My analysis has been directed towards a specific type of motif in the literature of *Staffrider*, a motif that I believed to have relatively promising connotations for the recognition of the issues of class struggle in the general context of this literature: the motif of the 'staffrider' figure. Other motifs might have been analysed. The concept of 'Africa'/'Afrika' in the broadly black consciousness-oriented poetry of the magazine is worthy of extensive analysis. I don't think, however, that the conclusions I have reached in my analysis of the 'staffrider'-type motif would have been substantially different, in their general implication, if some other motif(s) had been selected.

The organized black working class movement in South Africa is of course weak and vulnerable, and involves only a small minority of even the industrial working class. It is nevertheless disturbing that the vigorous, township-based literature of *Staffrider* has so little to do with this movement, although this is perhaps only too understandable in view of the 'petty bourgeois' ambience of the dominant genres – poetry and the short story –

in *Staffrider*. To conclude, I would like to reiterate two shortcomings of the literature of *Staffrider*, in relation to recognition of working class struggle.

In the first place, *Staffrider* literature conceptualizes and opposes the apartheid State in terms of *racism*. A popular-oriented assault on the racism of the State is, of course, very necessary, and is perhaps capable of winning some important ground back from that won by racist oppressors. On the other hand, behind the Afrikaner Nationalist agents of the apartheid State can be found the interests of not only local capital, but also of giant transnational combines, of interlocking international structures of capital. An ideological assault on the racism of the apartheid State does not penetrate to the existence of this structure of interests, although these interests are as committed to the exploitation of the working population of industrialized South Africa as are the immediate agents of the State to its political oppression. It seems important, therefore, for writers to broaden the scope of their ideological armoury.

In the second place, *Staffrider* literature seems to operate at quite a remove from the loci of class struggle. It is noticeable that *Staffrider* stories, even when they refer to highly volatile situations in which the 'whole community' seems involved, tend to follow a fictional course that is oriented upon specific, individual trajectories – rather than giving sustained attention to structured, organizational developments of the 'popular will'. The preference for locating 'popular' action in the region of informal interactions between individuals of a relatively free-wheeling type also means that the 'characteristic' sites of the development of organized working class consciousness are left relatively untouched. I can't think of any material in *Staffrider* that deals with anything like the emergence of organized working class action – or with the history or the typology of such actions. Between the 'informal' and the 'formal' there seseems to be a divide that the writers just can't cross. But then, for writers to commit themselves to the formal development of working class consciousness would obviously involve an enormous change of image. So far, as the recent symposium at Gabarone showed, writers of 'imaginative' literature are not, on the whole, ready for such a change. The issue, for the majority of them, poses itself as between an insulated aestheticism and a full-blooded commitment to 'the people'. The question of the role of the working class, and of the responsibility of writers to this *class*, has scarcely surfaced.

Notes

1 Introduction, *Forced Landing*, Ravan Press, Johannesburg, 1980, p. 5.
2 Joe Forster, 'The Workers' Struggle – Where Does FOSATU Stand?', *South African Labour Bulletin*, Vol. 7, No 8, 1982, pp. 71–3.
3 Cf. Keyan Tomaselli, 'From Laser to the Candle', *South African Labour Bulletin*, Vol. 6, No 8, 1981.
4 K. F. S. Ntuli, 'Magawulana', *Staffrider*, 1, No 1, Johannesburg, 1978, p. 8.
5 Motshile Nthodi, 'Staffrider, a poem', *ibid*., p. 28.
6 *Call Me Not a Man*, Ravan Press, Johannesburg, 1979, p. 5.
7 *Ibid*., pp. 19–20.
8 *Ibid*., p. 18.
9 *Ibid*., pp. 46–7.
10 *Ibid*., pp. 48–9.

INDEX